Being Real
An Ongoing Decision

Being Real
An Ongoing Decision

Bruce Scott, Ph.D.

Frog, Ltd.
Berkeley, California

Published by Frog, Ltd.
Frog, Ltd. books are distributed by
North Atlantic Books
PO Box 12327
Berkeley, CA, 94712

Editors: Carly Newfeld, Mary McAuley
Book design and typography: Roger Knox
Cover design: Roger Knox
Cover illustration/concept: Pola Lopez
Originally published by Eagle's Way Publishing

Printed in the United States of America on acid-free recycled paper

Publisher's Cataloging-in-Publication Data

Scott, Bruce S.
     Being real: an ongoing decision / Bruce Scott.
  —1st ed.
     p.   cm.
     Preassigned LCCN: 98-70611
     ISBN: 0-9662806-4-4

    1. Self-realization. 2. Spiritual life.
  3. Interpersonal relations. 4. Scott, Bruce S.
     I. Title.

BF637.S4S36 1998   158.1
                              QB198-576

10 9 8 7 6 5 4 3 2 1

Acknowledgements

I am grateful to a young man named Jonah for daring me to be absolutely real—a decision that, once made, cannot be broken. Jonah only spoke to me when I had no pretense, no social face, no empty smiles, no false identity, and no vacant words. He helped me expand my beliefs about psychological labels to reveal the visionary that often lies beneath so-called abnormal behavior. His presence demanded I evolve my limits of perception or exclude him from my self-defined normal world.

My thanks to Arnold and Amy Mindell, Carlos Castaneda, Dan and Joy Millman, Roselyn Bruyere, John Johnson, Taisha Abelar, Florinda Donner-Grau, Carol Tiggs, and Sara Lonsdale. When in their presence, and by how they teach and live, I've been able to see them in me. I have learned what it looks like to be in the present, and to live with clarity and intent.

To Meigra Simon, shape shifter, sorcerer, dancer, singer, the woman who lives and teaches with me, able to nudge me alive whenever I believe I am powerless and lost in self-doubt. A woman who lives out her life purpose with clear intent and loves through her actions.

To those friends in my life who continually remind me to keep moving internally and externally: Jo Warley, Kerry Sissem, David Schwartz, Chris Willet, Laurie Swett, Katje Wagner,

Bill Reese, Gene Rumrill, Gwen Marie, Zoey Helenski, Janet Steinberg, Ellias Lonsdale, and Rachel Cobley.

And to all the people who played out the roles of enemy when in fact they were my allies and teachers. They showed me that I could either live forever with anger, fear, and blame or change my perception and emotionally reach beyond where I believed I thought possible. I needed them and I am grateful for their part in my life.

My thanks to Jessica Dubroff for being the girl who could fly and to Lisa Hathaway, the mother who opened her arms to the sky. Thank you to all the children I've known who live in this multidimensional world without apology and without doubt—my greatest teachers.

And to our little one, the little person who remains official-ly nameless as of this writing, I bow to you with great respect and admiration. For coming to me in a dream before your birth to inform me that you'd have a name when you, Meigra, and I see each other equally. You have come into this world to show the way and it turns out you are the way.

My thanks to Carly Newfeld, editor and friend who worked with this book, committed to bringing life and realness to every word and sentence. Her involvement filled out those places that called for clarity and thorough integrity.

And to Mary Eileen who read through the pages with the eye and heart of a warrior, tapping into the rhythm of the words. As a literary exercise and one of sorcery, Mary fine-tuned the writing to maintain and amplify the intent. To Roger Knox, friend and artist, who designed the pages, provided a visual invitation, and created open space for words.

For providing humor, perspective, and a stop-in-my-tracks reality, I humbly and graciously acknowledge Ellen Kleiner, editor, coordinator of the publishing process, and an invisible planetary secret.

I am grateful to the people who had asked for or were called into reading the original, raw version of this book, who then shared with me how their lives had been changed, their perception emboldened.

And my gratitude to the many people who have come into my life who no longer want to pretend that something meaningful is happening when it is not. I've learned, like the real people in this story, that a commitment to being real will allow the unraveling of all influences that limit our own creative life forces.

Contents

Introduction

Long ago, as a young child, I wondered if the day-to-day existence I knew was all there was to being alive. Consistently, a soft voice inside me questioned, "Why be alive if all there is to do is go to school, work, earn money, spend money, find a mate, get colds, and eventually die?" It all seemed so uninteresting.

I watched my parents, relatives, schoolteachers, and most other adults around me alter their voices and facial expressions while in the company of others. In the presence of little people like myself, their voices became higher, their pronunciation more exaggerated, and their eyebrows more rounded. "What has happened?" I'd wonder. "Where did they go?"

As I grew older, I noticed that I, too, was behaving differently around other people. I had learned to believe that the way others lived was how I was to live. I had become a social being, and in the process had lost most traces of my realness, my authority, and my willingness to be different—to live *from the inside out.* Then I got married, completed college, had children, worked, graduated from more schools, got divorced, and became a psychologist. I also developed headaches, backaches, fevers, runny noses, and a variety of miscellaneous physical symptoms. My face, meanwhile, having taken on the habit of pushed smiles, held tensions that reflected the uninteresting way of life I had adopted.

"Where did *I* go?" I wondered. "How could I have left myself to follow a path I knew would lead to an empty existence?" It didn't make sense. Nothing made sense. My life force was waning, and my energy rapidly depleting. I had to change or I would die. I wanted to soften inside. I wanted to feel an internal quiet and to be free of my anger, hurt, lostness, confusion, stuckness, blame, and judgments, and of occasionally believing that death would be easier. I knew there was more to life than paying bills, being busy, getting things done, acquiring merchandise, looking good for others, and pretending I knew what I was doing.

Before long, I began asking new questions: Why do I seem so busy, rushed, anxious, and unable to slow down? What am I doing? Why am I here? How am I not *being real* in my life? What is real? I decided to stop being busy and trying to please. I stepped out of the world of achievement and success, stopped running toward the future, and gave up the notion that I had to "become somebody." At that point I dropped into another reality deep within—a place that was unfamiliar, often scary, unpredictable, incapable of offering guarantees for the future, and forcing me to risk living without knowing what I was doing.

Right away, dramatic and tragic life events began to shake loose my socially conditioned expectations, as well as my need to be nice. At the same time, in my role as a therapist, I befriended hundreds of women, men, and children in deeply personal ways, stripped of the masks they often wore. Their realness awakened mine—an awakening that I knew was critical if I was to have an awareness free enough to grasp the truth in everything.

To be real in all situations became my calling—a task that required excruciating honesty, as well as a fierce commitment to the practice of paying attention. For this, I had to drop all illusory identities and experience the discomfort of acknowledging that I really didn't know anything. I had to *risk dying in order to live*. That deliberate challenge is what this book is about. In portraying my years of awakening, it blazes a trail out of the so-called world of reality and into a universe filled with many realities, no ranking order, no pretense, and an ever-delectable freedom.

Reading this story requires a new kind of listening. Here, you will get to listen to yourself, be yourself, and magnify your own authority. After all, there are no rights or wrongs in this landscape—only a commitment to awareness and a willing-ness to live without ego or apology amid the mundane dis-tractions of everyday existence. Dropping in close to the ground with yourself will help you assimilate, page by page, information you can embody in your own life about the power of intent, magic, clarity, and activating that which is real.

As for the characters, they are flesh-and-blood people of dif-ferent ages and colors who live in real ways, unalarmed by daily events. Each one demanded that I acknowledge who I am and what I bring to the world. They would not let me hide behind psychology, the past, or excuses of any sort. With them, I could no longer pretend to be nice and, in fact, had to see that guilt, obligations, and false ways of being were destructive forces that served no one.

Jarid, a young man labeled schizophrenic, taught me to embrace all beings and events as normal. In his silence he showed me how to communicate with the real me, the person who did not need to maintain an image as a writer and psy-chotherapist. He taught me that the only difference between client and therapist is which side of the room one sits on. As my perceptions became more fluid, I learned that there is no such thing as abnormal, only *unfamiliar*.

Lupe, an eighty-six-year-old Huichol medicine woman, insisted that I take myself seriously, be responsible for what I see, and live respectfully. Maria, a Navajo woman, showed me how to slow down so that I could feel. Leo Garcia, an age-old acquaintance, helped me to connect events of forty years ago to the present. And Meigra, my partner, evolved into a major guide in this story and in my life, informing and transforming our everyday relationship. Interacting with these extraordinary people, as well as many others, moved me from the everyday, easily believable world into the one that existed beneath my denial—the world of the intangible and the unseen, the sometimes terrifying and the always unfamiliar. I had to *become familiar with the unfamiliar.*

Interwoven throughout the story are several life-changing nighttime dreams that proved to be potent sources of information. I needed to live out all these dreams, one by one, before I could complete the chapters in which they are described.

To alter my life, I had to *change* it, not work on changing it. I had to leap into a terrifying abyss that required me to see everything everywhere without judgment. I had to break the illusion of how I thought I was supposed to live, and instead risk living daily from an inner authority, with no attachment to being right. I had to trust my perception and allow it to take priority over the opinions of others. To cross all these thresholds, I needed to liberate the voices of the past that were not mine, that had chained me to social and cultural beliefs, holding me captive in a daily trance.

The intent of this story is twofold: to show that the way out of such a trance is through the dissolving and expanding of beliefs, and to portray how everyday relationships can illuminate and transform the perception of hopelessness, powerlessness, and being victim to anything. Once out of the trance, physical symptoms can also change. The events in this story are presented to open windows, doors, and gateways to visions revealing that there is more than the everyday, ordinary world to use as a reference point for what we call reality. Indeed, so-called psychological dysfunctions can dissolve the moment our perception changes.

With renewed vision we can see, for example, that the teachers in our lives are rarely those who have made teaching a career within an institution. I found my teachers in the least likely places. Sometimes they were walking the streets in search of food and shelter; at other times, they were bedridden with life-threatening diseases, undergoing the dying process to come alive. Often, they were children who appeared at the most unexpected times to teach me silence of the heart. A young African child, simply by his presence, helped me recognize that as a middle-class white person, I have the privilege of moving through the world in a relatively safe way. He taught me to take even more seriously the need to respect and stand for the little people we call children, and to do whatever is required to dissolve the artificial divisions between people of different races who are judged, excluded, and appeased.

A Mexican migrant farm worker in the San Joaquin Valley of California taught me that realness and wisdom are natural occurrences. American Indians, especially many Native people of Alaska, brought me home to myself and opened me to a universe I could not touch with my fingers or see with my eyes. From them, I learned to laugh with others, rather than at them. I even learned to laugh with myself, and to understand that everything in life is about relationship.

If you decide that being free from the trance of daily existence is essential for you, then walk with me through these pages. As you read, trust your body to let you know what is real—it always tells the truth.

This will be a journey inward—as far into the interior as you are willing to go. It may even take you to places you've never been before and change who you believe you are.

1

The Tiger Speaks

A tiger was chasing me through dark, wet city streets slick from rain, with only the puddled reflection of streetlights to complete the eerie setting.

I was terrified, running faster than my legs could move. My hands clawed at the air in front of me, seeking all the forward momentum I could bring to escape.

From behind me, I heard the tiger's breath. I felt its presence, its pursuit pushing me forward. Its pure intention activated my strength to move, transforming panic into action. I didn't turn around to look.

I sensed it. I could feel its shadow. The pads of its clawed feet echoed each time they touched down to spring forward again, bringing the powerful animal within a few yards of making contact with my body.

I was alone except for the tiger closing in. I felt the distance shrinking between us. I moved through space, unaware of touching the ground, surrounded only by terror. My thoughts scanned ways to distract the tiger. I was hopeful, even in my seemingly helpless state.

With only seconds to decide, I saw a possible way out— a distraction. Just off the darkened path to my right, a dog sat quietly, calmly observing what I considered to be a life-threatening chase. Her eyes, instead of revealing any hint of the terror in mine, had a serene, wise, almost satisfied look.

Ignoring my conscience, I slowed my pace, allowing my hands to reach down, grab the dog, and quickly set her on the sidewalk directly in the path of the tiger. I prayed she would serve as an edible distraction, slowing the tiger enough for me to escape.

That didn't happen.

The tiger simply passed through the dog as if she were only a puff of mist with fur, consuming her whole. It continued toward its ultimate prey.

I felt the imminence before contact. I saw images of instant darkness, a sharp light of momentary pain, and a cavernous mouth opening to inhale my body. I felt in my terror a larger force, and the tiger ready to pull me in.

I was about to surrender, give up to death, when in an instant, the terror ceased. There was none. It was gone. I had no fear. In that moment, death and life were the same.

I was in another world, fearless, neutral to the outcome.

I became action itself, like a knife piercing steel.

It was my turn! No judgment. No fear. No way out.

I had one option. I stopped running. I shifted all my intent and purpose to slowly, gracefully spinning with perfect balance, my muscles sensuously working in unison. My physical strength was amplified. I had no doubt.

With the timing of an Aikido master, and with perfect coordination, I faced the tiger, setting my feet solidly in place.

I was ready. I was relaxed. I was the moment.

I looked into the blackness of the night with only the shining wetness of the streets for illumination.

Out of the dark the immense figure appeared, filling my vision. The tiger leapt from the path, springing high into the air directly toward me, its front legs outstretched, reaching for me, a monstrous, shadowy figure traveling through space almost in slow motion.

Within seconds the outline of the huge creature evolved into full, solid form, its power, intent, and immense energy locked in its eyes. I watched as its open mouth approached my face. There was no more space between us.

We made contact. Distance ceased as we merged and blended into each other like a hand slipping into a glove. There was no separation. I became the tiger's eyes and the tiger's eyes were mine. I awoke from the dream as the tiger and I dissolved into one form.

I sat up in bed fully awake, stunned into another reality. My mind took over, producing familiar thoughts defining the alleged real world. The day "dream"—the one of work, worry, and schedules—slowly took form, like a ship emerging through early morning fog. I stood up and stretched.

My stretch was different. I had never felt my body like this. My arms and hands reached for the ceiling as I stretched up on my toes. An image of a cat filled my mind.

I had to face one of my greatest fears that day. I had been invited to give a talk that evening on Future Psychology and Heightened Awareness before five hundred college students. I had been worrying about it for weeks. I was scared about appearing in front of large groups of people, even though I'd been doing it for twenty years. This time I was presenting information personal to me; I had not shared these insights in public before, and I feared being seen as foolish, being dismissed by an audience of rolling eyes.

I questioned why I continued to place myself in front of strangers, year after year, always anticipating and feeling fear weeks beforehand. "Why do I keep doing this?" I asked myself. "I'm not trying to prove anything." I wanted to blame something external to justify my fear: "They probably won't understand, anyway."

I was aware of how familiar this sounded. Fear and doubt were old habits. I believed that I needed guaranteed preapproval from others with no emotional risk involved.

I recalled a scene from my high school days, thirty years earlier. I was standing before two thousand people, about to ask the students to vote for me as their student body president. I pretended to myself that I wasn't afraid, believing that no one would notice if I pretended well enough.

Shaking inside, I stepped up to the microphone, placing one hand on the adjustment knob and the other hand over the microphone itself. Shrill, high-pitched feedback saturated the auditorium, forcing everyone to cover their ears. I was startled and embarrassed. Cautiously, I returned to the microphone, bypassing any attempt to adjust it. Instead, I adjusted my body by bending my knees and slightly hunching my back. I had to hold my head up awkwardly to see the audience.

"Dear Mr. Principal," I began, "Mr. Faculty and all the audience in the people."

I stopped. There was an ominous silence. By the time I'd heard what I'd said, two thousand people had erupted into laughter. I turned red and dripped sweat in embarrassment. I thought of running from the stage, believing the momentum of humiliation would cause me to dissolve, never to be seen again by anyone.

I stood facing the audience, my shirt soaked with perspiration, trembling with fear but determined to finish the speech. The laughter continued as I waited in silence, waves of panic urging me to run away. I stood still and stayed quiet. The laughter soon subsided, and the entire auditorium joined me in silence. I leaned into the microphone again and completed the five-minute speech in a monotone, my voice shaking.

After that embarrassing experience—and learning, later in the week, that I had received only thirty of two thousand votes—I asked myself why I had received so few votes. In a flash I realized that I had been trying to protect my self-image, look intelligent instead of foolish, hide my fear instead of acknowledging it. I wanted people to like me and take me seriously, and I thought that was the way to do it. This was my first awareness that presenting a false image of myself did not work and wouldn't get me anywhere.

That week, I had made a commitment that I would only present my real self to others, even if it meant being banned from the universe forever! The early morning tiger dream reminded me of that commitment.

I drove to the college in the afternoon, knowing I would stand before hundreds of people even if I wasn't sure why, and even if I was afraid.

I entered the small auditorium thirty minutes early to become familiar with the space, projecting myself into what I was about to do before a group of people I didn't know. I stood behind the heavy wooden lectern and imagined the audience sitting there and what I would feel like with all their attention. By doing this, I took the emotional charge out of the event before it took place. I moved the lectern over to the side so there would be open space between the audience and me.

I felt my insides trembling as I spoke with the first few people to arrive. Making these personal connections before standing alone in front of a thousand pairs of eyes, I began to feel more at ease.

As I waited for people to arrive, I heard the familiar voice inside asking, "Do I have any useful information to offer? Why would anyone want to hear what I have to say?" The auditorium soon filled with students, teachers, and mental health professionals. The "professionals" wore suits and ties along with facial expressions that questioned whether I could tell them anything they didn't already know. I realized I was indulging my fears by discounting some segments of the audience.

Everyone was seated; I listened to myself being introduced as I sat quietly, perspiring in my jeans and tee shirt. I had decided, years before, to dress in clothes that were comfortable, though, perhaps, not always appropriate. To risk appearing inappropriate, yet not rebellious, demanded that I access a realness and presence within me that could penetrate judgments about my external appearance.

The introduction ended. People applauded politely and the room became silent. I walked to the edge of the stage, stopped, picked up the portable microphone, and breathed fully.

I knew that once I uttered the first word, I had to continue until I finished the talk, just as I had once known, during a parachute jump, that I could worry all the way down or fall in faith, but either way, whether or not the chute opened, the ground would still be there.

I smiled inside, remembering that thought.

As I stood at the edge of the stage, I searched out the eyes of people who appeared receptive—open or, at least, neutral eyes. Mostly, I saw silent anticipation.

Some faces were connected to bodies that appeared to be asleep, lost in the lifelong ritual of showing up somewhere, for something, and not knowing why.

One woman began to doze, her head inching slowly toward her shoulder. She was the inspiration for me to begin. I decided to take the leap.

"It doesn't matter which choice you make," I began, hearing my own voice amplified and echoing in the large auditorium. "One is freeing; the other is secure and familiar."

I was quiet for a minute, allowing the silence to fill the distance between us.

"Standing before you, I realize I am as afraid of receiving your respect as I am of being dismissed. I didn't know that."

Eyes lit up. Bodies sat taller. I hadn't planned to say that. It was not in my notes.

"I have no title for this talk. I'm not even sure what it's about yet. It does have something to do, however, with the trance we all live in daily and don't know we're living in. Actually, most of what I say here is outside our normal belief about what is real. It is outside the reality which you and I construct, that we've been taught to believe."

"We are taught what to believe, you know," I repeated. My words came slowly, so I, too, could feel them as they took form. My fear guided rather than controlled me. I decided that I didn't have to look good or be right; I only wanted to reveal what I saw. I didn't need anyone in the audience to agree with me.

"As children," I continued, "we believed everything we saw, heard, and imagined—even imaginary voices of imaginary friends. Our view of the world was expansive and infinite, before we learned what we should believe."

I felt the interest rise in the room.

"The daily world most of us move in and react to is only a small, tiny piece of what exists and what has yet to be discovered. We are more often operating in a belief system and in a body that is only partly informed, and has only a limited portion of the facts and information readily available, outside the usual learned information system.

"Just outside the belief limits of our vision and thought process is a breathtaking, awesome, wondrous environment every bit as tangible, colorful, and full of information as the ordinary, daily world we live in. There are visual and auditory horizons that extend way beyond the one we normally see as the sun sets."

"For some of you," I added, in response to quizzical looks, "what I say here may not make sense. None of this information may seem right to you, and if that is so, it doesn't matter; I don't require that you see what I see. I do not expect you to. I doubt it myself sometimes. But if you stay with me awhile, you will recognize something. For others of you, what you hear may only be a reminder, and inside, you may hear yourself say, 'Yes, I know that.'"

I heard the shuffling of feet as I walked slowly from one side of the stage to the other. I felt the tension in the room, much of it my own. There was an urgency in the air, the kind of urgency I've felt when struggling to comprehend something I didn't believe I could comprehend and simultaneously judging myself for having that belief.

"Recently," I continued, "a twenty-two-year-old man officially labeled as schizophrenic stood directly in front of me, his face only inches from mine, and said, 'You think I'm standing in front of you. I'm not. I'm really standing behind you. You are just projecting me out here in front of you so that you can learn about a part of yourself.'

"His eyes penetrated my soul as he spoke. The impact of his words startled me, bringing my ego to its knees. My mind attempted to convince me that he didn't know anything, that his words were meaningless. His eyes did not leave mine for a second. I was so moved by his words, which I didn't even yet fully understand, that tears formed involuntarily. I looked at him and all I could say was, 'Oh my God!'"

The woman who had been dozing was now fully awake, her face bright and alive.

"That twenty-two-year-old man," I continued, "taught me that there's nothing wrong with me, that there is nothing wrong with any of us. Everything is wanting to happen. The world is not out of order.

"Open to the possibility that the beliefs and understandings you have about normal, abnormal, right and wrong, good and bad, are no longer relevant.

"We have no more time to explore our history—our mother, father, brother, sister, teachers, or any past traumatic event. And, we don't need to."

I heard sounds of discomfort in the auditorium as solid belief systems came into contact with question. "Place yourself into a world where all behaviors are normal, all human beings, thoughts, fantasies, physical symptoms, and fears are normal. Even abnormal is normal. Imagine you haven't named things in your world yet—that the only descriptions for objects in your environment are descriptions that originate from within you. What would that look like, feel like, and be like?"

I paused and heard someone mutter, "He's crazy."

I appreciated that the person gave voice to what others might be thinking, and I went on.

"Assume that nothing makes sense, everything is unpredictable, and planning for the future means not knowing what's going to happen next week, tomorrow, or even the next hour, and that this feels exciting to you—it's even a relief.

"Believe that your education and necessary survival information come to you in dreams, through direct contact with and observation of others, and when you are completely silent inside. You might even ask yourself what education means and what it is for."

"Huh?" someone responded.

"What if your answer turned out to be that it is for more than to find a job, or to make money and be a formally educated person? What if education has little to do with what you've been told? What if?"

"A story comes to mind, one I haven't told before. I will tell it to you now, although I am not sure why. I suspect we'll all find out by the end of it."

Everyone, including me, settled in to hear a good story.

"This is a 1967 story. I'd completed a second college degree. I had a wife, two children, and a home. I'd been a high school teacher for two years; I'd had a white-collar job with an oil company.

"I was doing everything right to make it in the world of jobs and money. I worked the real world believing it was the only world. I was formally educated and was doing all the right things. I thought I was being a good boy. Yet, doing it right wasn't feeling right. I applied and was hired for a job as a counselor with an experimental Bureau of Indian Affairs (BIA) project. I'd only seen American Indians in the movies, yet I was hired to coordinate a counseling program for a people and a culture I knew nothing about.

"The Bureau transported Indians from tribes and reservations all over the country to an abandoned air force radar station in the hills of a hot valley in central California.

"On paper, the intent of the BIS was to provide help to Indian people of all ages, offering a boarding-school vocational training. Theoretically, graduates would leave reservation life and poverty and go to work in big cities. What I observed, however, was a painful absence of respect for the Indian people.

"When I learned that the real intent of the program was not training but relocation, providing a way for the government to regain control of reservation land, my life changed.

"Simultaneously, all my values, beliefs, and goal-oriented thinking came to an abrupt halt. It became starkly clear to me that the formal education I had so valued had not taught me respect and trust for my own judgment, or that of others. Education had not encouraged me to follow my instincts and intuition or to honor, above all, relationships.

"The money I had sought and the education I had endured satisfied neither my heart nor my spirit. I began to learn what was important to me, and that everything in life is about relationship, that television, clothes, a reputation, and security can be slippery illusions.

"The material world I'd believed was necessary for survival disintegrated, and out of that dust emerged a less predictable, less sure me, but a more real and solid person."

Someone in the audience sneezed a funny sneeze, and laughter broke out.

"Since that time in 1967," I continued softly, as I walked to the edge of the stage, "I've found it easier to question all that I believe to be true. What if I'm my own hero, and my own leader? Then what?"

I sat down on the edge of the stage and breathed deeply. I liked being closer to the people in the front row.

"Decide," I continued, "that women and men no longer project enemy status on to the other gender, that you will no longer blame others for anything because no one is really doing anything to anyone else, ever.

"Imagine that therapists, psychologists, and psychiatrists charge by the quality of your insight and sometimes they pay you for what they learn about themselves.

"Assume that schools become places of wonder, mystery, excitement, cooperation, and enlightenment; that teachers and students share their life experiences with each other from a place of mutual respect; that grades are replaced with the belief that life is a process of learning and, in its natural state, learning does not have to be taught. Instead, you know that all people are wanting to grow, learn, and use themselves completely."

I saw many smiles. We were all more at ease.

"We might even all agree," I whispered into the microphone, "that life comes complete with built-in wonder, excitement, and thrill."

Someone jumped up and yelled "Yes!" then sat down, embarrassed.

"Imagine that children and adults of all ages, races, sizes, and sexual beliefs," I continued, "want to know more about each other—not to judge and separate but to discover one another, to view each other with wonder, even to see a part of themselves in the other person.

"Imagine that."

Two people in the back walked out. My instinct was to question myself. Was I losing everyone? Was I all alone with these thoughts? Did the two people who left represent others who wanted to leave? Were the remaining people too shy to leave? In a microsecond, all my self-doubt came to the surface.

"Oh damn, I'm a fraud," I heard the voice inside me say. "I have nothing important to say. I'm just fooling myself." I allowed the thoughts to fade in favor of going on, fool or not.

"This imagined world is happening now, in this room," I continued. "In physics, energy follows thought; how you perceive things is how they are. How you view the world, yourself, and each daily event is exactly how it will be for you."

I smiled, realizing that I was saying things I hadn't heard before. I felt the excitement of being my own audience.

"What you believe is true," a female voice yelled from the back of the room.

"Yes," I responded.

"The present collective belief about human behavior and psychology requires a polarity: those who are identified as having problems and those who allegedly fix the problems, the healers and experts who perceive themselves as more together.

"For this polarized system to work efficiently, there must be a sufficient number of problems to fix, and you must perceive yourself as not together. You must believe that in the future you will have it together, and that later you will be happier and more satisfied with your life. Not now. Later. Tomorrow, you must hope, will be better. Today isn't."

The person who had jumped up earlier stood again and yelled, "Yes, yes, yes!" then sat down, smiling.

Her enthusiasm was contagious. It seemed as though the entire auditorium was speaking the same language. It didn't matter if everything was understood or whether we were all in agreement. What did matter was that we weren't competing to be right: there was nothing to prove.

"Current psychology and cultural practice," I said in a relaxed and smiling voice, "is based on what could and should be. It is based on what we think is missing from our lives now, and how we believe that our life is not happening as it should be. It is about how we want to feel and be in years to come."

Maybe I was meant to hear it, maybe not, but I heard another voice say, "He's criticizing everything I believe in."

"There are cultural beliefs," I went on, "about personal relationships, global chaos, family dysfunction, racism, sexism, addiction, violence, disease, and sexuality. Among these beliefs is that all of these things are outside our individual control—that we are powerless.

"Today's psychology is based on tomorrow: on what could and should be and what might happen in the future. It is about how you want to feel and be, eventually.

"Future Psychology is about mystery and what wants to be revealed in any given moment. It is based on how much information you are willing to handle—you must call it forth.

"It's not even about psychology. It's more about perception and stepping back from who you think you are. It's about making a decision to not have to know.

"Future Psychology requires an internal shift where you feel and see, for yourself, that there is nothing wrong: there is nothing to fix and nothing to heal. You see the world in yourself instead of yourself in the world."

I found myself looking into an audience of receptive eyes.

"What is happening in your life now is right for you; you are always doing what is right and don't know it. What I say here, I am not attached to. I do not have to be right. I do not need your agreement. This is not the only way to see the world. It may not even be a way. I have no need to convince you of anything. This information may make sense to you. It may not. Either one or both are correct."

"Huh?" I heard again.

There was a tingle in my spine. It shot up and out through my eyes.

"There was a time when I thought I knew how people should behave, feel, react, and express themselves. I knew what normal and abnormal were. I just knew for sure what appropriate, mentally healthy behavior looked and sounded like in the standard-human-being-person.

"I believed I had the answers for others and that with my professional training, guidance, and encouragement, I could, single-handedly, cure, heal, and bring about a fully functioning human being, based on my beliefs of what one looked like."

"Yes," someone spontaneously interjected.

"I learned to believe that my body was a home for disease, headaches, backaches, and a variety of pains and illnesses requiring store-bought drugs to numb, hide, and kill any unusual sensation or symptom.

"I expected to get sick; it's what humans do. My body seemed to belong to unseen germs, viruses, and fate. I believed that my mind and my emotions were destined to be depressed, moody, and negatively affected by traumatic life events. It was inevitable, I thought, that something awful would happen to me, or that it had already, when I was little; that I would have to devote decades toward healing the hurts so I could live without hurting and feeling victim to life itself. That's what I believed."

A few people started to applaud.

"I no longer know what is right or normal for other people. But I do know how to help them find out what is right for them.

"A woman once told me that she had abandonment issues from childhood. As if on cue, she began to recite her childhood story in an attempt to explain the current condition of her life.

"A minute into her story, I asked her how she abandons herself now, today. Startled by the question, she stopped, and an expression of wonder crossed her face. Her eyes went blank as if in a trance. We both sat in silence until suddenly she began to laugh. Her laughter became contagious, and soon we were both laughing out of control. We couldn't speak.

"When one of us managed to squeeze out a word, or looked at the other, we'd begin laughing again amidst incomplete sentences.

"Unexpectedly, she stopped laughing, stood up to gather her belongings, and turned toward me with only a soft, relaxed smile remaining. Standing directly in front of me, she said, 'My abandonment issue is not with events of yesterday; it is how I abandon myself every day when I believe someone else's perception first, before I believe my own. It is when I say yes because I'm afraid to say no. It is when I do something from habit instead of from heart. It is when I ask a therapist to tell me what is real and true, instead of asking myself and trusting the answer. It is when I see myself as a victim and blame someone for something.

'I abandon myself when I believe I'm powerless and affirm this with my own thoughts. I abandon myself when I believe something is missing in my life, when I believe I have no control, no power, and act as though I'm not in charge. I abandon myself when I see a parent yank their child around and I say nothing.

'I have no one to blame. Nothing is missing in my life, nor has it ever been missing.'

"She walked toward the door, opened it, and said, 'I take myself back. I am home. We will meet next time as friends over tea.'

"Quietly, she closed the door behind her. From down the hallway, I heard her scream, 'I did it! I'm free!'"

"If you choose to view the world differently, as she did, what would it look like? One different view might be to see that everything is about relationship. There is nothing wrong. No one is avoiding anything. There is order within chaos and you don't have to know what you're doing. It helps to recognize that relationships serve as a practice field for awareness and personal insight, that there are no boundaries or limits even when you attempt to set them.

"To be in life this way requires an inner discipline: paying attention to every thought, feeling, and physical symptom without self-judgment or analysis. You learn to get out of your own way, stepping out of beliefs and learned theories and, instead, observing yourself and others from a sense of wonder. This way of being in the world requires recognizing that perceived life difficulties don't need long periods of time to change. What used to take months and years to resolve can happen in minutes."

We were all quiet.

"'In the Beginner's mind,' Shunyru Suzuki wrote, 'there are many possibilities. In the Expert's, there are few.'"

I stepped back from the edge of the stage. A few hands came together in polite applause followed by a rolling wave of applause. A few people stood up. Soon, everyone was standing, applauding, smiling. A surge of shyness shot up my spine, leading me to the brink of lowering my head like a child in a classroom, trying to hide by not looking. For a moment, I wanted to become invisible.

I encouraged myself to take it in and feel the acknowledgment completely. I stood tall, bringing myself fully into my body. I smiled back into the applauding eyes, receiving their appreciation and feeling.

I thanked everyone and walked off the stage like a tiger.

2

Banana Man

My father, a fifty-six-year-old man with facial skin as smooth as a child's, leaned through the open window of my car to kiss me on the cheek. My hands rested on the steering wheel as I moved into his kiss, receiving it fully.

I placed my cheek next to his and whispered, "I love you." I hadn't said that to him before. I didn't plan it. The words just came out. He stepped back in tears.

I was twenty-three years old. I don't remember his verbal response. I do remember his cheek next to mine. A few days later, he died of a heart attack. I saw him buried and I thought that was the end of my life with my very funny father.

"Why are you telling me this story?" Meigra asked. I'd met Meigra two years earlier. We'd been together ever since. She was the first person I'd ever been with who I was willing to follow anywhere. She met me, unafraid, her full self always present. She was her own person.

"I'm not sure," I replied. "He died thirty years ago."

"Must be about something that will happen tonight," Meigra suggested.

"Maybe. His favorite place, when we moved from New York to California in the 1940s, was Carlsbad Caverns, here in New Mexico."

"Strange, huh? Let's close our eyes," Meigra said. She fell asleep instantly.

We were camping in the mountains of New Mexico; our tent was waterlogged from the continuous rain. Lightning was exploding all around us, and thunder cracking the air, both exciting me and teasing my fear of instant death. Hesitantly, I followed Meigra into deep sleep, not sure I'd see another day.

A burst of lightning struck nearby, and a thunderous crack startled me to sit up in fear for our lives. I anticipated the tall tree by our tent toppling, crushing us beneath the canvas.

I was scaring myself and I knew it. I opened the tent flap to look outside. Mysteriously, the sound and light storm had disappeared. There was only darkness and calm; a breeze was blowing through a moonless sky. I could see only black shadows within black shadows.

I had to pee and, to do that, I had to leave the tent. "If lightning doesn't get me," I said to Meigra as she slept, "then something in my imagination will." My physical need pulled me out of the tent toward a small clearing twenty feet away.

As I stood urinating, my head turning quickly, first to the right, then to the left, searching for monsters and stray lightning bolts, I focused on relaxing to avoid thinking myself into panic. Standing alone in the dark, silent night, I felt a soft pinch on my right hip. I spun around to see if Meigra was playing around.

No one was there.

I froze, scanning my mind to find a rational explanation for the pinch. The only logical one was that somehow, Meigra had snuck up behind me, pinched me, and run twenty feet to the tent in less than a second. To appease my fear and allow my body to move, I accepted that explanation.

Before the improbability of that illogical thought took hold, I bolted for the tent. I dove in, nearly missing the opening, and scrambled for my sleeping bag, believing I was safe from everything when beneath covers with my favorite pillow.

"Meigra," I called out, recalling that she was never afraid of the same things I was.

"What's happening?" she asked sleepily

"I was standing outside," I answered from beneath the cover of my sleeping bag, "about twenty feet away and you pinched me."

"No I didn't," she replied, "I've been asleep. I haven't left the tent."

"Stop playing around," I insisted.

"I'm not playing."

"If you didn't, then who did?"

"Who did?" she asked back, without taking on the responsibility of my distress. I appreciated that she took the event seriously rather than laughing it off.

"This may sound crazy," I blurted out, sitting up quickly, "but my father used to pinch me playfully in the same place, with the same pressure, when I was little—but that's absurd."

"It may be absurd," Meigra insisted, "but that doesn't mean it didn't happen."

I looked into her eyes and saw that she was serious. "Thanks, Meigra," I said, "I'll go to sleep with that intriguing thought." I let it be and fell into a dream.

In the dream, my father stepped out of an elevator that had just descended from upper levels. He walked into the empty courtroom where I was standing. He came over and stood in front of me, looking into my eyes.

"What do you want?" I asked. "Why are you here?"

Silence.

When he chose to answer, it was less a direct response to my question than information I was to hear. In a voice reflecting the highest authority imaginable, he said, "Your life is about justice and fairness."

The force of his words traveled throughout my body, down to the soles of my feet. I was mute; there was nothing to say. I heard him. He did not linger to see if I had heard him. He didn't need to; his intent was clear. Therefore I had to hear him. I had no option. As the dream was ending, he turned and walked to the elevator, entered, and pushed the "Up" button. The doors closed and he disappeared.

I woke up and nudged Meigra awake.

"You remember asking me why I was telling you the story of my father?" I asked excitedly.

"Yes."

"'Cause he was just here," I said.

"Here?"

"Yes, in my dream. At least, it seemed like a dream."

Meigra listened attentively to the details of my dream. After a brief silence she simply said, "Yes." The way she said yes, I knew there were no more words.

We got dressed, packed up our belongings, and continued traveling toward Taos, New Mexico. We had decided to move to Taos, not knowing exactly why.

Arriving in Taos for the first time, we walked into Dori's Cafe and Bakery, a small coffeehouse on the edge of town, tucked away behind trees and off the main street. The coffee-house appeared to be more for locals than tourists, since it was some distance from the main part of town. We'd found it only because we weren't looking for it.

While Dori was preparing our order, she casually asked where I was from.

"California," I answered.

"Oh yeah?" Dori said. "I grew up in California but probably long before your time. Been in Taos for thirty years."

She was making our sandwiches with her back to us.

"Where'd you grow up?" she asked.

"Los Angeles, but I left there in 1960," I replied.

"I grew up in L.A. too," she said, "What high school did you go to?"

"Manual Arts High," I answered, assuming she'd never heard of it.

"Manual Arts?" she said in a surprised voice. "I went there too, but again, probably long before your time. What junior high?"

"Audubon," I answered.

"Me too," she said, her voice escalating into excitement as she halved our sandwiches. What grammar school?"

"Angeles Mesa," I replied.

Dori turned around to face us, a sandwich on a plate in each hand.

"Me too," she said. "What's your name?"

When she heard my name, she jumped into the air, sending the plates and sandwiches flying. She ran around the counter and hugged me. "I'm Doris Boles," she said excitedly. "I'm Doris Boles."

We hugged each other in disbelief.

Doris and I had first met in the third grade and hadn't seen each other since the first year of high school, forty years earlier. While we asked each other questions, Dori was making new sandwiches, on the house.

"Where have you been the last forty years?" she asked.

"Where have I been the last forty years?" I repeated, both to myself and out loud for Dori to hear. I wanted my answer to be thoughtful, one that would translate four decades of time and space into something meaningful, bringing us both into the present. I had no interest in reciting year-by-year events, relationship highlights, or the usual activities that mark one's life. I wanted us to meet in the present.

I didn't push for an answer. I let it come on its own.

"I think I've died a dozen times, Dori," I replied instinctively. "The world you and I grew up in doesn't exist anymore for me."

I knew Dori would either join me or think I was strange.

"I know what you mean," she replied.

"Actually," I continued, "most of how I was even a year ago is now meaningless. I no longer know exactly what I'm doing anymore, and that's okay with me."

Dori handed us the sandwiches and sat down. "You know," she said, "I don't have any memory of or interest in the past anymore. Even now as I sit here with you, I'm deeply moved

but it has something to do with why you're here and . . . and
. . . I don't know."

Dori looked around the room to see how private our conversation was. "You were special to me when you were twelve
years old and you are now," she said in all seriousness.
"Showing up now, for whatever reason, is just the right thing.
Your being here is reminding me of something I'd forgotten
long ago. I can't even tell you what it is yet, but I feel it inside.
You carry something within you that calms me when I'm in
your presence."

"I believe you, but I don't feel it," I replied.

"That's good," she said. "You can almost have greater
impact when it lies innocent within you. I don't know why, but
I want you to meet someone. I want you to call him."

"Who is this person?" Meigra asked, curious.

"His name is Jarid. He grew up in Los Angeles, was a child
actor. He was a rock singer in a garage band, a high school
dropout with straight A's," Dori answered.

"He had always been meticulous with his dress and appearance. He used to surf; he read metaphysics, the Bible, the
Koran, mystery novels. His parents supported everything he
did. His mother was a hands-on healer, and his father,
although they were divorced in a friendly way, was a long-haul
truck driver."

She paused. "I don't know him well, I only know that you
must meet one another."

The next day I was walking on a hot, dusty road with a not-
so-normal person who wore clothes that hung everywhere but
directly on his body. He had been identified, in the opinion
and diagnosis of a university-trained psychiatrist, as a schizophrenic.

We had agreed to meet on the Gorge Bridge, a 650-foot-high
structure of steel spanning the Rio Grande that provides walkers, as well as drivers, a spectacular, sometimes scary view of
the canyon and river below.

I had arrived first, just before dark, at the east end of the bridge. I parked my car and walked along the footpath to the middle of the span, the highest point above the Rio Grande. The setting sun was barely touching the land, inching toward the edge of the world. The sunset rolled up slowly, like a window shade opening to the night, casting long shadows. The red sky filled my senses.

A strong wind blew around and through me. Dark thunderclouds were perched everywhere; lightning formed a 360-degree curtain of excitement.

I thought I saw Jarid walking toward me from the west side of the bridge, about a hundred yards away. He seemed to match the physical description given to me, except for his clothes, which Dori had described as meticulous. He walked a walk I had never seen before, as though he were completely autonomous, unentangled in the personal world I was so familiar with. Even far away, I had the feeling he was really right next to me—that physical distance wasn't really an essential issue with him.

It was as though earthly physics did not apply to Jarid. I felt his presence long before I could actually see his face clearly. I stood at a place on the footpath that protruded over the canyon, scary but thrilling.

Jarid walked right up to me until he was only a few inches from my face, a distance that normally would be too close for comfort. Our eyes met in a strange recognition. I had the feeling that, even though I had never met him, I knew him well. I wanted to be scared; instead, I felt mysteriously at ease.

Just to be sure, I asked, "Jarid?"

"I'm Jarid."

It was easy for him to look into me. His eyes commanded, "I'm here. Are you?" His gaze was accompanied by a slight, knowing smile.

He seemed to scan my energy body, as though I were part of a Star Trek episode. We stood there for several minutes, our eyes being the only form of contact. I felt a burning sensation around my heart, something I'd never experienced before.

Lightning danced around us, sending out feelers seeking receptive points to strike and energize. The bridge and the horizon became backdrops for the brilliant, explosive display.

The wind pushed against us as we steadied ourselves by holding onto the railing of the steel structure sixty-five stories above the river. I felt the bridge vibrate as a car drove by at high speed, heading into the desert.

We had yet to say hello. Instead, his eyes still holding my full attention, Jarid slowly shuffled in a circle around my body, returning to his original position directly in front of me. He moved closer so that our eyes met at the same level, only inches apart.

He held my attention with his piercing eyes.

"There is no more time to work on things. There is no past to heal," he said in a voice of absolute authority.

I knew exactly what he meant and, simultaneously, I didn't know anything. The dilemma didn't matter. This was not a rational mind experience. His words would never make sense. Being in his presence was an emotional relief. I had no questions.

Jarid's eyes were clean, exact, softly penetrating, and true. I felt his meaning, but I had a difficult time completely believing that the experience was happening.

He was seeing in my eyes what I was seeing in his. My face remained calm and receptive to his intense look. My body was stunned into shifting and changing its perspective.

Jarid began walking toward the west end of the bridge and into the desert sagebrush. I ran to catch up with him. He didn't seem to notice whether I was there or not.

As we walked together on a narrow road, he performed physical antics that would, by everyday standards, be considered bizarre and probably crazy. In one move he abruptly stopped walking, stood with one leg wrapped around the other like a vine crawling up a pole and, without bending his knees, reached down to touch the ground.

Untangling his legs, he stood up and gracefully spun around several times as though being pulled in circles by an unseen force. I followed beside him as he walked forward again.

A minute later, without rotating his body, he turned his head in my direction, his eyes reaching for and finding mine. With a smile that seemed to know the whys of the universe, he winked, looked away, and did a double take to check my response. My dazzled expression satisfied him.

"Hummm," he said, as though I hadn't done too badly.

We walked side by side in easy silence until, without warning, Jarid slowly crumbled to the ground, his limber body going limp like a string puppet being placed in its box. On his knees, like a Muslim in prayer, he kissed the dirt road respectfully.

He remained in this humble position for several minutes, then simply stood up and continued walking without comment, as though our pace hadn't changed.

"I had a dream last night about exactly what you're doing right now," I said to Jarid excitedly.

I expected him to say, "Like what." Instead, he had no response at all. He said nothing. I was so excited by the similarity of the dream and what Jarid had just done, that I decided to tell him, even if he wasn't interested.

"The man in the dream could do anything with his body," I began. "He could twist and distort his body in ways no one else could. You couldn't touch him if he didn't choose to be touched. Because of his unusual behavior, the police came to arrest him but couldn't get hold of his body because of his ability to move swiftly and lightly."

Jarid appeared indifferent as we walked.

"In the dream," I continued, using dramatic hand gestures, "each physical movement was a teaching. The man wasn't resisting arrest; he was demonstrating the principle that you're always free, no matter where you are. The authorities or police couldn't understand that."

Jarid was silent.

"The dream man understood the why of everything, including the universe," I went on, "so he knew how to maneuver his body to elude those wanting to arrest him; he was practicing an undiscovered form of physics. As the dream figure man, a man in his early twenties, and I were walking together, I asked him . . ."

Jarid interrupted, "You asked him, 'What is everything in the world about?'"

"Yes, how did you know that?"

"What else would you ask him?"

"Well, he didn't answer," I said.

"So you asked again, what's it all about? Right?"

"Yeah," I said, "and still the man did not answer. But then something changed. I didn't need the answer anymore. I wanted the answer but I didn't need it. When I asked the same question from wonder instead of fear and urgency, he answered me."

"Hmmm," Jarid said. I expected him to ask what the dream man said.

"The dream figure said that he understood the law of the universe which allowed him to perform seemingly impossible feats. I was surprised, even in the dream, how easily I could get such big information simply by asking.

"He said that when I'm truly willing to know what everything is about, I simply must ask questions clearly, without a specific agenda and from a wondrous place. Especially, he repeated, the question has to come from a wondrous place within me, with no fear attached.

"The purpose of a question," he said, "is to wake me up, as well as the person of whom I ask the question. If there is fear in the question, I will receive a fearful answer. If inside me, the answer doesn't matter, then I will have replaced judgment with respect, and the answer will be expansive and illuminating."

Jarid rolled his eyes, implying that my information was basic. I knew he was right, but I still didn't get it completely.

"The man," I continued, "told me that when I'm in a place of wonder, I'd be ready to know the answer and I could hear him without confusion. The dream ended with him advising me that there is no purpose in speaking when you can't be heard. He called himself the Banana Man."

Jarid spun around in place and lightly stepped from one foot to the other, moving forward at the same time. About twenty feet ahead of me he stopped, turned in my direction, bowed, and fell to the ground smiling. Then he stood with his back to me.

I felt tingly and hot all over.

"Jarid," I asked, "are you the Banana Man?"

Acting as though he hadn't heard my question, he formed exactly the same body configuration as the man in my dream. With his chin nearly touching his knee, he looked up with an expression that said, "Of course! So?"

"Jarid," I said, "this is too much."

In the fading light, we walked in silence through the high desert sagebrush along the canyon rim. I was with a seemingly crazy teacher, the kind of teacher I had never found in a classroom.

Occasionally, Jarid's attention would be drawn to a specific object nestled in the sand: a bottle cap, a leaf, a matchbook, an item unidentifiable. As if performing a sacred ritual, he'd bend over and pick up something, inspect it, then tell a brief story about its history and purpose. Sometimes, he'd put it in his pants pocket.

"What's this?" Jarid whispered as he knelt down to pick up a pebble. He placed it next to his cheek, licked it, and returned it to its original resting place on the sand.

"Why did you lick the pebble?" I asked, intrigued.

"It was hot from the sun," he answered, his voice reflecting the respect he felt. "I cooled it off some."

Even though we were about the same height and weight, and I was thirty years older, Jarid's physical presence was almost overwhelming. Sometimes, I felt small and emotionally young around him, especially if I got lost in comparing us. Something about being with Jarid challenged the internal list I carried of lifetime accomplishments—the last refuge for believing my self-image.

An unbridled, vital energy radiated from him. Yet his words, if heard literally, made little sense. From the ordinary, every-day, common point of view, nothing Jarid said was logical or resembled anything anywhere near normal.

"Normally," I said to myself, "Jarid would be identified as abnormal, schizophrenic, delusional—anything but wise and brilliant, possibly a seer of things I could not yet see. Now I know why Dori wanted me to be with him."

I heard the conservative, traditional voice inside me say things like, "He needs medication, hospitalization, profession-al help." Then I heard another voice—the one that gravitates toward the unusual, the unknown and has no limits, rules, or social constraints. This voice, the explorer, wants to embrace all inexplicable experiences, especially if they are sponta-neous, instinctive, and probably not okay with most people.

Since childhood, I've cherished my explorer tendencies, the ones that helped me expand my perceived limits about people and life, the ones that helped me see weirdness as part of a much larger world. The explorer didn't need to make sense, and wasn't supposed to. Walking in this setting, I was pre-pared for the unusual. As I looked into the darkened canyon, listening to the river below, I heard another voice within me speak. For a second, I tensed, frightened at hearing a voice from nowhere in particular, without the usual body to visual-ly relate to. Then I listened.

"Stretch your awareness to include the illogical," the voice said. "Stretch your feelings beyond what you think you know. Jarid is your teacher in the form of an identified ill person. Listen with your instinct, not your mind."

"Oh come on," I said out loud. "This isn't Star Wars."

Jarid must have heard me. He turned his face toward mine and smiled.

There was now a full summer moon to illuminate our path. As we walked, I listened not only to Jarid's occasional words but also to my outwardly silent judgments, my attempts to find a box to fit him in. I was now hearing more voices coming from inside me, voices that brought me to the brink of believing I was crazy, out of control, and would go berserk at any moment.

Just as I thought I would physically panic, my mind emptied. I had no thoughts. I was blank. I was aware only of Jarid, the moon, and the terrain. That was all that mattered. I was staring at the moon, wondering if a werewolf would jump out from somewhere. The illogical washed in like light into a darkened room.

"The illogical is translucent," Jarid said, more to himself than directed at me.

"What?" I asked, distracted and puzzled by his comment. He didn't answer and I didn't pursue it.

We'd been walking for hours, turning around now only because we'd reached the edge of a canyon wall, with nowhere to go but five hundred feet straight down.

I was physically and emotionally exhausted. Jarid turned and faced me. Like a cobra, his eyes locked in on mine, as though he were looking deeply into the world through me. I was surprised at how clearly I could see his face in the moonlight.

"Don't ever interfere with another person's path," he said softly, then repeated, this time with a penetrating seriousness, "even when you think you're standing up for someone out of justice and fairness, don't ever interfere with another person's path."

Apparently seeing my dazed response, he reached out and gently placed his hand on my shoulder. "You do too much work for other people," he said. "Don't. Stop it. If you are to be useful to someone, you will know. They will call you to them in some way. If you attempt to fix them, make them more like you believe they should be, you are denying them the experiences they need, and have asked for.

"Just as each and every event in your life had to happen the way it did to bring you here, the same is true of others. Let them be. Be useful only when you are asked, and when they are ready."

I took a step back. I needed more space to absorb his words. "I know I am having illusions," he said, as though he could see I needed calming, "but the world is an illusion."

My body began to tremble gently and, for the first time, I felt cold, even though the temperature must have been near seventy degrees. We stood at the edge of the canyon, looking out through darkness toward the horizon. It seemed to be, at once, only an arm's length and also a hundred miles away.

Under his breath, and barely audible, as though speaking directly to the night, Jarid said, "Don't shame those who need help. The fear and anger you see in me, I carry because I can. They are not a burden: it is my work. I am not a victim to my life. My work is to live myself completely, no matter what others may think of me."

He looked at me as though he expected me to know what he meant. "We are all given emotional and spiritual tasks in this world that seem uncomfortable. This discomfort is to help you realize that what disturbs you the most is what you most need in your life until you decide not to be disturbed."

He didn't stop. I heard my thoughts trying to convince me to discount him, to not allow myself to be his student, and wondering how a person thirty years younger could know more than me. Yet, he was teaching me, and I was his student. I was being humbled and knew it.

Jarid gazed into the desert, his profile silhouetted against the full moon. A soft breeze filled the space between us.

"You can recognize the outer world disturbance as exactly mirroring what you need to see in yourself," he continued, "When you are around other people or events that disturb you or seem crazy, you are getting a chance to work with yourself. When there is someone in your life bugging you, that is their function. They bring up from within you exactly those things that disturb you. They become your teachers."

My mind recoiled, seeking justification for itself and its thoughts, as it was slowly being disassembled, belief by belief.

"The people who trouble and disturb you," he said, as if revealing an immense truth to all living things, "will literally change in front of your eyes if you want them to. How you view them and react is up to you. They are being who they are. What you do with what you see is up to you. No one does this for you. No one is supposed to do it for you. Not therapists, not close friends. No one."

He leaned into my shoulder and whispered in my ear, as though the information he was about to reveal was so delicate it would break with too much volume.

"What you do," he said, "with those in your life who disturb you—in this case, me—must come entirely from inside of you. It is an action of your spirit. It is your ultimate inner discipline—an emotional martial art. To act from a place inside you that you've never acted from before, requires the ability to observe yourself being the way you are at any given moment, observing as an unbiased witness. It is a form of meditation, the martial art of emotions. You do what you do and you observe yourself doing it."

We started to walk back toward the bridge, hours away. As if on cue, I stumbled over some brush and fell onto my hands.

"You do what you do and you observe yourself doing it," he said, as I picked myself up. His rhythm didn't change. He used my actions to make his point.

"There is no intent to analyze or change what you observe," he continued. "You simply notice. That's awareness. Your greatest protection is your awareness—not guns, police, or security systems. Awareness is your greatest protection. That's your work."

He paused to notice my reaction.

"You, however," he said with a smile, "in any given moment, believe you should be doing something else, other than what you are doing." I was humbled, and I was listening. Jarid was coherent, insightful, expressive, and clear, the opposite of how

I would have described his behavior an hour earlier. I couldn't understand what had changed. Where was Jarid when he wasn't with me in this way? Where was I when I wasn't with him in this way? How could he spend almost twenty-four hours a day, one dimension away from the world most people live in, and then, in an instant, become a wise and brilliant visionary? "I know," he said, somehow having heard my thoughts, "you wonder if I've been playing mind games with people, right? Because you can understand me now? Maybe you can hear me now because your mind is no longer in the way. Is that possible?"

"How do you know all this?" I asked, "and how come no one can see who you are?" His face softened, and, almost inaudibly, Jarid whispered, "You know, you know," then stepped back.

I thought I knew what he meant, but I wasn't sure, at least not sure in the usual way that I'd been sure in the past. Knowing what he was saying was like trying to describe the taste of chocolate without tasting it.

I began yawning, though I wasn't tired and I certainly was not bored. I was losing energy as if I'd run ten miles without stopping. My mind was closing down. My thoughts were about eating, sleeping and watching television. I was antsy. My body felt like it was being squished between two walls.

Doubts about what was happening between Jarid and I dominated my mind. Then I remembered the last line from a dream I'd had a couple of days earlier: "Believe your doubts. Believe everything. Let your doubts be stepping stones through the swamp."

The words reminded me to respect the doubt without having to take any action. Some unidentified voice inside me said that doubt isn't a bad or wrong thing. Doubt is like a warning light reminding me to pay complete attention to what I'm doing.

I was feeling claustrophobic, overwhelmed by all that was happening, as if being squeezed into too tight a space all at once.

I noticed Jarid staring at me and, although it was dark, I believed his look to be one of compassion. I even anticipated that he was about to speak. I couldn't prove it. I could feel it.

"When you feel compressed," he said, again dazzling me with his ability to hear my thoughts, "expand your consciousness beyond where you believe you can. The compression feeling is your expanded consciousness in conflict with old consciousness, or what you believe you cannot do."

I knew the truth of what he said but couldn't believe he was able to do what he was doing—listening to my thoughts. I soon realized that Jarid only spoke when I wasn't thinking thoughts. He spoke in the silent moments between my internal debates. That's why he had nothing to say to me most of the time. I must have had a momentary internal silence because Jarid began talking nonstop. "When you're being aware," he said, "which means you are paying attention to everything, go inside and expand your consciousness, your attitude;. Empty your mind. Shift to a beginner's mind."

Jarid's voice seemed to carry the authority of a thousand years; his clarity was seductive. As much as I wanted to doubt where his wisdom could have come from, I couldn't doubt the truth of it. I knew he could feel my discomfort and how his words challenged the limits I placed on my imagination.

We were now walking at a faster pace along the canyon rim. The moon, beginning to set, still illuminated our way.

As he stood facing me, I asked, "Are you someone who sees so much in people that it's too much to absorb and live with in an ordinary, everyday state of being?"

"Huh?" he responded, and I laughed.

I either had to discount Jarid or expand myself so I could see not only what I see but what he sees. I was afraid I'd go crazy if I accepted the fact that he was brilliant instead of weird. I had to get bigger myself or discount him.

Could it be, I wondered, that those people I judge as being on the fringe, disturbed, mentally ill, and psychotic represent parts of me that I ignore, fear, and repress? Do I console myself by only seeing others as strange, unusual, and disturbed?

"This may be a crazy question, Jarid, " I asked, "but how am I schizophrenic?"

He started to walk faster, this time directly in front of me. He wasn't ignoring me; he was simply indifferent to the question.

"How am I schizophrenic, Jarid?" I asked again. "I hear voices inside all the time, but I call them thoughts and legitimate concerns. If I really pay attention, I realize that I have a constant dialogue going on in my head with people I rarely see or haven't seen in years. Usually, I don't speak out loud to them but sometimes I do, without realizing it, and I scare myself."

Jarid stepped up the pace, but what I was saying was informing me even if Jarid had little interest.

"I must be crazy, too, Jarid. I just haven't been found out and diagnosed yet. I'm still disguised as a normal person operating within a normal range, able to observe myself enough to selectively choose my behavior so others won't be too uncomfortable."

I thought Jarid was still ahead of me until I felt a tap on my shoulder. Startled, I turned to see him at my side, leaning so close I feared he'd accidentally nudge me over the canyon edge.

With his mouth only inches from my ear, he began to whisper so quietly that I could barely hear him, yet I knew that to ask him to speak up would disrupt information I might never hear again. I sensed that I had to slow down inside and listen with soft ears, even if I thought I couldn't hear all he was saying.

"You tend to personalize things; I don't," he said, sounding as though he was speaking in slow motion. His words were alive and without blame. He wasn't just informing me of something, he was drawing something out of me—directly out of my body.

"You experience self-doubt and blame yourself," he continued, still whispering. "You think that your thoughts and self-scolding are yours only, believing they are a very personalized, individual thing. This feels true to you, but you are also picking up the environment and the people around you. Everyone hides amidst their self-doubt and self-blame.

"All of what people carry hidden within them comes through you. It comes through me. It settles in like rain. All of what happens in your life is not yours alone."

Hearing that, my eyes blurred with tears.

"You work on behalf of others," he said. "Your personal life difficulties, dramas, and crises are necessary for you to develop and define yourself."

I was fading, lost in the language and scope of what he was saying. I'd read about these concepts; now Jarid's words and presence demanded that I bring them into my life and apply them.

"You are stepping out of the world of the known into that of the unknown," he continued. "For some people—those who need to know why they do what they do—this can feel difficult and uncomfortable. They are conditioned to having to know why. What you must do now requires not knowing why and not needing to.

"It is in this silent void, where there are no 'shoulds' or 'oughts,' that your perception shifts and your relationships change. This way of being—entering into inner magic places, and recognizing everyday relationship difficulties as part of your practice—will change your life.

"You will feel quieter. Calmer. You'll feel more at home inside, more inspired. Your relationships with people will change now. Your emotional responses and reactions will be different, and you'll be surprised. You may find yourself asking how you just did what you did. Physical symptoms will move, change, disappear, and reappear, minute by minute."

Suddenly, I felt tightness in my neck and around my shoulders. I was bombarded with a variety of physical symptoms. My lower back was pulsating. My head hurt. My eyes felt as though they'd been looking directly into the sun. My hands trembled, and my stomach cinched up into a knot. I was

afraid I was going to die or, at least, become completely inca-
pacitated and fall over.

Jarid leaned into my shoulder even more, almost pushing
me forward along with him. He didn't pause, even though it
must have been obvious that I wasn't doing well. Then he
moved slowly around behind me to whisper in my other ear.
Smiling, I had the thought that maybe each ear was designed
to receive specific information. Even less audibly than before,
and more slowly, he went on.

"There is a belief that when you're around other people—
family or others in your life who don't seem to change—and
you see yourself as having tried everything, your just cause to
change them is hopeless. You then either give up, feel frus-
trated, or write them off. Instead, what you must do is change
your perception."

"Why don't they simply change," I thought to myself, laughing at the absurdity, "instead of me having to change my perception?"

"You, in particular, must change your perception because
you can," Jarid insisted over my internal humor. "It is you that
must change to internally embrace and allow others to be who
and whatever they are. When you do that, they change."

I thought, "This must be what going crazy is like," but I did
not know what crazy meant anymore. I could feel Jarid smiling beside me. I could actually feel the smile without seeing it.

"When you think you might be going crazy," he continued,
as though he were hearing my thoughts through my ears,
"you are. Going crazy is a good thing. "It's much worse to go
sane. As your awareness wants to expand and grow, just like
your body, you go through extreme states; at least, to you
they're extreme. Some would call you psychotic. You have sui-
cidal thoughts, think you are worthless and that nothing matters anymore. You believe you are always on the verge of a
panic attack.

"Truth is, nothing does matter—not the way it has always
mattered to you before. When you notice that what was mean-

ingful yesterday may become meaningless tomorrow, then you are on the right track.

"If you don't freak out at the possibility of freaking out, or label your experience as something wrong or negative, the belief in you that fears chaos will, within seconds, reveal a changing inner structure. This is what is happening. Your inner structure—everything you've been taught to believe and live by, the foundation and reference point for all you do—is changing. It is breaking up."

"But . . . ," I began, as I attempted to intercede. I wanted to scream, "Wait a minute. I'm feeling too much. I can't handle all this." Again, Jarid was ahead of me.

"You will know all this instantly," he said, "as you allow yourself to ride through feelings more extreme, frightening, intense, and exhilarating than you've ever allowed yourself to feel. That's why race car drivers race cars, why football players play football, why musicians play music."

"What? What are you talking about?" I said, reacting in a tone lacking composure. I believed Jarid's mind was drifting, that his attention was gone. I couldn't imagine what race car drivers and football players had to do with what we were talking about.

"What do those examples have to do with feelings?" I eventually asked more calmly.

"Those activities," he answered, "allow them to feel completely, to feel everything completely through, fully. The drama of their physical movement brings out the feeling, the energy. Feeling is feeling, no matter how you access it or how you find it. No one feeling is any different from another. Only the identity of its source varies."

Jarid must have perceived my self-judgment comparing my ability to do one thing or another better or worse than someone else. I could tell by the way he took a quick glance in my direction and shook his head.

"You never come out right with that one," he said. "Can't. The very act of comparing implies that you've already judged and discounted yourself. Even if you conclude that you're good or better, that decision is only valid until the next moment. It's an endless game nobody wins, ever."

"How about this?" he said in a voice full of challenge. "Assume you don't need to succeed at or resolve anything."

"What? What else is there?" I asked. "My whole life is based on succeeding at or resolving something. What else is there but to succeed, resolve something, or become somebody?"

I thought Jarid would laugh at me, since I was already laughing at myself, embarrassed. I didn't think such thoughts were still in me. He didn't laugh. He simply looked up at the moonlit clouds, as though waiting for me to come back to the present moment.

Even if I'd felt justified, I couldn't continue questioning what he was saying. I collapsed back into my body, feeling like I was buried in mud, holding my head just high enough to breathe.

Jarid stepped back from me, still speaking in a whisper. I relied on faith that I could hear him or, at least, would hear what I needed to hear.

What he had said—the beauty of his words and vision— touched me so deeply, I couldn't hold back a gentle stream of tears. I was outwardly embarrassed, inwardly relieved.

"Everything in the world is wanting to happen," I believed I heard him say. "Everything. When you live from an attitude of wonder, the changes you struggle for suddenly appear, without struggle."

I had to walk faster to keep within hearing distance.

"You are not here to change people. You are here to open up to the whole system, to emotionally embrace everyone and everything. This is where the greatest edge, the most perceived difficulty exists. This is the place where you recognize that nothing is wrong. You know that everything, everywhere is wanting to happen."

I watched Jarid as he walked in his unique way, sometimes twirling, sometimes trudging along as though he were hundreds of pounds heavier than he was. There was always a lightness around him, no matter how he appeared.

When he was some distance away, I heard him say, just loudly enough for me to hear, "The only thing I owe you is my freedom."

I cringed when I first heard his words, believing them to be selfish and cruel, unconcerned about others.

"Oh, that's not selfish," I blurted out, realizing what he'd actually meant. "If all I owe others is my freedom, what I'm really saying is that my every action comes from within me and has no hidden agenda, demands no reciprocation, and carries no expectations. Whatever I do, then, can only be freeing for me and the other person. I am not pulling on them emotionally. That's it, isn't it?"

Jarid's only response was to walk at a faster pace.

It was near dawn as we approached the bridge from the west, at the point we'd started from nearly ten hours earlier. Jarid walked out to the center line of the concrete roadway and began performing physical movements which could only convince an outsider that, indeed, he was a bizarre, strange, and possibly dangerous person.

I watched, appreciating how different he was from anyone I'd ever known, living from an entirely different set of rules. Separating now, after a night in the desert—a most intimate and meaningful night—was surprisingly sad.

Being with Jarid felt like I'd been taken somewhere by a force not in my control, having to rely completely on trust and faith that the force had good intentions. His spirit was so rare and different. I wanted more of his stimulating, unpredictable energy.

As we were about to part, I realized I wanted to embrace him, wanted a final connection to complete our time together, yet I was hesitant to reach out. At the same moment, Jarid abruptly interrupted his movements at the center of the roadway and walked briskly over to where I stood. Standing in front of me, he gazed into my eyes, his face expressionless.

For the first time, I noticed a sweet shyness in him, a mixture of, "Yes, I want to hug you" and "I'm embarrassed."

"Enough," a voice in me said. "Hug him already. He's only human. You waste too much time thinking about it. Hugs don't come from your mind."

"But this can't be an empty, obligatory hug," I argued with myself. "It has to be honest, shyness and all. The hug has to come from mutual respect."

Jarid reached out and put his hand on my shoulder, his eyes all the while searching mine. With perfect timing, we simply embraced. His body shifted sideways slightly, creating a side hug, the kind people offer when their bodies are shy. We were close and, simultaneously, distant. I felt both our discomfort and our comfort.

His face close to mine, he whispered in my ear what, at first, sounded like nonsensical statements. "I got past the atom state and I stopped there. Dream backwards. There is no reality without good and bad. The fire is bigger than God. I can't lie to one person ever."

He concluded by adding, "Don't try to understand what I just said. You can't. Someday, you will."

He disengaged, shuffled backwards a few steps, turned, and walked toward his pickup truck. He opened the passenger door, slipped in, turned on the radio, and simulated conducting the classical music that was playing.

3

Rapture Theater

Slowly I walked the length of the bridge back to my car and sat down inside. I wondered which direction to take and decided to drive into and toward the reddening sky. Driving off, I could still see the ghosts of darkened, far-off mesas teetering at the end of the world, silhouettes changing form from the activity of darkness to the emerging light.

I had no limits. My mind was quiet; I had no thoughts. My body seemed free of weight. I felt I had just spent a night with God and now I was alone in the universe and it didn't matter. Nothing mattered anymore and everything mattered, but in a different way.

The empty, black, mysterious highway ahead of me prompted me to accelerate. As I did, my headlights captured a sign on the side of the road with a message that seemed to have been placed there specifically for me to read at this particular moment: "You are only alone in your dreams." The letters were so large that I had time to read it twice before passing it at high speed. At first, I thought it was a Christian message, or an advertisement for a psychic service or even a dream therapist. There were no names or phone numbers on the board.

I drove through the desert into nowhere as the darkness dissolved into light. The driving, the motion, the speed into an

41

unknown nothingness felt liberating. I pulled off the road and stopped to watch the sun rise. I was in a void, an altered state. I was alone with myself.

As I watched the vastness of the world changing before my eyes, I wondered again about the meaning of life.

"Boring," I heard the court jester voice inside me say. "Don't wonder about life again, this is it. While you're wondering, you're missing the color."

I turned the car around to head home, away from the ever-brightening western sky. It was late, I thought.

"Late for what?" the voice asked. I laughed at the absurdity of my mind.

The next ninety minutes of endless highway and lengthening shadows carried me easily toward home. The final two miles of dirt road leading to our tiny high desert house comprised, primarily, potholes, ruts, and symmetrical washboard style bumps—a perfect design for dismantling any type of vehicle.

This road, more than anything else in life, had the ability to anger and irritate me on a daily basis. The shaking and vibration seemed to have me by the throat—a universal trick to humble me into patience.

I arrived home to a darkened house with only the reddish reflection of the sun painted on the window glass. I entered quietly through the squeaky screen door so as not to wake Meigra. I undressed and slipped into bed.

Instantly I was asleep and lost in a dream. I was awed at what I was dreaming, and even more surprised that I could observe myself dreaming from within the dream and continue to dream in an awake state.

In the half-awake, half-asleep state, I reached for the tape recorder I kept beside the bed and, in a whisper, recorded the dream as it was happening. My awake self said it was not possible to record a dream while partly awake. My half-asleep self had no rules about recording dreams.

In the dream my close friend Sara, a woman I'd known for

many years, was an usher at the entrance to an old movie house called the Rapture Theater. She greeted me, tore my ticket in half, smiled her radiant smile, and led me inside. Soft blue lighting filled the interior space. The floor was thickly carpeted, and the walls and ceilings, intricately carved, reminded me of a medieval castle. I felt as if I were walking into a womb.

Sara led me to my seat, one of a thousand in the cavernous theater. I was the only one there. My eyes cherished the sensuous lighting. My fingertips absorbed the soft, thick, velvety texture of the electric-blue upholstery as I took my seat.

Sara gently squeezed my hand and smiled. She turned and walked down the dimly lit aisle toward the huge screen. She walked up three stairs leading to the small stage and stepped into the white movie screen, becoming the projected image of herself on the screen as though she were the movie.

Her movie image filled the screen as she turned to face me, an audience of one. Behind her were dozens of other Saras standing in single file like dominos on end.

I watched in awe as the original, largest image of Sara looked directly at me and smiled. Suddenly, Sara's projected screen image slowly fell forward, face first. Behind her, all the other images fell forward and flat, exactly like dominos. I sat in silence for several minutes, staring at the screen as though I were watching a slide show with only one slide. Nothing moved, there was no sound. Slowly, very slowly, the original Sara arose, while the other images remained fallen, stacked.

She walked out of the screen, off the stage, down the steps, up the aisle to the row where I sat transfixed in wonder, and sat down beside me. She was translucent. I could see through her as if I were looking through a finely woven white curtain covering an open window, a thin veil revealing a muted outline of the trees just outside moving to the gentle breeze.

Sara faced me, a joyous, excited smile rushing from her eyes directly to my heart.

"I did it. I died. I did it! " she said.

She took my hand and led me outside the theater, where we

found ourselves standing in a cemetery by a grave. Holding hands, we watched her old friends lay the dozens of flattened images of Sara, layer upon layer, into the grave. The images were stacked like cutouts of a person, all grayish, all the same.

The friends grieved. We didn't.

Sara and I stood some feet away, watching. She looked at me with her heartwarming smile and said again in a low whisper, "I did it." I felt my heart burn with a type of ecstasy I'd never known. To my right stood Jarid, neatly dressed, completely coherent. Sara and Jarid nodded in familiar recognition of one another.

"I've been waiting for you," he said, as they acknowledged each other. With Jarid at my right and Sara on my left, we laughed and giggled together. I could feel their warmth radiating through me. I believed that originally, Sara and Jarid had both been in the everyday material world on a mission and now they were back together again in another dimension. They didn't have to share their stories and exploits with each other—in Sara and Jarid's time, they'd only been apart for minutes. In my time, it had been years.

Sara took my hand, looked into my eyes with the softest, most serious expression, and said, "In this place there is nothing to cry about. No sadness. Nothing. That is what the crossing over is. It is crossing and moving into this other form. It is not material, not physical. Nothing has been lost or gained. Just changed. The body is ready to change."

"Where do you go now?" I asked.

"There is nowhere to go," she replied. "I've just moved over a few inches to another dimension."

With those words, Sara, Jarid, and the entire scene slowly dissolved into a blank screen.

I awoke into sunlight streaming through the bedroom window. I felt as though I had moved from one dream into another, much like the motion picture film technique of dissolving one scene into another without a defined border. I sat up feeling alive and bright, with a sense of well-being.

As I showered and dressed, the mood of the dream did not dissipate or fade. It stayed with me. I believed that I had observed the act of death and understood it completely. It was as though I, too, had died and didn't quite know it yet. "What if I have died?" I asked myself. "How would I know?"

I had to tell the dream to Sara, soon. In my everyday, awake world, Sara was dying of cancer. I questioned whether I was being arrogant to share such a simple dream with a woman who was fully living her death.

With some hesitancy, I called her on the phone and told her I'd had a dream about her. Before I could continue, she demanded I come over immediately.

"But you're in California," I reminded her.

"I know where I am," she replied. "It's important for you to fly here to tell me in person. This is for you as well as for me." Sara always told the truth. I drove the three hours from Taos to the Albuquerque airport and flew to California that afternoon.

When I arrived at her home, Sara came running down the steps of the wooden porch and into my arms. "I'm so glad to see you," she exclaimed as we hugged. "Tell me the dream, tell me the dream."

Her body was thinner than when I last saw her, her face narrower, yet her eyes glowed as they always had. Her physical appearance implied that she was ready to die within a few days.

Her eyes had no death in them. They were bright. Just like in the dream, she took my hand and held it in hers. She whispered, "I'm really so glad to see you." Her words filled me.

Sara and her husband, William, lived in a redwood forest several miles from the ocean, thirty minutes from the nearest town. Over the last few months, when Sara felt the severe pain of her cancer, she would walk outside and scream, and dance, and sing into the trees to give expression to the symptoms rushing through her ever-disintegrating body. The forest became her ally, providing the space and receptivity to hear her without argument or false sympathy. She did not have to convince the giant trees that her unconventional actions were valid, or that she knew what she was doing.

Sara led me to a shaded grove of redwood trees and sat with me on a stump that had been there for hundreds of years. "Tell me the dream," she said excitedly.

Swallowing with embarrassment, I hesitated. She noticed my discomfort and gazed into my eyes softly, her eyes moist, encouraging me to take seriously the information I was about to reveal to her.

As I told her the dream, she inhaled deeply, her body revealing the joy of being seen, realizing her journey was not hers alone.

When I got to the part about her realizing that she had died, Sara instinctively jumped up and with the grace of a ballerina, danced in a circle, joyously calling into the sky, "Yes, that's right, I died. I did it! I died."

Sara concluded her dance at my feet. She extended her hand and, looking into my eyes, said, "Yes, yes, yes. I've died."

Gently, she pulled me to a standing position.

"Come. Walk with me through the woods," she said. "When I am with you, I discover what I know. I want to tell you things I've never known before. "Come," she said softly.

Hand in hand, like sister and brother, we walked deeper into the woods. Being with Sara had always been easy. There was no tension between us, there were no masks to hide behind. The trees surrounded us, creating an atmosphere of mystery, a mystery that would be present even if we weren't there to witness it.

"When someone close to me dies," Sara said as she squeezed my hand in mutual recognition, "must I grieve? When I don't care anymore about being right, am I crazy? When it no longer matters how many friends I have, am I strange? Do I need question myself if something was meaningful to me yesterday and isn't today?"

Her questions led to silence. We both knew the questions were also the answers.

The ancient trees absorbed my fears and took me away from my independent, self-conscious self. I had no words to speak. The quiet was infinite. Sara's voice slipped out of the silence, and with her left hand she softly encouraged my head to move closer to her so that I could hear.

She laughed at herself as she spoke slowly and thoughtfully.

"The world that I grew up in," she began, "the world that I learned from and judged my life by, is no longer a reference point for me. It never was. But I thought it was. That is why life never seemed to quite work. There was always something missing, a sense of not quite doing life right."

The words stopped. Quiet filled the forest. As we walked arm in arm, words seeped into my thoughts that were fresh, previously unspoken by me. It was as though wise insights were being infused into my body from outside.

I thought about taking notes in case I forgot what I was thinking, then I laughed at the idea. The magic intensified.

Sara's words were a simultaneous echo to my thoughts.

"Living, by using the everyday world as a reference point or a guideline for what is right," Sara continued, "requires that I constantly compare myself to others to determine whether I am together, or doing life correctly. I've even taken on what others think I should believe and value—the right and good way to be. This way is not original, and neither is it mine. It is based on the expectations of others and the remnants of needing approval from an outside source."

Listening to her, I felt a sense of relief. A weight lifted; my shoulders softened. The information was freeing. Her words kept coming like a waterfall of rapids. "The life I used to live was solidly based on public opinion, general consensus, and the need to look for external signs that affirmed my place in the world. That way of being in life was the source for all my self-judgment and all my self-doubt, and encouraged me to feel separate and isolated from others and the world in general.

"The beliefs of others determined how I was supposed to feel about death, money, God, relationships, emotions, age, body size, people who are different.

"The hopeless, sad, and powerless feelings that I experienced when I heard painful human stories existed within me. They were only activated by the information coming from people outside me."

Like Jarid, Sara suddenly stopped and turned to face me directly. Her abrupt action captured my attention. I was ready for whatever was to come next.

"I've learned," she said, emphasizing her words, "that I can either become emotionally immobilized by the immensity of problems and earthly human tragedy, or mobilized. It is always my choice."

My thinking stopped. My mind went blank. Sara smiled.

A rapid, quiet, buzzing vibration radiated throughout my body. I found the sensation stimulating and mysterious.

"What's going on here?" I asked Sara.

Her only response was an innocent smile.

The trembling vibration intensified until I became afraid of losing all control and going crazy. It was no longer stimulating and mysterious.

"What's happening to me?" I asked again.

"You'll live," she replied, "I think."

I was scared at losing a familiar control over my body. Sara could see that some information was needed.

"When you take in new information, your body reorganizes," she said. "Your willingness to change and open to dimensions not yet familiar to you, or in simpler terms, to live differently, requires that your body make changes, causing you to feel sensations that are new to you. New feelings and sensations are what most people would do anything to avoid. Not knowing what is going on can be frightening."

"Yes, I'm frightened," I stuttered.

"The buzzing vibration is the change happening," she said.

"There is nothing you have to do. I've been there. Just hang out with it. The worst that could happen is you'll die. And who knows? You may already be dead, in the process of coming alive."

"I feel better now," I said sarcastically.

"I thought you would," she answered with a smile.

Sara's lightness was reassuring. She rarely defended herself. Instead, she could hear beneath the content of words and respond to what was really being said.

"Part of the belief I've carried for years," Sara continued, "is that my life is not within my control, that my reaction to tragedy and pain is a given, even expected, part of the human condition.

"I know now, there is another way to live life, and it has little to do with the present way. It requires no longer using all the information I've grown up with as a reference point for what is correct."

At that moment, a large hawk eased through the trees directly toward us at eye level, then soared upward in spiraling flight toward opening sky, in absolute silence. Our attention flew with the hawk. Watching it soar, I wondered what its perception was. How did it relate to other hawks? What did it know about human beings? What was it thinking? Was it thinking?

Playfully, Sara stepped behind a tree so that only her head peered out from behind the trunk. Her gaze penetrated the self-consciousness I carried. She was so authentic, her mere presence caused any falseness within me to rise to the surface so rapidly that I had no time to mask my feelings. My heart beat faster and my eyes softened to tears.

Sara's eyes peered into a place in me held dark, a place that now demanded I trust the darkness, things unknown to me, and not fear the fear.

"You do not need to understand anything to be with me," she said, responding to a thought I was about to have.

"This other way of being alive," she continued, stepping out from behind the tree to take my hand, "has nothing to do with separation, and yet it is based on separation."

"What does that mean?" I asked.

"Separation, as I define it, is autonomy. Autonomy has a completely different meaning than to be separate. I used to be afraid of the word "separate." It implied I'd be alone, lonely and sad. But to be autonomous is to be self-defined, acting as my own leader. It means that every action I take or word I speak comes from a solid, real, defined authority within me. Feeling and being autonomous are a relief."

"Why is being autonomous a relief?" I asked.

"Because I do not have to depend on your opinion," she replied, "or the opinion of others in my life. Being autonomous, I am free to listen to and follow what I intrinsically know. Opinion is meaningless. Instead, I risk being wrong, foolish, mistake prone, and even wise."

"Then you really have to believe yourself," I commented.

"Whether I believe this or I don't," Sara added in a serious tone, "doesn't matter. It is what is happening anyway."

Her hand took mine as she gently encouraged me to walk along with her.

"To live a different way," she continued, "means separating out what is real for me from that which is not real for me, and knowing how to tell the difference."

"Have you. . .?"

"Yes, I've learned the difference," she interrupted. "I've learned to locate and listen to myself. It's easy. When I free myself from the emotional entanglements of others, I hear a different language. I hear myself as clear, direct, specific, and sure. I use myself completely as a reference and as the primary source of information."

Sara turned and looked into my eyes again. I felt uneasy, self-conscious. She put her hands on my shoulders and told me to stand in place no matter what she did. Slowly, Sara walked around behind me. I started to follow her with my eyes.

"Don't turn around," she demanded, "no matter what."

I heard her footsteps crunching the leaves as she moved into the distance. I wanted to turn and see what she was doing and where she was going. Then I heard nothing. My eyes followed a squirrel jumping from limb to limb. I waited for the next sound. Finally, I called out.

"Sara? Sara?"

She didn't answer.

"Sara, what's happening? Where are you?"

Suddenly, she was directly behind me. Again, she demanded I not turn around. I heard her shuffling around in the leaves. My curiosity almost forced me to turn anyway, against her wishes.

Out of the quiet, and from behind me somewhere, Sara spoke. Her voice was firm and clear, distinct from any other time I'd heard her speak.

"The first step to living differently," she said, "is to live your life through your heart."

"What does that mean?" I asked, still not daring to turn around.

"I used to think," she replied, "that it meant being nice, kind, compassionate, giving, sharing, and always available to others."

"What do you think now?"

"Shhh," she said. "You ask to fast. Pause between breaths."

"What . . . do . . . you . . . think . . . now?" I asked again.

Ignoring my attempt at humor, Sara replied, "Living my life through my heart means speaking, deciding, or taking a difficult action only after asking myself whether it is for the highest good of everyone concerned. This means that sometimes I say 'no' to someone in a big way, knowing that they may become profoundly disturbed, agitated, or even angry with me. Saying 'no' or respecting my own authority can be risky.

Living through my heart bypasses being nice, polite and seeking to be seen as a good person.

"Instead, I say what needs to be said. I speak words that need to be spoken. To do this, my intent must be clear. I must feel my own integrity even if no one else does. Without the aid of any more books or groups or other wise persons, I practice believing myself, even if I am wrong. Even if I am right. I practice this every day a hundred times with a dozen relationships. As I practice, in what can seem like trivial ways, every day, I begin to believe myself. Then I am speaking for all humankind in my every action, my every word."

Sara slowly stepped out from behind me to stand by my side. She appeared physically weak and drawn, even though her eyes were bright.

"Let's go back," I said.

She nodded yes.

We walked back through the woods without speaking, her arm intertwined with mine, allowing me to provide support for her body, which was quickly weakening.

When we reached the house, I helped her up the stairs onto the porch. We stood facing each other, ready to say goodbye, tears wanting to flow. I reached into my pocket for a beaded necklace I had been given twenty years earlier by a special person, an American Indian woman I'd befriended in New Mexico.

The woman, a respected tribal elder, had passed it on to me with the knowledge that it had been in her family for generations and she wanted me to have it. She hadn't said why she gave it to me, and I hadn't asked. "You will know why I give this to you when you can hear yourself," she had said as she handed me the necklace.

The necklace had a beaded red, black, and white pendant attached to leather strands for tying around my neck. For twenty years it had been the only material item I possessed that meant something to me. I'd often imagined that had my house caught on fire and I had time to retrieve only one item before leaving, the necklace would have been that item.

As I held the necklace for Sara to see, I told her the story behind it. I handed it to her and said I wanted her to have it. She closed her eyes, and with her fingertips she touched and felt each bead, seemingly taking in its story.

When she opened her eyes, they were filled with tears.

"She saw your spirit and you see mine," she said. "I receive it." And she held it to her heart.

Three days later, Sara died.

4

Flying without Wings

I slept well and long the night of Sara's death.

Just before slipping into a deep sleep, I remembered Sara's words a few days earlier: "I discover what I know when I am with you."

I entered into a dream in which I was running faster than humanly possible from people who were chasing me. My running became flying, and my pursuers and I transformed into a flock of swallows in human form, with me in the lead position.

In the dream I flew through the open window of a church and hovered several feet above and behind the minister while she was giving a sermon to her congregation.

The minister did not register my presence, yet the members of her congregation seemed to recognize me in a way that I did not fully comprehend. The people had knowing smiles around their eyes, and the expressions on their faces were soft and receptive. I felt intimacy, magic, and wonderment.

As the dream evolved, the minister saw me, experienced my presence as an interruption, and demanded that I leave her church. The dream ended as I was realizing that I was Christ, and telling her, in a clear voice of authority, who I was, and to look at my hands for proof.

I flew out through the open window of the church into the dark night, and gradually wakened from the dream watching the warmth and light inside the building disappear into blackness, as I opened my eyes to the rising sun in the tangible daily world.

As I awoke, I heard words simultaneously in the dream and in my waking state: "Being Christ is so mundane and personal." For a moment I existed in parallel worlds.

I got out of bed immediately, without my usual struggle to acknowledge the day. I felt bright and alive and could feel Sara's presence, as well as the mood of the Christlike dream. I dressed, and drove the six miles to the ocean near Santa Cruz to run along the beach.

As I drove, I reflected on why I liked to run. I had begun running two decades earlier after living through a life-changing divorce. I discovered that running each day was the one thing in my life that was consistent. When all my learned beliefs, familiar structures, and emotional pilings were suddenly removed, running became my thread to life and living. It was the one thing that was mine, the one thing I could always control. When and where I ran was always my choice.

Moving my body taught me that I alone was in charge of my movement and direction. The motion itself was a reminder that I was alive and that my body was well. Only my mind had the power to pull me back into thoughts of the past and events whose value had long ago been extracted.

For twenty years I had run almost every day, but this morning something seemed different. At first, I simply noticed a different mood, a mood that was so unfamiliar it would have been frightening had I not been surrounded by the lingering images of the dream an hour earlier.

I had familiar reference points around me: the ocean, dolphins swimming a few hundred yards out, sandy beaches, a pier off in the distance, the cliffs, Yet, something was different.

"What if I was in another world," I wondered, "like in a Star Trek episode? A world that looked just like Earth physically but existed in a different frequency—perhaps a different, parallel world? What if the dream I'd just had was a doorway into another dimension? What if I had died and didn't know it? How would I know?"

My feet touched down gently, displacing the water from one spot to another in the wet sand. I ran teasingly along the breaking, receding water's edge. The shiny surface of the sand reflected the early morning sun as the foamy water, slipping back into the next wave only to be thrust forward again, played at my running feet.

The wet granules of sand felt sensual, alive, and stimulating. I had the urge to stop and roll in them but chose instead to keep moving. It might be too cold, I thought, to get myself wet in the early morning. I was embarrassed by my own thoughts, as though I didn't want to acknowledge my own sensuality.

"What a revelation," I said to myself out loud. "If my own thoughts embarrass me, no wonder someone else's opinion of me can have such a significant impact. It isn't their opinion that bothers me, it's my opinion of me.

"Who can I blame then?" I asked no one in particular.

"I can't play dumb to myself anymore?" I mused, laughing at my own insight. "That means I have to be my own authority, my own source of information with no buffer between me and ignorance or wisdom. What a scary thought."

My attention moved toward the pier just ahead of me. Several children nearby, silent and content, were digging holes in the wet sand.

Watching the children, I felt free for the first time of having to place anyone on a pedestal and outside of me. In this emotionally pristine moment, I couldn't think of anyone who I believed had more authority than myself. A different perspective maybe, even more clarity, but not more authority. I was realizing inner authority, not authority over others. The mood of the dream about recognizing myself as Christ flashed for a moment as if to confirm my thought.

As I continued to run, I began to feel my spinal vertebrae individually moving. In my mind's eye, I could even see them. I could feel my lower back, and the often tense lumbar vertebrae, gradually soften, moving freely to become a strong foundation for my upper body—something I'd never have believed could be possible.

Usually, my lower back was the first point to weaken, to give out to the gravity of being alive. Now it was the origin of support. I could feel for the first time that I wasn't having to hold my body up; instead, it seemed to rest on itself, lightly, as though I were suspended between gravity and reverse gravity.

In the shimmering water at sunrise I noticed the dolphins swimming closer to shore, circling directly perpendicular to my running form. Their circling seemed mystical to me, yet I didn't need to know what that meant.

I smiled as I watched them jump and play. My own body seemed light. My thoughts were light. The dolphins seemed to be living completely in the present moment.

I was envious.

I realized as I watched them that, for most of my life, I'd been waiting for the present to take place, except when I was a young child. Before kindergarten, everything that existed had been real. I knew instinct. I knew spontaneity. I knew truth. I knew a soft heart. I was a dolphin in human form.

As I ran toward the rising sun, just out of reach of the breaking waves, I came alive as though waking up from a lifelong sleep. I realized that I had lived my life waiting. I had believed I had to learn to live in the future to placate the school authorities, appease parents, and think I was doing the right thing, the right way. When I scanned the years from kindergarten to the present, up to and including that day of running, I had always been waiting.

I realized that I had always experienced waiting as a physical sensation lurking in the background, almost unnoticed, yet something I'd come to believe was a regular, normal way of feeling. Waiting had settled in my body and felt like a full-time sense of urgency. It was like an internal split between living everyday life from a natural, instinctive place within me and attempting to live correctly based on the opinions of others.

I had become so busy waiting for and anticipating the next moment that I had forgotten to be grateful for—or even notice—the present moment.

Several dozen seagulls landed in an orderly fashion to my right, along the water's edge. Three days earlier, I had walked with Sara for the last time, and together we had watched a hawk soar above the redwoods. Like then, I wondered what life must be like from a bird's point of view. Do seagulls indulge in a constant cycle of introspection? Do they try to figure out who they are and where they belong, tediously compartmentalizing every aspect of life? I already knew the answer.

My body began to feel sluggish as thoughts endlessly bubbled up to the surface from some dark, musty place within me. The thoughts and words had a life of their own, as though someone else were speaking through me. I listened without self-judgment.

My legs were now running on automatic. I ran and listened, listened and ran, intrigued by an inner dialogue that was taking place somewhere within me. The inside, silent voice presented information in a tone that was not admonishing, offering, involuntarily, truths extracted from a deep, heartful place. Some new place was opening within me: my eyes teared and my throat tensed as I heard the silent voice within me.

This morning, my thoughts were not the regular worry thoughts so familiar to me. I knew these were different because I had no control over their content. I simply listened.

"You've waited for life to get better, to feel more secure, to know what you want to do, and to find the right person. You've looked for, sought after, waited, hoped, and dreamed—never quite satisfied.

"Consistently, through the years, you've felt a continuing, low-level anxiety within you like a subtle shimmering, a tiny vibration that gently rattles your entire body and feeds your continuous round of thoughts. You are most aware of this when you are silent—when you are physically and verbally quiet. You have come to know that there is something else within you that needs further attention, beyond psychology and outside of smart answers.

"The familiar body feeling, the anxiety, and the constant mind dialogue has always continued, even after each future project was completed, after each school paper was turned in, after each fearful life-event had passed, and after being hired for jobs you knew for sure you could never get.

"The anxiety followed you into long-term relationships with women you thought would never go out with you. It followed you after your divorce and separation from your children. It was present after each college class you taught that you just knew you could never teach . . ."

Suddenly, I snapped back into the reality of running along the beach. I was knee deep in water, unaware of how I got that far into the ocean.

"A perfect metaphor," I thought. "Completely unaware of how I was able to get in so deeply without noticing!"

A few feet away, two children were watching me. They giggled openly, appreciating my clownish act. Their laughter was contagious and a giggle surfaced in me, too. I joined them in laughter as I exaggerated my predicament by clowning my way out of the water. With soggy shoes and remnants of the children's laughter in the background, I scanned the horizon.

The dolphins had disappeared. I stood at the water's edge in the shade beneath a fishing pier that extended a quarter of a mile out to sea. I watched a wave heading for me, slicing through the pier supports and rushing toward higher ground, meandering in and around the pilings. I wondered where the wave originated, the exact spot where it formed. I played with the waves to see which one would come closest to sloshing into my already wet running shoes. Directly above me, nesting in every possible resting place among the timbers supporting the pier, seagulls filled a seagull world concealed beneath the pier.

I wondered aloud what it would be like to live under a pier. "You wonder too much," I laughed to myself, as the next wave hit me directly in my belly, knocking me off balance.

I stood up to drain. A few feet away from where I was standing, I heard a noise. At first I thought it was another bird, but when I turned to see what it was, there was nothing there.

Because of the early morning hour, the beach was empty except for another person running in the distance. Still, I felt an odd presence around me, much like I'd often experienced as a child when walking home at night, alone, after watching scary werewolf movies. The walk home led me through dimly lit streets casting thousands of lurking shadows. My young mind imagined every conceivable monster, knowing it or they were going to pounce on me and scare me to death, before eating my little seven-year-old body.

Now, decades later, I was standing under a crumbling pier, alone, tasting this same, irrational fear. There was no one else around to hear me, see me, or save me. The seagulls that had been nestled quietly beneath the structure suddenly and simultaneously flew off, the noise of hundreds of fluttering wings startling me as they made their abrupt departure.

As the sound of their wings diminished into the distance, I focused on the waves breaking at my feet, noticing that no sound accompanied their motion. The quiet disturbed me. I expected to hear something, yet I heard nothing. I listened acutely, alert to potential danger, wanting to hear something, yet scared that I might.

I looked around in all directions to see if there were any friendly people nearby. I attempted to calm my escalating fear by talking out loud, reminding myself that I was safe, that I was a mature, grown-up human being.

I saw a couple strolling, but they were nearly half a mile away and walking in the opposite direction from the pier.

A large cloud moved across the sun, dimming its brightness and intensifying the mood. "It's time to move from beneath the pier, " I thought, ". . . and Now!"

Even my thoughts were trembling.

Before I could take another step, my eyes were drawn to a small, dark figure, half hidden and scampering from one wood piling to another.

The ominous presence around me grew larger, activating an acute awareness, beyond childhood fears, of the dark or grotesque figures that never showed up. This was real. I sensed that something was about to take place that would change my life forever, one way or another. I was scared but not terrified.

I noticed the waves breaking and receding at my feet, but still I didn't hear them. All I could hear was silence. Everything else was filtered out by this mysterious presence. Slowly I began backing away from the place where I'd seen something move. The drifting cloud cleared the sun's path, freeing the remaining light, and shadows reformed with a new intensity and contrast.

As I was about to clear the last piling of the pier leading to the open, sunlit sand, I heard a brief scuffling sound a few feet behind me at shoulder level. More cautious than scared, I turned, willing to see what immense scary object, animal, or force was waiting for me. Startled with relief, what I saw had no intention of doing harm.

A small, black child about seven years old was perched on a wooden outcrop just above my head. He was sitting on the back of his feet with both arms wrapped around his knees. There was a look of recognition on his face.

I was not frightened, although I thought maybe I should be. Instead, I felt at ease, internally quiet, almost blessed. "Blessed" was not a word I'd ever used before, yet it defined that moment.

Within seconds of our eyes meeting, the boy slowly and gracefully reached down toward me, softly wrapping his arms around my head and delicately entwining my upper body with his spindly legs, sliding down slowly until I could see his eyes. The moment was delicate, fearless, light, powerful. I felt his arms and legs, his entire body slowly spiral around me, clinging gently, weightless as a spider spinning a web.

I welcomed him without question. His eyes, his presence, the way he reached toward me had softened any remnant of caution. I could feel a cry of ecstasy behind my eyes and my heart. This was something not of my mind, not rational, not even of a world I was familiar with.

He moved without sound, softly, in a continuous spiral until he came to settle in my arms, his arms resting on my shoulders, his feet around my waist, our cheeks touching. We were sweet. I did not know what was happening, and it did not matter.

I walked and walked. My heart burned with a sensation that was new to me. This gentle child held on with a touch that seemed to be infusing me with calm. He was almost weightless, yet his presence brought tears to both of us. I felt his tears running down the back of my neck. Our differences in age and size meant nothing. I started having images and thoughts that he was my brother, my best friend from long ago, or perhaps an angel.

He slowly shifted his body around to where he was directly in front of me, his cheek next to mine, his arms around my neck, legs hanging around my waist. We hugged and held each other, not speaking. It was like a dream.

Suddenly, he released his legs and arms from around me and leaped onto the sand. He turned, looked at me softly with watery eyes, and ran down the beach toward the deep red horizon.

For a moment, his abrupt departure left me dazed, spinning with emotion and thought. I watched as his shadow disappeared into the distance, and sat down to rest on the cool, early morning sand.

I became aware of how content, satisfied, and peaceful I felt. Everything seemed right with the world. My earlier anxiety and endless mind dialogue no longer existed. I was simply at home with myself inside. There was nothing I had to do.

My heart remembered the only other time I had experienced this graceful, peaceful place.

Twenty years earlier, I had been hiking in the high Sierras of California with my seven-year-old son, Eric. The narrow trail meandered through huge redwood forests, alongside steep cliffs, eventually emptying into an expansive green meadow illuminated by brilliant sun from a clear blue sky. Stepping into the sun-filled meadow with a young boy beside me was like entering a timeless dimension, not of this earth. Eric and I were awed by the vast silence. Holding hands, we walked to the middle of the meadow and sat down next to each other.

I fell back into the grass, stretching out fully, facing the sun. Eric lay beside me, our bodies touching. I fell asleep.

I awoke, hours later, feeling the warmth of the sun penetrating my entire body. With my eyes still closed, I felt Eric's warm body stretched across my chest, his heart against mine, his legs dangling over my side, his soft cheek on my shoulder, asleep. He was so light, I barely noticed his weight. That moment was all there was and all that ever existed.

His presence, his undiluted, pure ability to be himself completely, brought me to a place inside myself I hadn't known existed. It was beyond ecstasy. I was quiet all over and inside too. I was in love.

That moment, with Eric lying across me, our hearts touching, in a space bigger than the world, illustrated what it is possible to feel and still be alive. I didn't want it to end;— wanted to hold onto the feeling forever. I lay very still so Eric wouldn't wake up, since I believed that he, my seven-year-old boy, was the source of the quiet place.

Eric opened his eyes, smiled, and came awake. He slipped off my chest and sat up, a glow of wonder in his eyes.

The memory of Eric faded. The coldness of the sand beneath my feet brought me back to the present and the feelings of having just been with the young, black child. I was in a different dimension, as if I'd stepped outside of a circle I had been in unknowingly all my life.

I knew that I had to leave California immediately and return to New Mexico. Everything appeared different after being with the little person. The once familiar surroundings appeared strange, unreal, and foreign. Even though I'd grown up in this part of California, all that had seemed familiar the day before seemed, now, not only unfamiliar but alien. For the first time, I felt alone and isolated in the world.

I had to leave. There was no one I could talk with, not in the way I would have wanted to talk or about the things I was observing. There was nothing to relate to.

People talked to each other on the street and moved around from place to place, but I did not see life in their faces or in their bodies. Nowhere did I see life, with the exception of a few young children whose eyes, when they met mine, shined with recognition. It was as if we recognized some mystery together, and we nodded in silent remembrance.

Something more mysterious than I could imagine had happened to me with the black child.

5

The Big Trance

I called Meigra in New Mexico several times, but there was no answer. Without reaching her, I boarded a plane back to Albuquerque and arrived at the airport near midnight.

I called Meigra from the airport. Surprised at my sudden return, she knew something significant was taking place and volunteered immediately to drive the three hours to pick me up.

As we drove back toward Taos at three o'clock in the morning, I told Meigra of my experiences.

"I know," she said, over and over again.

"How do you know?" I asked. "I don't even know what it is that is happening."

"I know," she repeated.

"You keep saying you know . . ." I started to say angrily, then caught myself, realizing that she did know. She saw something I wasn't seeing.

After a long morning of sleep, Meigra and I put on our hiking shoes and walked out the back door into the warm desert air. A late-summer thunderstorm had passed over minutes earlier, and our trek began on a muddy dirt road that cut through a series of arroyos.

The blue sky was overflowing with luminous, brilliant white clouds. Wherever I looked, I saw the vast breadth of the

Sangre de Cristo Mountains, endless sky, ancient weathered mesas flattened against the horizon, and a carpet of fragrant sagebrush dotted occasionally with an island of trees. The 360-degree horizon extended into forever with only the sagebrush as a reminder of the earth beneath my feet.

We moved quietly, absorbing the silence. Without words being spoken, the remnants of anxiety surfaced within me—the anxiety of being alive, usually hidden by the distractions of daily life and the constant barrage of doing.

The visual landscape was so much more expansive than my constricting thoughts that I became aware of a familiar emotional distance forming between Meigra and I.

I breathed in the horizon, the soft colors, and the silence. I liked our being able to walk together side by side more than anything else we did. Yet, I felt the subtle gap between us dominate my entire mood.

I listened to my thoughts begin to blame Meigra for something or other—it didn't matter what, only that the thoughts were distancing in themselves, like some strange force that didn't belong to us.

I liked Meigra, and I had no known reason to feel distant from her, yet I did. I had everything to be grateful for, yet to be grateful in this moment would have been a stretch I was unable or unwilling to make.

Suddenly, while in the midst of my rapidly building internal case against Meigra, I realized that I wasn't there. I just wasn't there. Everything that was familiar a moment before, wasn't anymore, just like I'd experienced a day earlier in California.

I noticed Meigra walking alongside me—she was still there! I saw the same clouds and the same horizon that I had observed seconds earlier. More than anything, I was acutely aware of the absence of any concern in me, even though I thought there should be concern. My body felt light and free of anxiety. I even tried to make myself worry, but worry wouldn't come. The distance I had felt with Meigra had completely dissolved. Nothing was missing.

There were no words to describe accurately the dimension I found myself in; this was a place free of language. The closest I could come to a verbal description was a sense of well-being, of peace, of a place inside where nothing mattered—a place of non-attachment. If autonomy had a sensation, this was it. I felt no entanglements to anything or anyone. I just was.

I had not been thinking about or seeking this experience. I didn't even know it existed. How could I?

"Meigra," I whispered. "Something is happening to me that I've never experienced before. I'm not here! Nothing seems familiar. I know that sounds weird, but I'm not here!"

"So what's new?" she replied with a mischievous smile. After a brief pause to watch my reaction, she added, "If you're not here, where are you?"

"I don't know. I'm just not here," I repeated.

"Right," she said, as though she hadn't heard me.

"Meigra, this is scary. It's scary, but I like it. I'm not here," I insisted, realizing I didn't know what was going on, so how could she?

I wanted Meigra to assure me I wasn't going to go crazy and explode into a thousand pieces. Simultaneously, I liked the mystery of not knowing what was happening to me.

Meigra took me seriously, even though there was nothing rational about what I was saying.

"If you're not here," she asked again, this time with a tone of wonder and curiosity, "then where are you?"

"God, what a good question," I said.

My appreciation for Meigra intensified with her willingness to join me in what could only be perceived as a nonsensical adventure. I was in awe of her ability to go crazy with me rather than try to fix me.

"I don't know," I answered, relieved. "It's like I've stepped into another room. I have no body weight here." I was attempting to put words to body sensations and visual images. It seemed I had become translucent, physically invisible, as though some force opened a door and I'd gone through it. Awareness was amplified.

Without thinking and without warning, I heard a voice. It was my voice, but it sounded detached from my familiar self. The tone was distant and the words came on their own, without me having to think them first.

As I listened to what I was saying, I was in the same state of wonder as Meigra.

"We've been living in a trance, Meigra," I heard myself say.

"We all live in a trance state most of the time and don't know it. We do it daily and nightly. It is almost all that we do. It is difficult if not impossible to notice when we are in the trance."

I was talking out loud, fascinated by the information I was sharing with Meigra. From a side road in the midst of the gigantic desert, a woman and her dog walked toward us. I stopped talking as we nodded hello. The woman's eyes locked in on mine. I said nothing. She smiled.

As she walked by and was moving away, my energy sprang forth in words that excited and stimulated both Meigra and I.

"This trance I live in is like a computer program," I continued. "It's unconscious. It's a belief system—a learned perception that rules my life. This trance is different from and larger than the more common one, where suddenly I discover I'm staring into space, oblivious to my surroundings. That's a trance too, but it's a smaller one embodied within this larger trance I see now."

Meigra was mesmerized. I was too. I was no longer in control of my own awareness, which in itself was emotionally scary and simultaneously exhilarating.

"The bigger trance is involved with an entire way of being in the world," I said. "It's how I react to people and daily events. When in the big trance, I see the world as difficult, struggling, divided, hard—with a beginning, an end, and with transitions in between. It is replete with limits.

"The big trance I live in most of the time supports the belief that I have to get things done, that I have to hurry, feel tension, be busy, become ill, and blame someone for something most of the time. It requires that I view the world as out of order and chaotic. The trance convinces me that even though I see what needs to happen each moment and what action I need to take each day, I pretend to myself that I don't. Then I am able to internally disguise even an uncomfortable event to fit my familiar comfort!

"The big trance has no sense of itself, no self-observer, and no witness. It has a life of its own like a so-called psychotic person walking the streets appearing to have no awareness of how he is seen by others."

I looked up from the endless horizon and saw the sky slowly dissolving into huge, multidimensional designs of moisture drawn together to form deep gray and white clouds. The immensity of the clouds filled my sight until only puzzle-shaped pieces of sky seeped through their edges.

"I think the clouds are following us," Meigra said with a tone of eerie humor.

"Remember," I replied, "when we were at Mount Shasta a few years ago and a cloud did literally follow us?"

"Oh yeah, the cloud story. I remember," she said in a voice that implied I was about to recount the story one more time.

We'd been hiking in the winter snow of Mount Shasta at eight thousand feet on a sunny, clear, and windy day. The pristine blue sky contrasted with the white snow. Directly over our heads hovered the only visible cloud in the shape of a large airplane wing.

We both noticed its unusual color, form, and texture. Hours later and miles away from the original sighting, we saw the same cloud hovering right above us, still the only cloud in the sky.

That evening, ten miles away from the second cloud sighting, I took a brief walk around our motel. My attention was first drawn to the full moon rising close to the horizon. When I looked directly overhead, I saw what appeared to be the very same cloud that we'd twice seen earlier.

This time, it was the only cloud in the sky, and it was hovering in place directly over me even though there was a strong wind . . . .

"Meigra," I said, interrupting the story I was recalling, "if I live in a trance most of the time and don't know it, then I must be out of that trance right now, to be able to talk of it. And you must be out of it, too, if you and I are able to speak and understand what each of us is saying."

"Say more," she encouraged.

"There isn't anything to say," I said, "but that won't stop me. I'll find words for this somehow."

I stopped trying to find words and began to track a pebble along the rutted dirt road, kicking it to see how far out in front of me I could make it roll without losing it to the brush along the roadside. With each kick, I expected the pebble to disappear into the sagebrush. During my physical movements, playing with the pebble, memories resurfaced of my nighttime walk with Jarid a few months earlier. Jarid was out of the trance! My body relaxed as the internal revelation flooded my consciousness.

"I'm out of the trance now," I said, as I picked up the conversation, minutes into our silence. "That's all I know. I'm free. I know I am out of it because I can talk of it and I do not see myself as separate from anyone or anything in the world."

Meigra gazed out toward the reddening horizon, which seemed thousands of miles away. I could feel that she was hearing and sensing what I was seeing.

"Out of the big trance," I continued, "everyone and everything is part of my dream; they are figures and images in my painting. It is as though I am the one forming everything in the world as it appears to be, at any given moment.

"From here, from out of the trance, I cannot be separate from anything. Since I am out of the big trance now, I can choose what signals to use or physical symptoms to be watchful for, to alert me to when I am caught in it. I can weave my way out of the trance by observing the signals."

"What are the signals?" Meigra asked. "What brings your attention to the fact that you're lost in a trance or a learned program?"

"There are warning signs," I answered without hesitation, "especially signs or signals that are a consistent life pattern."

"What are they, what are they?" she asked excitedly, amplifying not only her curiosity but mine as well.

With each of Meigra's questions, and as I listened to my answers, I felt as if I were emerging from within layer upon layer of the trance state. All of my cultural learning was unraveling and simultaneously being replaced by the simplicity of my own innate wisdom. I felt awed and humbled.

My voice dropped into a quiet, clear place. I stopped walking, turned, and faced Meigra. Our eyes met in mutual respect as though we both knew something unusual and sacred was happening.

"Some signals," I began, "that give me a clue that I'm in a trance are when I'm feeling lost, bored, energetically flat, distant, alien, dissatisfied, incomplete, and separate from others. My signals are when I'm consistently envious of others, when I think I'm not fulfilling my potential, when I believe I'm not where I should be at any given time, and when I think that something is missing in my life.

"And that's not all," I said excitedly, anticipating what I'd say next.

"I know I'm in a trance when my thoughts recycle about any particular subject matter, when I'm worrying about money or a relationship, when I'm fearing tomorrow or being afraid of endlessly being afraid, when I'm always in the next moment instead of the one I'm in.

"I'm in the big trance when I feel powerless and guilty, when my mind is restless, and when my body seems to be one step ahead of itself—when I'm concerned about losing awareness, being hurt, fooled, used, or taken advantage of. I'm in the trance when I feel suspicious or unable to relax, soften, or locate any place of peace within me. My final signal is when I believe myself to be hopelessly out of control of my state of being and I'm hoping that tomorrow will bring a sense of peace. These symptoms grab my attention and drag me down into what others call depression."

"You've got my attention," Meigra interjected.

"And you're not depressed," I added.

"I can always be depressed later," she replied, "when I've got more time."

I nudged her shoulder, appreciating her humor.

"When I'm out of the trance completely," I continued, "if only for moments at a time, I will know I'm out by experiencing complete well-being in my body and mind—when I feel calm and at peace, with a realization that everything and everyone in the world is okay.

"Out of the trance, I realize that everyone in the world belongs in the world, and I have no judgment about anything. No one is separate from me, and I am not alone. It is similar to viewing the planet Earth from a another planet millions of miles away. My perspective and perception are different because I am not here."

The sky seemed to get bigger, and everything around me was more expansive. The mountains in the distance loomed larger and darker.

"When you are in the daily trance state," Meigra asked, interrupting my observation of the environment, "how can you know you are in it, while in it?"

"That's it!" I replied without pause, getting the meaning of my own words in an even clearer way. "The daily trance is so very seductive and familiar that it takes a committed, heightened state of awareness to even notice I'm in it, and even more personal commitment and faith to step out of it. I must have a willingness to be alive differently."

"To be alive differently? Heightened state of awareness?" Meigra said, repeating my words in a questioning, somewhat teasing voice, purposefully challenging the language I used.

"It's the ability," I interjected, "to recognize the state you are in so that you can shift in and out of it at will."

"What does that mean?"

"I don't know for sure," I replied. "I feel it."

We were both still for a moment. A warm glow filled the space between us. In the softness of the moment, nothing was missing.

I broke the silence, gently.

"To shift how I view the world," I said, "means I'd have to be willing to give up my justification for feeling the way I do at any given moment. I have the choice to feel any way I want to."

"That's a stretch," Meigra replied. "When I'm seeing my life as not working, for whatever reason, am I willing and able to change my perception to see life as working? Whoa!"

"And then again, how do I even know if I'm in a trance?" I asked. "Maybe life really isn't working! How do I remember to even notice the symptoms, signs, and signals as a reminder that I'm in the big trance?"

Meigra slapped her hands on her knees as she doubled over, almost convulsing in laughter. I'd never seen her laugh like that before. It would have been contagious except that I was still inside the trance, attempting to figure out the trance! Her laughter brought her down to the road, knees first.

I observed her movements with a smile, still holding a self-proclaimed insightful, thoughtful role, but I wanted to cry. I felt her lightness, her ability to see the absurdity of serious internal struggle. The space around her was so big, I could feel the tears in me just below the surface. My throat tightened at their potential release.

Meigra rolled onto her side as her laughter dissolved to a soft smile. Stretched out on the dirt road, her body position seemed out of context. She looked at me, then slowly sat up, her knees on the road, hands solidly resting on her thighs. Her eyes were fierce like those of an Amazon warrior—direct, intense, final. She leaned slightly forward, her entire body alive with passion.

"You know what is true and real," she said with authority. "You always do. You can move in and out of the trance state whenever you want to—a hundred times a day if necessary. You no longer need to be blocked, stuck, or lost in anything. You know this to be true for yourself. Speak what you see inside. Don't play the game of ignorance."

I was awed by Meigra's strength. As my stomach churned, I knew what she meant, and I knew enough to know that part of the trance belief is to think I don't know the answer—to convince myself that I am confused and need help from somewhere else, and someone else, to find clarity.

Meigra sat staring at me, waiting for me to take in her words. Her physical stance was solid, unflinching. I had no choice but to join her.

"I got it, Meigra," I blurted out so suddenly that she jumped. "There are three major signals that tell me when I'm in a trance state."

"There are?" I whispered aloud, surprised at hearing the words that had just come out of my mouth. I wondered, myself, what the three signals were. I witnessed myself standing back to observe myself as I spoke.

"By simply paying attention to the signals," I continued, "I can shift the trance state, moving through and out of it. It will feel like waking up! Simply waking up."

Meigra stood and casually brushed the soil off her jeans, then turned and placed her body directly in front of mine.

"What are they?" she asked, her eyes demanding information.

"I'll tell you in a minute," I replied, "as soon as I know."

"I'll wait," she said.

"What happens just before I'm about to recognize any one of the signals, is that my mind intrudes with thoughts in its attempt to hold me firmly in place—to divert my attention from leaving the trance. My mind presents distracting thoughts in question form, such as, 'What will happen to the future if I don't worry about it? If I'm not thinking and worrying, then what? Who will be on guard to protect me if I'm not afraid all the time? If I'm not suspicious and afraid, might not something get by and I'll be fooled?'"

I felt Meigra's complete receptivity. Her face was alive with wonder.

"The three major signals that will remind you that you're in a trance are . . . Yes? Yes?" Meigra encouraged.

"Impatience."

"I'm not impatient," she answered. "I just can't wait any longer."

"What are they?" she asked again, this time more seriously.

"The first signal," I said, "that reveals I'm in a trance is a sense of pride, any pride. But there's a fine line between pride and the appreciation and acknowledgment of myself. Pride requires that I be separate from myself, with a need to have others appreciate and like me at the expense of being real. Pride has a needing pull to it.

"Self-appreciation, however, whether expressed to others or quietly, to myself, has no better-or-worse-than feeling to it; there is no comparison or competition in it. It recognizes that I'm expressing my real self in that moment, unattached to being right or looking good. There is the highest internal sense of integrity."

"Yes, yes, that's right," Meigra said enthusiastically. "I feel that."

"The second signal that reminds me I'm in the big trance is believing myself to be or seeing myself as separate from any-one or anything. It's a feeling: I am separate, yet, when out of the trance, I see the connection. I am the connection. I know this sounds crazy. There is no fear in my body or anxiety in my thoughts; a sense of well-being prevails. When in the trance, the perception of separation is filled with fear, dis-tance, gossip, judgment, comparison, and so-called tangible differences.

"The third signal that lets me know I'm in the trance is a belief that something is missing in my life or that it won't hap-pen as I'd always believed it would. If I'm thinking that something is missing or might not happen in this lifetime, I'm lost and out of present time. I'm believing life to be hopeless and myself to be powerless. I have no energy. Thus, being depressed is part of the trance."

"Yes, yes, yes," Meigra said as she jumped up and down. "That's true."

"The belief is usually so strong that something really is missing or not happening as it's supposed to, that this signal requires slowing down inside to full stop, then pausing for a minute and listening to all the thoughts. There is no one in my life to help me on this one except myself. I must tap into an internal discipline that has no need for the approval of others. Few people in the world believe that what is happening in their lives is supposed to be happening, that it's all right on time, and that everything is on schedule.

"To work with this particular signal, my dialogue with myself might be something like, 'I'm thinking something is missing in my life, but if I'm thinking something is missing in my life, I must be in the trance.'"

"Wow," Meigra exclaimed.

We walked in silence, watching the moonrise slip through a hint of red color flowing over the horizon. Neither one of us spoke for quite a while.

I interrupted the stillness.

"Right now, Meigra, as we walk, if you pay attention to these signals, including this moment, you'll find you're out of the trance state within seconds. Simply being able to recall the signals requires you be out of the trance. When you're out of it, you'll know it immediately. There won't be any fear in your body or any sense of struggle. You won't be able to worry. Worry doesn't exist outside the trance. You couldn't worry even if you tried. While out of the trance, notice what you feel and perceive. Become familiar with your level of awareness, because, soon, you, I, or both of us will be back in it!"

"Why do we go back into the trance?" Meigra asked, somewhat puzzled.

"I don't know why; that's the way it is. That's the game. This is all about practice. After a while—days, weeks, months, or even years—you'll be out of the trance more than in it. Eventually, it will be unbearable, intolerable, to be in the trance at all."

"It's unbearable now," she replied.

"If it was truly unbearable," I said, "you'd never be in the trance again for one single moment. The pain of pretending dumb would be excruciating.

"Being in the trance becomes intolerable and painful because the trance state has no sense of itself, no self-observer, and no witness. You have to become your own witness. You're completely on your own. You have to lead yourself in and out of it or you become a victim to everyday events and a lifetime of despair."

"I've noticed," Meigra said

"You may also find," I continued "that much of what was meaningful to you yesterday is not meaningful today—that the lack of authenticity in relationships becomes glaring. It will no longer be possible to be around people where there is no energy, life, movement, or ability to speak of what is real."

"That doesn't leave many people left in my life," Meigra replied with a hint of sarcasm. "Does this mean I'll have to tell myself the truth, too? That's pushing it."

I liked the fact that Meigra could be funny in the midst of my being serious. Her humor added perspective.

"It means we'll have to listen to our intuition, not our minds," I continued, "especially since intuition comes through the body and has no words to it. Intuition has no logic—it is never rational. It's a body sense where you can feel and know a definite 'yes' to a question. If there is subtle physical discomfort or tension, the answer is always 'no.' Then, without judgment or accusation, I know to simply move on to being with people and in relationships where the concept of being out of the trance is a possibility and is acknowledged.

"It is at this point that I often hesitate for fear of hurting the feelings of others. If I stop here and continue pretending, no one learns to be real. My intent is to become the 'real' I want others to find in themselves. It is not to hurt or cause harm.

"All of my actions originate from an internal awareness that what I do is for the highest good of everyone concerned. Out of the trance, I am real."

"Just like the Velveteen Rabbit," Meigra said, smiling.

"Yes! Just like the Velveteen Rabbit."

6

Cracking the Mood Distortion

The next morning I awoke to a male voice speaking in Spanish, "Ah, la sombra mas importante de todas, la sombra mas importante de todas," followed by Meigra's voice, "Ah, the most important shadow of all, the most important shadow of all."

I opened my eyes to Joe Jimenez, Meigra, and our little boy sitting by the side of my bed, which for this night had been a couch on our front porch. It had been a warm night and I'd slept outside.

Joe was an old friend, a Nambe Pueblo Indian I'd known for twenty years. We'd worked, traveled, and experienced the despair of divorce together. We were like brothers. By being in his life, I learned about sharing, respect for children, and what it was like for him to live with an Indian spirit on Indian land in a white man's world. Joe spoke three languages: English, Tewa, and Spanish—ewa was his native language. Joe had lived all his life in the New Mexico world of Indian, Hispanic, and white people.

Joe and Meigra had their eyes closed and were slowly rocking back and forth, Joe repeating, "Ah, la sombra mas importante de todas," and Meigra responding in English, "The most important shadow of all."

Our boy, almost two years of age, whom we had yet to name, looked deeply into me, his eyes clearly communicating something too clear for me to comprehend.

I had assumed he would be a teacher for me when, weeks before his birth, he appeared in a dream to inform me that his name would be revealed to Meigra and I only after we could recognize him as already complete, and when Meigra and I held one another and ourselves with the highest respect. His exact words were, "See me fully and you are free."

I knew this meant we would have to make daily leaps of faith to trust that he knew what he was doing and was not simply an innocent, helpless, newborn baby, tiny and powerless.

I remembered the message of that dream as I looked into his bright face and clear eyes—a definite contrast to how fuzzy I was feeling.

I attributed my fuzzy, distorted state to having been immersed deeply, minutes earlier, in a dream about two men, who looked exactly alike, lost in conflict, yet both saying the same thing.

As the observer in the dream, I moved my body to stand between them, and simply because of my presence, their conflict ended and they became one. I awoke, realizing that conflict is not about words but about pulses of energy, which create an illusion that there is something to argue about, when in fact there can never really be anything to argue about if no one needs to be right. I was still too groggy to understand the insight.

That was the state of awareness I brought to Joe, Meigra, and the boy as I opened my eyes. Gradually I sat up, bracing myself on one elbow, in wonder at the sight of the three people whose attention, by this time, was fully on me. It seemed as though the three of them were in collusion to transport me somewhere or teach me something.

I yawned.

The boy, without taking his eyes off me, smiled—the kind of smile that demanded realness.

I felt the usual heaviness of the morning hours, the worry thoughts, imaginings about money, time, things to do, even though I had nothing I had to do. Often, when I had nothing that needed to be done, I worried that I should have.

Again, Joe repeated, "Ah, la sombra mas importante de todas," and Meigra added something this time: "The most important shadow of all is the one you carry into your waking life. It is time to change that. It is an old way of viewing the world; it serves no one and saps whatever energy you have in these early hours."

The boy's eyes remained in mine. I stretched to get more awake for what was coming.

I had wondered for years why waking from sleep had to feel heavy and less satisfying than sleeping and dreaming. I laughed to myself as I had the thought that all the beings in the world gathered together each morning by my bed to have a group meeting and I'm the only living person not invited!

In the midst of their gathering, I wake up feeling left out and fearful, while my mind busily attempts to explain away, with a dozen reasons, why I feel the way I do—rationalizing that life doesn't work and that I'm never quite doing it right anyway.

Meigra stopped rocking. She placed her hand on mine and said, "The mood you carry when waking up in the morning from your dreams and into your life of worry began when you were five years old."

"Five? What happened when I was five?" I asked, believing her observation to be silly.

"Not yet. No questions yet," she replied.

"Since you were a child, you have been determined to end the habit of waking each day with heaviness and facing the plight of being alive."

She squeezed my hand for emphasis. "This shadow, this mood has plagued you forever."

It was true. So many mornings I woke up with thoughts that seemed so tangibly difficult compared to the neutrality I'd just come from in sleep or dream. Even if the dream content was nightmarish, I still knew it was a dream and, for whatever unknown reason, that brought a sense of relief.

I smiled at my own questioning. Why not fall into sleep knowing that my waking life had been just a waking life, then feel equally relieved and relaxed as I dozed off. Why did one feel more real and tangible than the other? What was the difference?

"What happened when I was five?" I asked Meigra again, hoping she'd answer this time.

Surprisingly, she did. "You changed your natural body rhythm at five. You gave yourself away. You left your body and 'went out of sync.'"

"I did all that?" I asked. "How? Why?"

Meigra placed her fingers on her lips to gently remind me to be silent. Then she and Joe stood and motioned for me to stand with them. "Come," they said, and the boy took my hand as we all walked down the back porch steps into the morning sun. The cool air was fresh. The chairs around the fire pit were damp with dew, and we wiped them dry before sitting. Joe and Meigra studied the horizon. The boy touched moist flower petals.

In a quiet voice, I asked again, "How did I give myself away and go out of sync?"

"You entered kindergarten," Meigra replied, her voice clear and matter of fact.

"I entered kindergarten? That's how my life went strange?" At first I thought she was kidding.

Meigra ignored my comment.

"You entered kindergarten," she repeated, "and you didn't stop getting up at the same time every morning for the next fourteen years, even though you didn't want to get up. You wanted to learn, but you didn't want to go to school. You thought learning and school had something to do with each other. You believed you were forced, that you had no choice. For almost six hundred weeks, day by day, over and over again, you dragged yourself from bed to do something you had no interest in doing."

I squirmed as I absorbed how absurd it sounded when she put it that way.

"You came to believe," she went on, "that you needed to force yourself to do things you didn't want to do and that your own rhythm, pace, and interests were silly excuses to avoid doing the same things nobody else really wanted to do either."

I looked at Meigra, awed by the simplicity of her observation.

"You gave your spirit away to please others," she added. "Then together, you and all those around you decided to blame the institutions and authorities for making you do things you didn't want to do. You saw yourself as a powerless victim. The big people ran your life, you thought."

The boy sat down on my feet and glanced up at me, smiling. As if to bring perspective to the seriousness of our dialogue, he drooled, laughing as it ran down his chin. I laughed too, breaking the intensity of the mood I'd slipped into.

Meigra squeezed my hand with a bit more pressure, as if to grab my full attention. "It never occurred to you to walk away and follow your own rhythm—to live a different life from those around you, one that originated from within you, a life that fit no category and needed no one outside you to validate it as worthy."

"It did occur to me," I said defensively, "when I was about seven years old, but I didn't know there was any other way to live. I had fantasies about joining a circus and disappearing forever without telling anyone, or going to Hollywood to become a famous person in movies. I thought if I could become famous, people would listen to me and be nice to each other."

"But you didn't join the circus," she repeated back. "You didn't disappear, and you stayed at home."

Meigra paused. "Now you know what it feels like and what happens when you follow the world and bypass your own nature."

"What?" I asked.

"Moods," she replied. "Moods, dark times, feeling stuck, and living with an unconscious belief that life is hard and ultimately doesn't work."

"You're talking about all moods," I asked, "not just those I feel in the morning as I wake up?"

"Yes, all moods."

"Moods are like trance states," she went on. "Remain in the mood long enough, without awareness, and someone with a license to judge you will call it depression, which is simply an extreme form of a mood gone wild. They may prescribe a pill to deaden and cure the mood or depression. You then devote the rest of your life to believing you're depressed, trapped forever by some unknown disease, thinking you have no control over your own perception."

"Moods and depression are a lifestyle, a belief system, aren't they?" I asked.

"Depression is like a room with many doors, all unlocked." she replied. "But because someone told you they were locked, it doesn't occur to you to reach out and open a door."

"Sounds so simple when you put it that way," I observed.

"It is simple," Meigra emphasized. "It is easier to believe that something outside of you is controlling your world than to recognize that the mood itself is calling you to change your perception—that what you see and feel originates from within your own mind."

Touching the boy on the shoulder, Meigra said, "The boy has no moods. He doesn't need them. He hasn't taken on the outside world as his enemy. He lives from his nature. Neither you nor I want him to be anything other than what he already is. Therefore, he is present with himself."

The boy let out a sound that pierced the air, not irritating, just stunning enough to make me pay attention.

"Moods happen," Meigra continued, "and stay in place when you're not present with yourself but believe you are. When you cling to and believe your thoughts and the accompanying mood, you are in the trance. But when you sleep at night and dream, you are free from moods and are truly in your own rhythm, out of the trance. When you are out of your spirit, not dreaming, you are in your shadow—sometimes called a mood."

I was beginning to feel bad about myself, realizing that for so many years I had obeyed the social rules rather than followed what was inside me.

Joe, seeing my expression, smiled, and drove in the last wedge. "After six hundred weeks of pulling your body and spirit out of bed and into a social world not of your making, with no room for imagination, dreams, or magic, your perception of life became heavy and moody. You weren't home any longer. You weren't home inside yourself."

The boy climbed onto my lap, sat down, and leaned back into my chest, resting comfortably. I relaxed.

"So now, when I wake up in the morning," I said, "even though I have complete choice as to when I get up and what I will do, I don't fully believe it yet. The residue of the past clings, forming a mood that I believe."

"Yes, that's part of it," I heard Joe whisper as he slowly stood, holding the arms of the wicker chair to balance his well-lived body. Without looking in my direction, he headed for the back door, no doubt heading for the bathroom.

"You don't ask questions that you don't already have the answers to," he said as he reached for the handle on the screen door.

He opened the door, and before it slammed shut he added, "Are you ready yet to wake up and be here?"

The door slammed.

"Maybe not," he said moments later, his voice barely audible as he moved more deeply into the house.

My body suddenly grew hot. I felt my face turn red and my pulse quicken. I wasn't afraid. Instead, I felt desolate, although the word itself was unfamiliar to me, and I wasn't even sure what it meant. I perceived myself as a borderless desert with no familiar landscape. I was the horizon and the foreground and the heat. I was alone but not lonely. Everything had the feel of long, long ago.

I felt drained of energy. My thoughts became fearful about future events. My mind attempted to resolve them before they happened, in an effort to prevent from happening things that might never happen anyway!

I didn't know anything for sure. I was in an altered state. My mind flitted back and forth like a bee deciding which one of a thousand flowers to pollinate first. I didn't understand anything. Nothing was familiar.

Strangely, I was feeling the mood I had hoped never to have again: a view of myself as weak and small. I was completely dependent on emptiness for my strength, yet there was something different this time. I was okay with feeling empty and even dependent.

The screen door slammed shut again as Joe exited the house to return to his favorite chair. I was sure he had used that door to keep me alert. He sat down.

"You have to live from your warrior nature," he continued as he whittled on a piece of wood, "but not the kind of warrior that first comes to mind for most people. I do not speak of the mythical warrior going into physical battle without fear, courageously slamming his body through a flaming door to save a young child at the last minute.

"The warrior I speak of does not carry a spear or a bow, or have a black belt in Aikido. She does not ride a horse at great speed through fire and thick forest to rescue a city under siege. She or he might be a warrior, but not necessarily. It depends entirely on intent."

Joe tested the sharpness of his knife gently against his finger. Still focused on whittling, he said, "The warrior I speak of is the person who wants to be fully awake and free, acting from his own inner authority. She might happen to be a martial artist, but most important, she's an emotional martial artist. The warrior acts directly, without time for confusion or excuses.

"He realizes that every relationship, however difficult, every physical symptom, every thought, and every mood offers information to develop his warrior nature. Even now, as you listen, the warrior in you notices your thoughts, including your doubts about what you're hearing now."

I liked what Joe was saying, and I was impressed with how easily he knew what was going on with me, but it wasn't bringing forth the life that lay dormant within me.

"Notice your thoughts now," Joe instructed, "but don't try to make sense of them. Simply observe."

I did notice. My thoughts were continuous, like a loop of film circling endlessly through a projector playing the same scene over and over again.

"You can always feel and act sad or scared," Joe continued, "but at the same time, you must pay attention to yourself feeling and being sad."

In the neutral moment of observing myself think sad, I wasn"t sad. Instead, I was the observer witnessing myself playing sad.

"The warrior in you does not look for consensus or agreement from others," he added. "He learns to act singularly, no matter what others may say."

My body grew hotter. I began to sweat and fidget.

"Following your nature," Joe continued, "requires discipline. Not the kind of harsh discipline you learned in school, imposed by others and requiring limits and boundaries. This is an internal discipline that comes entirely from you, voluntarily, and has no limits or boundaries. It is a learned discipline that requires a lifetime of practice. The discipline is to observe, notice, and pay attention not only to others, but to yourself simultaneously. It is not passive."

Joe looked up at me and repeated, "You cannot be passive."

He was quiet while I absorbed his words.

"This discipline is an action," he began after a brief pause, "a moment-to-moment decision to be awake, alive, and here, especially when the last thing in the world you believe you can do is be here or be present. It is the warrior nature, or if you choose, it is what's required of you to come alive in this world. No more, no less. It is that complex and that simple."

Joe and Meigra sat back in their chairs and closed their eyes to rest. The boy sat contentedly on the ground, transferring small stones from one location to another.

What happened next I had not anticipated.

I watched the three of them doing exactly what they wanted to do, their inner calm apparent. The more contented they appeared, the more thoroughly dark my mood became. It seemed ironic, since I was wondering how to move in and out of moods more easily, that I found myself in one now, unable to escape.

It enveloped me like a thick fog, rolling in to completely obscure familiar landmarks The contrast of watching Meigra, Joe, and the boy be so light deepened my state.

I hadn't planned on this. I witnessed a mood take form in my own body and with the alleged cause of the mood, Meigra, sitting right in front of me. A moment ago I had perceived her as my friend and teacher; now, she was my enemy. I was trapped and powerless to stop it. The mood had a life of its own and came into my awareness much like a videotape playing at half speed. Meigra was resting, her eyes closed, yet my thoughts transformed her into a suspicious character. I had no doubt that I was right in believing what I was thinking about her. It wasn't logical or sensible, but it was a justifiable belief. I expected to be in verbal combat with her soon.

I acted on the belief.

"You look angry, Meigra," I said, pretending it to be an innocent comment, knowing it was highly charged.

Instead of reacting angrily or defensively to my double-edged assertion, Meigra turned to look at me. Her eyes were soft, and her response did not fit my perception. I wanted to reach out and hold her. Instead, I responded to the familiar hardness I felt inside, to the distrust and the pattern of believing her to be my opponent.

Without physical movement, Meigra appeared to step back into a larger perspective, voluntarily joining with me to observe rather than to enter into battle. She was clear, complete, and able to remain detached, aware that my mood and abrasiveness had nothing to do with her. Whatever was going on was clearly mine, and she knew it.

Her response was new to me. Usually, we'd get emotionally entangled and our moods would merge, creating an even larger, tension-filled environment with two equally lost souls, each believing the other one to be lost. This time, Meigra's defined view of what was hers and what was mine helped magnify my escalating mood. I felt as if I were a human cell dividing under a microscope.

The sky was clear blue—a crisp contrast to the brightly colored flowers surrounding us. Branches from nearby fruit trees formed a garden just above our heads. It was the kind of scene that evokes a natural serenity. Yet, I was far from serene.

I slumped back into the canvas chair, thinking myself stuck, lost, and hopeless. "What does anything matter anyway?" I thought. "Who cares? Nothing is important."

Joe glanced over at me, rolled his eyes, then smiled, penetrating the synthetic posture I'd molded around my body.

"He's gone," he said without taking his eyes off the piece of wood he was shaping."

"Now we have to go retrieve him."

I knew that he meant I was perceiving life from a deep, dark place, but I didn't know how to break free from it. I felt stupid—once again, lost to a state of mind that seemed so justified and out of my control.

Meigra spoke first.

"What's going on?" she asked me, her gaze direct and unwavering.

"I don't know." My body caved in even further on itself. "It doesn't matter anyway . . . "

My thoughts sought reasons for their own existence, willing to include events of long ago as proof that I had good reason to feel the way I did.

"Why am I feeling down or sort of, kind of depressed?" I asked myself inside. "Is it because I'm not doing something productive today? Is it my relationship with Meigra? Is it because my life is really not going anywhere? Am I just fooling myself again?"

I sat in the slumped-mood position for as long as others around me could tolerate it. Meigra, aware of the stagnant emotional environment, suggested we turn on my tape recorder and record exactly what was happening, as it was happening.

"Put it on tape," she said.

"What an odd suggestion," I replied.

She was asking me to record how unhappy I felt, with all the embarrassing words and silence that accompanied the mood.

"Well, at least its not videotape, " Meigra teased.

"Now that would be humiliating," I responded. I almost smiled, but held it in check.

"I feel emotionally lethargic, flat," I volunteered in a sub-dued monotone, ignoring her taping session idea.

I wanted Meigra to do more for me. I believed that Meigra or Joe—or anyone other than myself—was supposed to make me feel better.

"A minute ago," I said, "I saw you as the wisest of humans, strong and clear, and now I see you as the source of how bad I feel."

"Hmm," was her reply.

Meigra sat quietly, receptive and undisturbed by my words.

"How could my perception change so fast and I be caught in believing both?" I asked, my voice carrying a plea for help.

"What's both?" she asked.

"That you're the source of how I feel, and my savior."

"Maybe I am both," she suggested.

"Yes," I heard Joe whisper.

"Clip the microphone on your tee shirt," Meigra insisted. "You want to record this. Hearing this later will change your life."

I knew she was right, but I resisted the idea because it was her idea! Whatever Meigra suggested, I didn't want out of the emotional hole I'd dug with my own shovel. I looked for reasons to hold my position and couldn't find any. Meigra was indifferent to my inaction, so with a sigh of exasperation, I clamped the microphone to my shirt and turned on the hand-held recorder even though the idea seemed so contrived.

"This changes everything," I complained, submitting completely to the mood.

"What happens?" Meigra asked.

"I don't know," I answered. "I don't know where anybody else fits in my life. I don't know where a partnership fits." I began to stutter. "I'm thinking . . . I don't know . . . what was the question?"

It was difficult for me to look at Meigra. I didn't trust her questions, and her every look was suspect.

I pressed the Record button. The red light went on. "Recording this seems to take away from the picture I have of being miserable," I said, fully expecting to be taken seriously.

Instead, Joe laughed so hard he dropped his knife. I interpreted his action as mocking, even though I knew Joe was seeing me work so hard and so seriously to sustain a mood of misery as a way to learn about moods.

I suppressed my own internal giggle—a giggle that seemed more an aberration than the origin of a hidden truth. I wasn't going to give in to coming alive and climbing out of the hole, even though Meigra and Joe were providing the ladder.

A very long silence followed.

I almost laughed but thought Meigra might interpret my laughter as meaning that I was no longer in a justifiable mood, withdraw her attention, and ask no more questions. Realizing that I had the ability to change my mood any time I decided to, but didn't, embarrassed me.

"So, I'm lost," I said, waiting for Meigra to construct a path.

"Go into what is happening right now," she said.

"Sitting here with you, I anticipate disappointment," I replied. "I expect that we'll soon be angry with each other."

"What else?" Meigra asked in a sweet whisper.

"Everything I've been doing seems so unimportant now," I answered. "Nothing matters."

I heard myself fighting to survive in the deepening hole.

"Everything seems so unimportant," I repeated.

Meigra was serene. No matter what I said, she was right with me. Secretly, I was in awe of her ability to stay with me without reacting. I wondered why I didn't tell her, why I didn't appreciate her out loud so she could hear it.

I dismissed the thought that I wouldn't be able to stay in my mood if I showed her that I liked her!

When I did speak, I accused her of getting into a debate rather than being helpful. I was being skeptical and doubted her intentions. I was using Meigra's presence to dance with words around what I really knew, but was unwilling to admit I knew.

"I think you're bored and angry, Meigra," I said.

She paused, allowing silence for us both to take in what I'd said.

"I'm not feeling any of that," she responded. "I'm right here."

Her presence was unshakeable.

"Well, what would really help is to tell me what you are feeling," I replied sarcastically.

I heard myself engaged in an endless dialogue about who said and meant what, an infinite trail of words without meaning—an auditory figure-of-eight.

"The chances are, Meigra, that all this resistance I'm having is an indirect way of asking for reassurance from you. I want to know that you're still here with me because I'm afraid to acknowledge what I know, and I convince myself that you'll be hurt by what I reveal, even though I don't know what is yet to be revealed . . . and . . . "

I paused to take a breath. Joe was laughing so loud that his whole body was shaking.

"Wow," Meigra said. "I don't know what that means, but I have a feeling it'll sink in after a while."

"Actually, I'm not sure you're with me at all," I said. "I feel like I'm just sitting here."

"You are sitting there," Joe said, laughing.

Meigra wasn't laughing.

"I'm here and I like what you're saying," she said, pulling me in with her clear voice.

I suspected that Meigra was being polite and playing the good listener but didn't really want to be with me. I noted that, had I been sitting across from me, I wouldn't want to be there either!

Meigra leaned forward, adjusting her body to a position that implied I wasn't to mess with what she was about to say. Her face was open, and for emphasis, her eyes reflected the dead seriousness of her intent.

"You're giving me all your power," she began, "as though I could stop you from expressing yourself. I can't, and I don't want to. I don't want power over you even if you give it to me."

"Meigra," I said in an aching voice, "this mood is all I have, and it's such a struggle to keep this going because I have no idea where I'm going."

"There is nowhere to go," she insisted. "Where you are is where you need to be. Your struggle is in believing you're supposed to feel something other than what you feel. You're always where you need to be. You're right on schedule. There is nowhere to go."

Meigra's presence was so big, I feared I'd lose myself—that she'd see how small and weak I was beneath my external hard veneer, and that she'd either leave or swallow me up.

"No, no, no," a voice within me screamed. "Don't give away anything. Don't let go. Stay with the heaviness of centuries. You'll lose yourself if you live."

I felt lighter.

"I want to talk more freely," I said in a more receptive voice, "but I question whether I bother you a lot of the time. I wonder whether I get in the way of other things you want to do."

Hearing myself say that surprised me.

"That's a scared little person talking," I observed out loud.

I paused.

"Ohh . . . this is me, isn't it?" It isn't you!"

Joe's compassion, combined with Meigra's respect for the part of me for which I had little respect, twisted into knots the belief that she was out to kill my spirit and stop me from being myself.

Meigra's facial expression changed slightly and I froze, presuming the worst, interpreting her expression to mean that she'd left emotionally.

"What's going on?" I asked in an accusing tone.

"I'm still here," she replied. "I'm Meigra."

Her voice was soothing and reassuring, leaving no room to misinterpret the integrity of it. I felt the emotional edge I had to ride in order to move back and forth between feeling powerful and, a moment later, powerless. It was relatively easy to be powerless, and it was easy to be powerful.

The difficult part was the leap over the empty space between the two—a leap that bordered on impossible. I would have to rely completely on faith. If I stepped off the powerless ledge, I had to step onto a ledge of power.

Meigra's ability to see through my suspicious accusations, over and over again, brought me to tears, which I consistently pretended were due to yawning.

I had no excuses left. Meigra kept on being there. The mood was breaking up. My voice changed, dropping two octaves to become softer; my words fell out rather than being shoved.

I felt myself come back into myself, safe, quiet, relieved, and glad to see Meigra still sitting there. Her eyes were moist and glistening, joining mine in silent gratitude.

"I love it when you're talking about what's happening within you," Meigra began before I interrupted.

"I got it. I got it," I said excitedly. "This may sound simple, even stupid, but it's not up to you to make me feel better. It's my mood, my dilemma, and it's up to me change it."

Meigra's look implied that my insight was accurate.

Joe's background laughter implied that my insight was obvious.

I looked over to a grassy area beneath a large cottonwood tree and saw the boy asleep on his side. His soft, open face reminded me that I could be that way too.

"Meigra," I said excitedly, "if how I feel is of my own making, that means I can't believe, anymore, that I have no control over my own moods."

"Huh?" she responded. "Untwist that one for me."

"I control my own moods," I translated. "I can't believe anymore that I don't. What will I do now? Not being a passive bystander to how I feel is outrageous. I mean, I've always been a bystander to my funky moods—to being down, even to being up."

"You mean," Meigra said, pretending innocence, "you're the one that is responsible for how you feel and you can change it? Unbelievable!"

I smiled, bypassing the impulse to be serious.

"But what if I'm justified?" I asked. Immediately, I began to choke and cough. When I realized what I'd just asked, I wanted to burst out laughing but gagged instead.

Meigra watched me in wonderment.

"This is crazy," I went on. "Who can I blame then? How will I spend all the time I'm usually in a mood, if I'm not in a mood? Hmmmm. . ."

"Maybe I can develop new enemies to sulk on," I suggested.

The mood had changed. Emotional struggle dissolved to effortless hope. My energy returned. I was alive again. I realized I had to change the mood for my own sake.

"What an innovative idea," I thought out loud. "To do it for my own sake."

Meigra rolled her eyes.

"To stay with myself and hold this awareness is difficult," I said.

"Poor thing," I heard Joe whisper. "Don't want anything to be difficult."

"I believe so strongly," I continued, "that I can't really stay in charge of myself like I am right now. It's so much more familiar to see you, Meigra, as the real problem."

"Okay," she said in a teasing voice. "Let me try it."

Meigra sat up, leaned forward with her arms outstretched, and placed her hands on her thighs, knees apart. She moved forward and said, with the look of a cobra about to strike, "I'm not your problem. I've never been your problem. How you see me is your problem."

I was silenced.

"There's no place to go with this in words," I replied.

"No, not words," she said emphatically. "It's about energy, feelings, and remembering that you're forming the beliefs you see in front of you. They're yours. Completely and totally yours. There's no one outside of you who can make you think or do anything. It is an illusion to believe otherwise. This is your dream and you can play the day-to-day drama of it for-ever, or step out and be here, be alive, be real, be yourself—now, now, and now."

Joe put his knife and wood aside and applauded. He even pushed himself up from his chair and applauded. "Bueno, bueno," he cheered. "Bueno, bueno."

I was stunned by the force and energy of Meigra's words. Her body stance and incisiveness cut through any remnant of self-indulging doubt that remained in me.

I tried to contain a smile. I couldn't. With a force of its own, the smile burst through, consuming my caution as I laughed uncontrollably. Tears ran down my face. I laughed in ecstasy and applauded along with Joe and Meigra.

"You know, Meigra, when we were making love last night . . . ," I began, and burst out laughing before finishing the sentence.

I couldn't take my eyes off her. She was beautiful. Her expression was soft, clear, receptive. She looked strong and bright. I felt warm just looking into her eyes. The tension and fear I'd had with Meigra dissolved as though a different person had stepped into her body.

I knew that my perception had changed. Meigra had never left her body.

"It's okay for me to feel good with you, isn't it?" I asked. "This is scary. Now I want to hold onto this feeling. I'm afraid if I lose it, it won't return."

"Shhh," Meigra said. "Be here."

We were quiet.

"Meigra," I said, "sometimes my day is full and complete after simply making one real connection with another person."

"I'll be darned," Meigra said. "Why, how could that be? You mean you sometimes just live?"

She paused to allow the sarcasm to sink in, then added, "Huh. So you're not responsible for the glaciers melting?"

I touched her hand, appreciating her lightness.

"Once I stop needing to have all the great things in my life happen, they happen," I said.

Meigra crossed her eyes, exaggerating an expression of looking dumb.

"When I stop seeking, I find I have it," I added, at risk of being mocked even more. "I'll never find what I seek."

Meigra's dumb expression dissolved as she burst into laughter. "That's profound," she said and doubled over, falling to the floor, continuing to make comment for her own entertainment.

"That was brilliant," I said as I laughed, too.

It felt good to laugh together. I couldn't imagine how I'd perceived Meigra, only minutes earlier, as the enemy wanting my soul.

Unexpectedly, I remembered a secret but not-so-secret awareness I'd had since childhood—In the midst of being hurt, offended, or insulted, I'd always known I had the choice to laugh, had I chosen to. Usually, I took the more familiar, serious role of being hurt and offended. I hadn't yet learned to believe the background voice inside, which told me that the blaming words and opinions of others didn't matter, that they had nothing to do with me personally.

Frequently, I could have ended conflict and anger, but I believed I had no right to feel neutral. I thought something must be wrong with me if, in the midst of a genuine conflict, I felt like laughing.

I could see Joe enjoyed listening to us talk and laugh together.

As Meigra and I spoke, images of people I believed were doing important things in the world, compared to me, filled my thoughts. Without telling Meigra what I was seeing, I interrupted with, "What could I be doing that's important compared to them?"

At first, she was startled by the question, since it was totally out of context with our conversation. She quickly recognized that my mind was beginning to recycle its thoughts. She looked at me as though she were watching a larva go through its different stages to become a butterfly.

"Part of the problem of writing or doing anything I love," I continued, "is that I might get done. If I get done, I might not be satisfied with it."

"What a crazy thought," I said before Meigra could.

Listening to my thoughts was beginning to exhaust me.

"Whenever I'm just myself," I told Meigra, "I feel content. When I start comparing—thinking I should live like my friend or my brother, instead of being myself—I become lost in a sea of doubt."

"You've discovered how to change your mood," Meigra said.

"It's such a delicate thing," I replied.

"It is a delicate thing," she agreed.

"It's not the difference in moods that matters," Meigra added, "but the act of transition itself. The transition is the delicate place. It's where you either get lost in the mood or keep moving. It's a discipline. It's a faith. At once, you must believe you're capable of doing more than you believe you can do or have ever done, even if you don't fully believe it."

"It's simple, isn't it?" I commented.

"Yes, it's one of those things that's so simple you overlook your ability to do it. Based on past experience, you believe you can't. The trick lies in your ability to move in and out of different states fluidly, without having to understand them. You must have clear intention."

Meigra took a breath.

"You just keep moving without getting hooked on a belief

that separates you from me," she said.

I sat back and relaxed my shoulders.

I felt like I did when I was a small child and the miniature Lionel train derailed. The wheels continued to spin but the train just sat in place with all the other cars backed up behind it. My father carefully put all the wheels back on the track and the train continued to glide along the rails like it was supposed to.

I had a good feeling inside, watching the train move effortlessly around the bends and over the track switches. I felt that way now. My chest felt soft. My shoulders were relaxed. A more familiar feeling began to seep in and slowly radiate throughout my body.

"I really like you, Meigra," I said. "I like you a lot. I like that we can hold hands and that my heart feels on fire. I like that when I unexpectedly see you driving down the road, my instant reaction is, 'Oh boy, there's Meigra.'"

I was embarrassed, and relieved that I was embarrassed.

"It's almost too much sometimes," I said, "to remember who you really are. You shake my whole system up. You're so present, I can hardly stand it. That's why I find fault with you. Then I don't have to stand it. Did I say that?"

My whole body energized. I felt like I'd just wakened from a deep sleep.

Meigra smiled a sweet smile. "I'm getting full, I'd like to stop," she said.

"Okay," I answered, my eyes watering.

I felt warm all over. I stood up as Meigra did. We reached out together and pulled ourselves into each other; our bodies melted together as we stood silently. Even though I was six inches taller than Meigra, it seemed like we were the same height.

"Moods lead you somewhere," I heard Joe say. "They happen for you, not to you. When you are in one, instead of waiting for it to go away, or to feel better, see it as something wanting to happen—information to be revealed. Even though you may feel uncomfortable, not understanding why you feel the way you do, or what is behind it, respect the mood. Respect it.

"Each mood has a physical sensation attached to it, like its own personal fingerprint."

Meigra and I held each other.

Joe continued, "Moods happen at your scared places, those places in you that are developing, where you can go one step further than you've ever been before.

"Sometimes, a mood is simply feeling more, saying something you are afraid to say, or even a willingness to be alive, vibrant, and in love. Sometimes the 'in love' is with a person. Sometimes it is with silence, or with music, or a feeling, or life itself."

Joe was silent.

"The other side of a mood is what we're doing now," Meigra whispered in my ear. "This is where all our feelings—and awareness—come together. This is what hides behind the fear. To get to this side, like you did today, requires that you allow the discomfort of feeling bad to exist—to respect it but not indulge it."

"Why?" I whispered, still holding her close.

"Because," she answered, "I suspect I, too, shall be in a mood soon, and I will have this information stored some-where, enabling me to move more easily through the mood and into the present where I can hold you close."

"Meigra," I whispered, "there must be more to do in life than paying attention to everything all the time."

"There isn't," she replied. "When you're not paying attention to yourself, you're in the trance. When you're not paying attention to yourself, you're not paying attention to anyone or anything. You are not here."

"Yes!" I agreed.

Meigra looked at me with respect. "When you step out of the trance, your awareness takes no break. Your daily practice becomes one of paying attention to each relationship, each person you meet, each conflict . . . in each intimate moment."

7

Gap of Awareness

"Where does one dream end and the other one begin?" I asked. "What is the difference between a night dream and this one, the day dream, with me standing here in front of you? Is this not a dream too? How do you know if you're dreaming now or not? Am I dreaming you and are you dreaming me? Whose dream is this anyway?"

"Bruce, Bruce," I heard Meigra whispering in my ear. "You're dreaming out loud."

"Am I awake now?" I asked instinctively.

"You must be, unless I'm asleep too."

"Maybe we're both dreaming the same dream," I suggested sleepily.

"Could be," she replied.

I sat up.

"Meigra," I said in a now awake voice, "how do I know if I'm dreaming now or not? How do I know for sure if I'm awake or asleep this moment as I'm talking to you? I think I was dreaming that I was talking to someone about dreaming, but how do I know if that is true? Maybe everything is a dream. Maybe I'm never not dreaming. This is crazy."

"It is crazy," she agreed.

Meigra sat up and stretched.

"That's what makes all this so interesting and alive," she continued, now fully awake.

Meigra could do that. When she'd wake from sleep, she'd be awake as though the next thing to do after being asleep is to be awake! I, on the other hand, handled the transition from sleep to awakeness as though walking through sludge.

Just then, the boy, who slept between us, awoke with a smile on his face. He turned first to Meigra, then to me, ecstatic in his sandwiched position. He reached for Meigra to nurse, his eyes calling in each of us.

Meigra held him against her breast and continued speaking.

"On any particular day everything in the world, to you, seems like it is chaos, and you attempt to make order out of it. The next day everything appears orderly and you make chaos out of it. That is the way it is. Life has a rhythm of its own, and you either move through your days and nights with that natural rhythm or react to it. The decision, each moment, is always yours. If you decide to react, the consequence is simply one daily conflict after another, either with yourself or with someone else."

"How do you know this, Meigra? You're brilliant."

"I know."

"And humble," I teased.

"I know that too," she replied.

"I'm in conflict much of the time," Meigra added, "usually in conflict with myself. Sometimes I think I'm a bad person or I've done something wrong, or I'm not doing something right. Then I argue with myself. I get lost in the argument. But since the argument is with myself, I can't win or lose, only persist. If I'm not careful and aware of what I'm doing inside myself, I will end up in conflict with you, blaming you for my inside conflict."

"If you want peace, you must give up the idea of conflict entirely and for all time," recalling something I had read.

"That's profound," Meigra responded.

"No! No, it's not! Conflict is necessary," I blurted out, startling myself with such an irrational statement.

A moment later, I thought that revelation absurd and felt stupid for saying it.

Yet, Meigra's eyes lit up at my words. She seemed intrigued, and encouraged me to continue without having to be logical.

"Conflict is natural. It is part of life," I said. "It is also what I would do anything to avoid.

"And, I know that entering into conflict, consciously, will change my life and allow greater compassion, intimacy, and a sense of well-being."

Meigra silently questioned me.

"I don't know yet how any of this works or why. I'm hearing this for the first time myself," I continued.

"Learning to work with conflict really does begin with the relationships closest to me, including myself, that often seem the most difficult, if not impossible. First, I have to make the decision to acknowledge, feel, and enter into a conflict consciously, and to use conflict as a tool for revealing the hidden truth."

"If you'd just be nice to me all the time," Meigra teased, ". . . there'd be no conflict."

"Uh huh," I replied. "If you are fortunate enough, Meigra, you'll have a person in your life with whom you have an ongoing conflict. You can use the conflict to deepen the relationship, and practice not only surviving conflict, but using it to expand the limits of relationship, especially with me."

"Limits?" she asked, "You said, a few days ago, that there were no limits, even when I attempt to set them."

"There aren't," I replied, "but in believing there are limits, we set ourselves up for conflict. A limit is a belief and beliefs always come into conflict. I have to change how I think to work with conflict successfully. Someone like Einstein may have said you cannot solve a problem from the same level as it exists. I have to move to another level of seeing the world to work with conflicts—especially, ongoing conflicts."

"And what is the other level?" Meigra asked with a provoking smile. "How does it actually work in a practical, everyday relationship way—you know, like our conflicts?"

"Great question," I answered, "and I don't know."

"What is conflict anyway?" Meigra asked.

"Conflict happens when I see and believe something to be true and expect you to believe it and see it as I do."

"Yes!" she exclaimed.

"I expect you to see what I see and I am determined to hold my position, no matter what," I continued. "It feels like a survival issue, as if my total being is on the line. I take a stand. I cannot move. I am lost in holding a belief. From my position, I believe you know what I am talking about but choose to be my enemy."

"That's really what it feels like," Meigra said.

"It is, isn't it?"

"This is the essential level of unconscious conflict," I went on. "This is what most people deeply believe in their bodies, including me, and then they live from that belief. No one escapes from this belief. It may be all we all know. It is the first level. The unexpressed conflict lives in the background. It permeates the atmosphere.

"At this level, no one wins. No one feels good. No one moves. Nothing changes. The conflict continues for weeks, months, years, decades—and in global terms, centuries. Our bodies become pained. We experience headaches, colds, back problems, stiff necks, or disease. The conflict becomes frozen in the body. It locks up and stiffens us."

"Keep going," Meigra encouraged.

"There are few people around us who demonstrate how to work with conflict as a useful tool and who see it as necessary.

"Conflict is too often brought to a halt at the first feeling of fear or anger, or as anxiety escalates. Sometimes, it's impossible for me to break away from being nice, or pretending that nothing is happening."

"Yeah," Meigra interjected, "that's why I so often see couples or families in restaurants eating in tense silence or making small talk. They seem to be all pretending together that something meaningful is happening, when in fact, they are all lost in deafening disconnection. No one is home and no one is speaking of it."

She looked down a moment thoughtfully, then said, "I've done it. I know."

"I do it too," I graciously acknowledged.

"You?" Meigra teased.

I almost chose to be offended but instead laughed at her quick humor.

"The world around us," I continued with fervor in my voice, "feeds the belief that conflict is hurtful, difficult, wrong, shouldn't be necessary, usually leads to violence—and is unevolved."

"I am left in conflict then," Meigra added, "not only with another person, but also—and most important—with myself."

"Yes," I responded, "and the other level, which allows conflict to be used in an expansive way, requires that I recognize that the difficult people in my life represent aspects of myself. And this is tricky. To work with conflict—any conflict with anyone—requires that I am willing to see that all those around me really, really are aspects of myself.

"I remember reading, a long time ago, that what we perceive in others we are strengthening in ourselves. I understand, now, that when I am willing to believe that others are part of my dream, and are aspects of me, then I have to stretch even further. I accept that conflict is not in my life by accident. It is there to help me expand into greater awareness and more intimate relationship with whoever I'm in conflict with."

"That doesn't sound very comforting," Meigra interjected.

"Conflict is rarely comfortable," I replied. "It's often unpleasant and can bring about nausea, physical pain, and panic-and-flee thoughts. Sometimes, I make a choice not to panic or flee.

"The symptoms only mean that my body is reorganizing as it discovers its real self, separate from what I've learned to believe is true."

"I could also simply eliminate conflict from my life completely and be done with it," Meigra suggested as she nudged my arm in mock humor. "I may not need conflict anymore. That is a possibility, you know?"

"No it's not," I said, nudging her back.

"Yes it is," she quickly replied, then just as quickly reflected on what we'd just said.

"Oh, I just proved your point, didn't I?" she asked.

"No, not really," I said.

"Yes I did," she said. "Geez, I did it again."

We nudged each other simultaneously.

"Conflict is as necessary," I went on, "as breathing and eating. In big and little ways, conflict is everywhere. I can't imagine life without it. It's the word itself, by its common definition, that's usually thought of as being bad, uncomfortable, difficult, and a social comment on the hopelessness of humankind. Actually, conflict is just another way of describing the gaps of awareness between people."

"Gaps of awareness between people?" Meigra questioned. "What's a gap of awareness?"

"The gap of awareness is the belief I mentioned earlier—that if you see something differently from me, not in the same way I do, then you must be my enemy trying to trip me up in some way. It is incomprehensible to me that you don't see and believe things the same way I do. Absolutely incomprehensible. That places me squarely in conflict with you."

"Sort of never ending, eh?" Meigra observed.

"From that point of view of being alive, it is never ending," I replied. "That is what that point of view believes. Beliefs stick together to not be disbelieved, ever."

"So, if life isn't hopeless," Meigra asked, "what do we do about it?"

"There are two levels of conflict." I answered confidently, even though I no longer knew how I knew what I knew.

"What are they?"

"The first level is being part of the conflict," I replied. "This happens when any two people, or even nations, believe they have been wronged, attach blame, and take a justified emotional position, waiting for the other party to recognize their wrongness. This level believes that conflict is inevitable.

"The second level is conscious conflict. The intent of conscious conflict is to awaken us. In this level, I know what I am doing. I realize there may well be escalated feelings—that fear may come up, and that the conflict may disturb the peace. I also know that, ultimately, conflict has purpose—t will lead to clarity and bring not only peace but increased power to both persons. From this perspective, I know that conflict precedes expanded awareness and a freedom from restricting need to hold a limiting belief. Thus I immerse myself in it, scared, shaking, and frightened—but willingly."

"Hmmm. What would it look like if we practiced that second level," Meigra asked.

"Yesterday, during that conflict we had," I began, "when I heard your blaming, admonishing tone of voice, I fought back and defended myself, meeting your blame with mine. I joined you. When I joined you, as if by habit, our conflict became another notch in my belief that it's hopeless to live with you or anyone.

"At that moment—just before the impulse to justifiably defend—that is the absolute moment, and the only moment, for me to take a different action than ever before. If I let that moment pass, I will be right back in conflict with you."

"What could you do instead of defend?" Meigra asked.

"What I can do next time is pause a few seconds to choose the thoughts I want to have instead of the defensive, hurt ones I've always had before. I will remember you are my friend, not my enemy."

"Oh," Meigra said. "That would be different."

"And I have to do it," I said. "I have to change my perception of you to change the conflict. It is entirely up to me to change my perception, and I can do that in the first minute by remembering images and incidents where we're liking each other and when I'm even in awe of you. One incident will do. In that brief window where the conflict lifts, my body tension and need to be right subsides. That is the moment where I must follow the calm instead of the impulse to hold any emotional position.

"When I hold that moment of calm, my heart softens, I breathe, and my face reflects quiet neutrality. Your face softens in direct response, and I will have changed our belief about conflict forever, knowing I can perceive you any way I want and that it is always within my control. We both can do this, even if we only hold the calm period for a few seconds. We'll know that we can do the same thing again. That's hope."

Suddenly, I started laughing uncontrollably. I couldn't stop. I felt embarrassed.

"What's funny?" Meigra asked.

"I just had the thought . . . ," I began, and curled into more laughter before I could finish the sentence.

Without knowing what we were laughing at, Meigra started laughing too.

"I think I've become one of those people I used to envy," I said as my laughter dissolved into tears. "I think I've become who I always wanted to be."

I felt cold and began trembling. I was acknowledging something I thought I had no right to acknowledge, think of, certainly not to say out loud, but I couldn't stop.

"I have to tell you this, Meigra," I said, laughing and crying at the same time. "It's been such a private, long-standing, background thought, that even I didn't let myself in on my own secret."

I was sure Meigra believed I was about to reveal some hidden sexual desire. Even I thought I was about to say something embarrassing. Instead, I reached out and took her hand.

"Meigra," I said, "I always used to want to be like me, like I can be now. But I only saw it in other people. I was in awe of people who could fluidly glide through their lives without getting forever stuck in anger, blame, and emotionally dramatic daily soap operas. I saw others as being able to see life from a larger perspective, with big vision, and outside of personal conflicts. Now I can do it. I'm them!

"Meigra, my entire body is brighter, I can feel it! There is no one who is more or less than me right now. I feel taller. I feel solid. I feel joy without tears. I respect myself as much as I respect others."

8

Lightning Vision

The heavens darkened as rain clouds filled with thunder and lightning crept slowly under the sky, reorienting my senses and deepening my involvement in being alive.

I could feel something about to happen. The moist air was charged with anticipation. Clouds and colors changed constantly. Cloud shadows moved slowly over the distant mountains, casually climbing and descending thirteen-thousand-foot protrusions into space, suggesting a relationship billions of years in the making, wise and all knowing.

My difficult thoughts dissolved into the mountains, clouds, and shadows. For a moment, I was out of my self-importance. Things elsewhere forced me to stretch beyond emotional self-indulgence.

It was Sunday at dusk. Meigra and I were alone in a house that was nestled by itself just below the mountains of the Taos Indian Pueblo in New Mexico. The approaching storm drew all our attention. Nothing was more important than witnessing the power surrounding us.

I thought I was being presented with a private showing of the first wide-screen production of Earth, God, and nature, all aligned with each other in a brilliance not yet duplicated by any motion picture projector. Even in the waiting silence, the sound was full, vibrating with what was yet to be heard.

We did not speak.

A lightning bolt slammed to the ground just outside the house. Dozens of others followed, forming a curtain of unpredictable light. The thunder, only seconds behind, burst open my senses, forcing an excitement I'd never felt.

The sound was all around us, lightning tentacles reaching for the ground everywhere, pulling my awareness up into the clouds and out into space. My senses were beyond stimulation. I felt lost in a vortex of lightning and thunder energy. I thought of taking off all my clothes and running out into the desert through the endless light, immense sound, and pounding rain.

I fantasized being struck by the lightning and incinerated into some other form, destined to handle the power and energy I could only observe and not be.

Meigra, beside me, was transfixed. We were each having our own personal response to this giant event. An hour passed as the sound gradually diminished and the light drew distant.

The rain continued.

I did not want this breadth of awareness and excitement to end. I did not want to return to my belief that life had to appear so difficult. Looking out the window into the darkened sky, watching the rain saturate the parched desert ground, I felt myself shift into another dimension.

For the first time in my life, I could see how I had been living and responding to everyday events, and I could see myself seeing myself respond to those events.

It was dark outside now. Completely dark. The rain was all we could hear. I was seeing without my eyes. There were no words for what I was experiencing. It was as though I were wired for radar, sonar, and telepathy all at once.

"Meigra?" I called gently so as not to startle her.

"Meigra," I called again.

She turned her head, her face reflected in the glass by a candle I had just lit.

"What?" she asked in a whisper.

"Where are you now?" I asked.

"I have no words to tell you," she answered. "I don't know."

"Me neither."

We sat quietly with the candle and listened to the rain.

"Meigra?" I hesitated, knowing I would disturb the mood, yet compelled to speak. "This question may seem out of context compared to the gigantic experience we're having, but it's a question that comes to me. I can't not ask it."

"Can't not?" she responded.

"Can't not!" I repeated.

"What would you do this moment," I asked, "if you couldn't blame anyone for anything ever again? You couldn't blame your parents, a husband, a wife, a child, not even yourself. You couldn't blame the government, the weather, the economy, or lack of money. What would you do with no one or no thing to blame for anything?"

"Hmmm," was her only response.

"And you didn't need to blame anyone for anything?" I added. "What then?"

"What then?"

"Yeah, what then?"

She stared at me with a look that penetrated any remnants of ego." I am left with the probability," she said in a commanding voice, "that nothing is wrong or missing in my life. I recognize that no one is doing anything to anybody, anywhere at any time. There are no victims, only a victim state of mind. That state of mind believes that the world doesn't really work, that it is out of order. What feels like internal life struggle and effort to make things happen is part of that belief."

"Yes . . . ," I started to say, but Meigra continued without changing rhythm.

"Struggle has a familiar body feeling to it," she continued. "It is also a belief. I've been taught that I need to struggle to survive, that I need to struggle to make it, as though that is the way to live life.

"I see struggle all around me. It's in the people I know and see every day. Struggle exists as an institution and is preached by governments, religions. The school learning process expects it and demands it."

"I know . . . ," I said, about to add my observation, but Meigra was impassioned and I listened carefully.

"School children are expected to have a hard time. They—and us, if you recall your school learning experiences—were expected to work hard, earn good grades, worry, compare, and fret. I came to believe that worrying and working hard were life itself. I felt guilty if I relaxed.

"School grades had a higher priority than getting along with each other, or even liking and believing my own perceptions. The grade became the goal; it took the place of thought and thoughtfulness, and for most people, struggle and anxiety were attached to comparing—feeling either better or worse than someone else."

"As I recall," I interjected, "my question was about not blaming anyone else. This sounds like that's exactly what you're doing now—blaming others."

"You don't hear blame in my voice," she replied. "Blame has a complaining tone to it. I'm not complaining. I'm illuminating and observing. I'm retrieving myself. Do you get that?"

"Maybe."

"'Maybe,' in this case, means you are getting it. Good, then I'll continue illuminating for you," she said as the candle brightened in apparent response to her words.

"See, the candle knows," she teased. At least, I assumed she was teasing.

"Grades," she went on, "implied smartness and dumbness. They separated me from others. I've carried a body and mind belief about struggle into most of my relationships."

An unexpected burst of lightning hit the pole just outside our window, about twenty feet away. I counted the seconds to the first roll of thunder. Seven seconds. I began to compute how fast sound travels to determine how far away the lightning was.

"What am I doing?" I asked. "I'm sitting here computing the distance of lightning. I don't even know how to do that."

"You often emotionally leave the room at times like this," Meigra said, yet I heard no tone of blame in her voice, so I consciously decided to not be offended.

"When you're on to something," she observed, "or close to seeing some bigger truth, really seeing deeply into what is happening in the world or with people around you, you judge yourself for what you see. It is as though you become afraid of the simplicity of truth and your ability to see it. It is terrifying for you to believe that you could see what others apparently are not seeing."

She placed her hand on my shoulder in what could have been interpreted as condescending, but it wasn't. Instead, she was emphasizing the need for me to hear what she was saying.

"Being afraid doesn't stop you for long," she added. "You just take an emotional break by computing the distance of lightning."

Smiling, she concluded, "Kind of like what you do when you get a flash of insight."

"That's quite a long, complex explanation for my simply counting seconds," I said, embarrassed and relieved at her clear perception.

"Did you just bust me?" I asked.

"Why not?" she replied.

"Actually, I do get it," I said, rolling my eyes.

I looked at the clock. It was exactly 2:00 A.M.—much later than we believed we could stay up and still be awake. I wondered why the clock time mattered anyway.

"What if the entire world," I asked, "came to some agreement hundreds of years ago that we all have to be in bed and asleep before midnight or we'll instantly decompose. And everyone lived their lives believing that?"

"What else do you see around relationship and struggle?" Meigra asked, ignoring my cleverness. I felt her implied demand that I stay present in the room and not count the seconds.

"As I become involved with people," I said, "especially in close relationships, I bring with me my own familiar feeling of inner struggle and that 'something is missing in my life' belief. Eventually, I project that belief onto my partner. She then becomes the alleged source of the struggle and what appears to be missing in my life, and the struggle continues."

"So what do you do about it?" Meigra asked. "What can you do about it? How can you not live in struggle?

"It seems," she went on, answering her own question, "that it is in our cells. If I'm not in some form of struggle, I feel uncomfortable. When I have moments of complete ease and quiet inside, I begin to worry about losing it. I like it so much, I try to hold on to it and the worry dissolves to struggle. It is almost as though I fear peace because I will lose it."

"We can't force ourselves to be at ease and quiet," I said. "Ease, and that quiet place inside me, happen on their own. I have to be available for them. My struggle is always inside myself. Feelings of hopelessness, despair, and struggle come from believing I'm powerless and at the mercy of world events outside myself. Nobody out there can make it better."

I stopped talking, feeling shy as I felt Meigra's full attention and respect for what I was saying. Being with Meigra this way was so satisfying that I became uncomfortable.

"I live in these feelings unknowingly," I continued through the discomfort. "You know, Meigra, these feelings are another manifestation of the daily trance we spoke about that morning I returned from California. I'm unaware that I'm living in a constant state of struggle and urgency. I call it keeping busy."

"What do you do with this?" Meigra asked.

"I begin with the understanding that struggle is in me and has nothing to do with outer circumstances. First, I must notice when I am struggling—any struggle at all. Even the most seemingly trivial sense of making an effort is struggle. No one struggle is more or less intense than another."

"Are you struggling now to tell me this?" Meigra asked perceptively.

"No."

"How come you're not?"

"Because I'm just here. I'm not thinking about what I'm about to say next."

"So," Meigra said with a mischievous smile, "when you're just here in the present moment, there is no struggle. You are being yourself without having to look good. Is that right?"

"Yes."

"So," Meigra said, physically exaggerating how smart she was, "let your first sense of struggle be a signal to pause and get quiet inside. Be quiet for a minute and let the silence bring you information, instead of trying so hard to know and be right. Use the pause time to notice your thoughts and body sensations. Become aware of your breathing."

"That's magic, Meigra," I said, appreciating her ability to transform confusing things into clarity.

"Struggle changes to quiet in those moments of pausing," I continued. "The shift to quiet and peace may last only a few seconds or minutes, yet a lifelong pattern is consciously changed by simply paying attention and taking a specific action."

"It's a matter of practice," Meigra said. "The whole process requires practice, practice, and practice. Soon, struggle becomes a signal to be at ease inside and allow answers and information to come to you. Your mind will often present what seem like valid reasons to keep the struggle and tension going. Your internal discipline is to notice the mind thoughts but let them pass on through."

"My words exactly," I concluded.

"Right! I thought they were your words!"

The lightning had moved off into the distance, leaving only an occasional, gentle illumination of the sky. The thunder was only a distant rumble. Rain had saturated the ground, and there wasn't any more rain in the sky. The stars and the moon gradually displaced the clouds. We both yawned at once and fell asleep on the couch in seven seconds.

9

Tracking Perception

"Get a piece of paper and a pen," the voice said. "Draw two columns. Label one column 'Oh Boy!' Leave the other column unlabeled. With your mind, scan the names of people in your life, past and present, including family, friends, and those closest to you and farthest from you emotionally. Do not censor or judge any name.

"With just your body response and not that of your mind, feel how you respond when you hear each name. If your body goes 'Oh Boy!' when you think a name, as though you feel happy and lighter when you think of the person, place their name in the 'Oh Boy!' column. If there is no such 'Oh Boy!' response, place their name in the blank, unlabeled column."

I asked the voice why I should do this.

"Do it," the voice demanded.

I agreed to the command, realizing I was about to learn something that I might not learn if I didn't agree to learn it now, at this moment.

My mind filled with names of people who came through my life, as though I were flipping through a personal telephone book. I scanned the names as they passed through. Like the ball coming to rest on a particular number of a spinning roulette wheel, the name Gene Rumrill came up first. Without judgment or letting my mind make up its mind, I felt my body respond with an 'Oh Boy!' as I said his name and saw his image.

I always looked forward to seeing Gene, and I liked thinking about him. I wrote his name in the 'Oh Boy!' column.

"Judy" was the second name to come up. I hesitated at even thinking her name. There was no body response. My body was neutral. I wrote her name in the unlabeled column without justifying or explaining to myself why.

Names rolled through my internal vision like credits at the end of a film, moving through quickly as I scanned them.

"Dari" was the next name that came into focus. "Yes!" I said, and I placed her name in the 'Oh Boy!' column.

The name of a close family member came up. My mind wanted to place his name in the 'Oh Boy!' column. I wanted him to fit there and felt that his name should be there. I even had thoughts about how wrong it would be for me to place his name in the other column. Yet, the voice reminded me to listen to my body response only. Like a leap into space, I placed his name in the unlabeled column. I almost changed it back again to appease the guilt I was beginning to think I should have.

The authority of the voice kept me moving.

"It requires courage to step out of the circle of pretense," the voice commanded. "Be willing to see the truth. Everyone will be free when this is done. Do this with everyone you know who is in your life.

"Continue until your list is complete," the voice instructed. "When you have finished the two columns, those in the 'Oh Boy!' column will remain in your present life. Those in the unlabeled column will be free to be who they are, in their own way, at their own pace. You will no longer need to spend time with them. They will no longer cause you emotional or physical disturbance."

"Why am I doing this?" I asked. "What's the purpose?"

"Some things are too spacious to say indoors," the voice replied. "Go outside and I will answer your question."

I walked outside into the sunlight and found myself surrounded by green hills and clusters of oak trees. I took a deep breath and sighed in relief, feeling the expansiveness around me.

"You need emotional space around you," the voice began, "to understand the concept of being real. Your body will always tell you what is real and what brings life to you. It will also tell you what has been constricted, limited, and condensed by being trapped in a particular view of living. This list defines the two."

"Sounds arrogant," I said, "to determine who is to be in my life based on my body response to them."

"Arrogance requires that you feel and see yourself as less than others," the voice responded.

"Less than?" I questioned. "I thought arrogance was about judging others to be less, with me being smarter, more special, or better in some way."

"When you see what you call arrogance, you are looking terror square in the eye," the voice replied. "A person perceived as arrogant believes himself to be separate, isolated, alone, unable to communicate the fear that clings within him. He cannot believe it himself, so he pushes a self-created image in front of himself, believing and hoping others cannot see that it is only an image, an illusion.

"What I have demonstrated to you, however, is not about judgment. This is about respect for life—all life. You have no choice. You have called into your life the people that you've come to know over the years. You've dreamed them. They're in your life to serve you, and you to serve them. Trust me."

"Trust me?" I repeated. I laughed so hard, I woke myself up still laughing, surprised that I had been dreaming.

My dreams and waking life were beginning to blend, with less tangible difference between them. The thought of no longer being able to distinguish between dreams and waking life could have been scary, but I didn't know whether I was dreaming that thought or not!

"It requires courage to step out of the circle of pretense." The words in the dream—if it was a dream—echoed within me. Jarid had spoken those words a few months earlier. They were some of Sara's last words to me before she died. Meigra frequently repeated them to me. I took notice.

The sun blazed a pathway through the window, illuminating the dust particles floating just out of reach of my nose.

"I breathe that," I thought to myself. "Yuck."

I had a strange feeling, as though I had been to another world doing other things and now I was here in the more familiar one. When I pulled the covers back, a pad of paper fell to the floor. I picked it up and noticed that it had two columns drawn on it with a list of familiar names in each column.

In the left column—labeled 'Oh Boy!'—nine names were listed. The other column, unlabeled, had twenty names written down. Remembering the dream, I looked at each name in the unlabeled column.

I recognized the truth of what I was seeing. The names in the 'Oh Boy!' column brought up a smile. Each name in the other column brought neutral feelings or a disturbing sensation in my belly. I realized that I felt a subtle tension in me when around the person, as though they weren't quite present; it felt very much like being in a room with someone when they don't want to be there but are pretending they do.

A sadness moved through me as I read down the list and realized a part of my history with many friends was truly history. I knew I could not actively reach out to these people again for now—maybe forever.

I wondered what prompted a dream like this in the first place. Why now? Then I remembered how much of my life I'd devoted to trying to make some relationships be something other than what they really were or were ever destined to be.

I couldn't let some people just be. I believed that if I did just one more thing, they'd be okay, or they'd be like me. "What would happen," I asked myself, "if I didn't take responsibility to fix them?"

"You think too much," I heard someone say. I turned to see who was there. Before my eyes could find a human figure, a woman's voice asked, "What is this about relationships that causes you so much disturbance?"

Startled, I spun around to face an almost translucent image of Sara. I couldn't speak. She stood there like a white shadow, glistening.

"Sara!" I said.

I looked at her in awe. What was incredulous to me appeared to be matter of fact to her.

"There are people in your life who disturb you. They are supposed to disturb you," she continued, completely ignoring my initial fright. "That is how you learn. The disturbers in your life ignore, avoid, verbally abuse, disrespect, and definitely don't understand you—they push your buttons. They don't show up on time, rarely follow through, and if they listen, they don't seem to hear."

Sara's words so fascinated me, I lost interest in how she got there or what she looked like. I wanted to question the experience I was having, but her intent to speak over my extreme curiosity prevailed.

"These disturbers," she went on, "are your parents, your children, friends, landlords, banks, your partner, and—what is most significant—yourself.

"The disturbers fill your thoughts, even when they're miles or continents away. Your day's mood can be set by the mere mention of their name. You will be irritated and emotionally drained solely by a mental reminder that they exist.

"The ultimate disturber seemingly has no redeeming value to be in this world. And you can't understand why they are. That is their gift."

"Gift?" I asked.

"Yes, gift," she repeated. "As long as you can be disturbed, there will be disturbers in your life. The real question is how can these people become the peacemakers for you."

She paused and smiled a translucent smile.

"What is going on here?" I asked as I was suddenly struck with the illogic of her presence. "How are you here? What's happening? This is crazy or I'm going crazy."

Sara said nothing. She simply stood facing me; my confusion didn't really matter to her, especially since she had my full attention.

"A disturber comes in both female and male form. Neither gender has fewer or more disturbers than the other. Equality exists in this realm without respect to politics, background, or financial status. Disturbing people come in all sizes, colors, and ages. They can be six months or ninety years old. Ageism does not exist here."

She must have noticed my eyes glazing over as I stared into space.

"Stay with me," she encouraged. "This information will change your life forever.

"Disturbers can live in your house, next door, or on another continent," she continued. "Distance does not matter. It is irrelevant. Their influence transcends the miles, steel doors, and concrete walls and can have the impact of substantial amounts of kryptonite. But you know that," she interjected with a side remark.

Embarrassed before I needed to be, I wondered if she could see what I was thinking.

"You know my thoughts, don't you?" I asked, not really expecting her to answer.

"I'm a disturber to other people too, aren't I?" I thought out loud. "I know how others disturb me. But how do I disturb others?"

"You disturb Meigra every day. Whenever she defends, justifies, or explains herself to you, you're there, in her face, so to speak, to push her to the edge—the edge at which she learns that there is nothing to defend, justify, or explain to anyone, ever. She sometimes hates you, simultaneously knowing that her reaction comes from within her and has nothing whatsoever to do with you. You are her gift, and her disturber."

Leaning closer, and with a playful expression in her eyes, Sara whispered, "And what a gift you are."

"The disturber does not need to be present to award its prize," she continued. "It could be someone you see every day or haven't seen in ten years. Time doesn't matter.

"The disturber has his impact outside of time, space, distance, or logic. He can drain your energy, fill your thoughts completely, and cause you to do and say things you can only imagine in your dreams. He brings out parts of you that you didn't know existed, and often wish didn't.

"One common example of a disturber, especially to you," she added with emphasis, "is the opposite sex, the other gender. Women—those creatures who inhabit bodies that look so different, behave so weirdly, and are so unpredictable and inexplicable.

"They appear difficult to deal with, understand, and communicate with. You think you cannot trust, believe in, count on, or even love them for any length of time. They are easy to blame.

"You perceive that these other gender types delight in deceit, manipulation, and being inconsistent. You believe they can't make up their minds and that they find commitment a ten-letter word. Some will say of these disturbers that they have always been that way and you just can't reach them, that's just the way they are."

I was getting uncomfortable. I felt hot all over, and my hands and forehead were beginning to perspire. My heart was beating faster. Assimilating the truth of Sara's words was challenging.

"As people who disturb you, women appear as the enemy," she continued, no longer whispering. "You believe that they want control not only of their lives, but of yours, too. You suspect that this is what is really behind their actions, their niceness, and their behavior, that they have a hidden agenda to stifle and suppress you completely, to keep you from being yourself.

"You believe that, as with insatiable vampires, blood is not enough. They want everything including your heart, soul, money, and ultimate control of your life force.

"They, these disturbers," Sara continued, "leave you feeling powerless and hopeless. In your view, that is their primary function—to leave you not only powerless and hopeless, but lost forever in a sea of self-doubt.

"The opposite-sex disturber plays the role well in your life. She is easy to spot and identify. Decade after decade, there is a voice in you that repeats, 'You're not going to pull anything over on me.'"

Sara playfully twirled in place, then reached for my hand even though she couldn't physically touch it. "You definitely see them as the disturbers, the ones who cause you so much pain, confusion, and self-doubt. You speak in circles to yourself. 'If only she were different' could be your life mantra."

I laughed at that line, then quickly realized the truth of it and felt embarrassed. I hadn't realized how long and consistently that thought had been lurking in the background of my life.

"So why do I need disturbers in my life?" I asked, sounding innocent. "What is their purpose? How do they serve me? How do they serve anyone?"

"I'll tell you how," she replied. "But first you have to calm yourself. Be still."

"I am calm. I am still," I said, my voice rising.

"You're not angry?"

"No!"

"You look angry."

"I'm not. Just tell me."

"Disturbers serve you by bringing to the surface those things uncomfortable to you," she said, smiling just enough not to provoke. "They bring up the anger, the self-doubt, disappointment, frustration, and all the judgment you carry. Whatever lives within you every day, usually without your awareness, is what brings disturbers into your life. Strangely, when you are no longer disturbed, they cease to exist."

"What? How do people who disturb me cease to exist if I'm not disturbed?"

"Jarid once taught you this, when he looked directly into your eyes and said, 'We project out there what we need. We give parts of ourselves distance so that we may work and integrate those parts. Your discipline is to remember that you are forming the beliefs that you see in front of you.'"

"I remember," I replied, "and I'm not sure I fully understood what he meant when he said that. But how did you know what Jarid once told me?"

"Doesn't matter," she replied. "No one else can disturb you, in any way, unless you want to be disturbed. You always choose your own response. How you respond depends on how you view the world and how you want to use your energy. No outside force or person makes you do anything you don't voluntarily choose to do."

Sara reminded me of a couple I had known: each had complained that the other was the problem. Together and separately, they had confided that the other one kept them from being themselves. "I can't be myself with him," she had told me. "I can't be myself with her," he had repeated.

Each believed that their perception was absolutely true—that the other person was to blame and that's all there was to it.

Remembering them, I saw how silly the idea was. Unless I am friends with a very large, muscular body-builder who lifts twice her weight in steel, chews on automobile tires, and literally has me bound and gagged in a dark cellar with rats and centipedes, no one is stopping me from being myself, whatever myself might be in that moment.

"The disturber person brings you to your edge," Sara continued, interrupting my thoughts. "The edge is the place where you must acknowledge to yourself that it is you that is scared, it is you standing alone in your own shadow."

She moved closer and placed a hand on each of my shoulders, allowing her forehead to gently fall forward against mine.

"And the shadow will chase you everywhere," she whispered, "until you turn around and see that you are the shadow."

I stepped back, uncomfortable with our proximity.

"How do I know this isn't all a dream right now, Sara? How do I know whether I'm awake and you're here in this translucent form or I'm dreaming, about to wake up only to remember you as a dream?"

"You're asking me this question now," she continued, "because it seems easier to ask it than to believe what you are experiencing."

"Why would it be easier to believe you before I believe me?" I asked.

Sara's presence sparkled. Her image resembled that of someone in a Star Trek episode being transported from one ship to another. She was absolutely present with me, yet always seemed about to dissolve into another dimension. Bright blue sparkles radiated from around and within her image. When she was still, the sparkles slowed to a more constant light.

"It's your training," she replied. "The culture around you does not support trusting yourself. Instead, it encourages you to believe external authorities, experts, other sources of information outside yourself.

"That is why, to be in relationship with people, including yourself," she said, exaggerating a slow, methodical voice, "you must slow down and be still inside. From that stillness, you will hear accurate, practical information.

"For the first time, you will feel what relationship feels like. To believe yourself and genuinely connect with others, you need to know what relationship feels like. You need to know what it looks like. Without stillness, you only know what it is supposed to look and feel like, and you become easily disappointed when your picture of it changes. At that moment, when the picture is not what you expect, you are no longer in present time with what is happening. Instead, you are struggling to retrieve what you expected to happen."

"That's true, that's what I've always done," I agreed.

"And it doesn't work, does it?" Sara responded. "Never has, never will. Can't. Real relationship is different from anything you've ever seen. You wouldn't know what it looked like. "

"What does real relationship look like?" I asked, challenging Sara to be specific.

"It is more than being with another person or simply living with a family," she replied. "People who have lived together for decades, married and with children, may never have been in relationship. You could be emotionally and physically intimate for years and still have no relationship."

Sara paused as if to study her next thought.

"You can live an entire life without ever having experienced relationship with another being, including yourself," she said gazing into space, "and you can live without relationship, believing you have it."

I found myself secretly comparing myself to others, to see if what she was saying was true for me. Voices filled my mind to convince me that I could do relationship while others could not.

Sara ignored my secret thoughts, which I knew she sensed either telepathically or by the obvious, pained expression on my face.

"There are clues," she continued, "that demand you see what is really in front of you and always has been. In relationships, there is always something wanting to happen at some level. It is not that something is wrong, bad, or missing; there is simply the next step waiting to express itself."

"What are the clues?" I asked.

"You will know something wants to happen when you experience consistent physical symptoms like headaches, colds, backaches, low energy, disease, and what are commonly called addictions. Actually, addiction only exists for as long as you want it to. By itself, without your belief in it, it's a myth.

"And there's even more, like there shouldn't be?" she laughed, speaking with a perfect New York Jewish accent.

"Wait," I called out. "What did you say about addiction?"

"What did I say about addiction? I said addiction is a belief, and as long as you believe it, it has you. Addictions keep you out of relationship."

"How?" I asked.

"You identify yourself as the addiction. Once you identify yourself as a specific addiction, you can devote the rest of your life to fixing it, recovering from it, talking about it, avoiding it—even meeting with others who have taken the same identity. With your life fully immersed in what is inherently wrong with you, there is little energy and time to be with other people in the discomforts, joys, and unknowns of real relationship."

"Why would I take on an addiction as a lifestyle to avoid being close with other people?"

"Why not?" Sara answered. "For some people, it's more familiar to feel powerless to some external substance or behavior than to be real. For them, being real can feel more painful than an addiction. Common emotional disturbances like self-doubt, symptoms of depression, powerlessness, despair, and numerous other debilitating thoughts and beliefs usually show up at the edge of being real—that place where you are willing to enter into the scary, often frightening unknowns of relationships."

"Is that why," I asked, "with some people, even though they are physically present with me, I feel like I must emotionally chase them in an attempt to make contact, as though no matter how far out I reach, I can't quite touch them?"

"Yes, that's it," she replied. "Relationship requires being completely present, attentive, and aware, and being exactly where you want to be in every moment. Relationship does not happen when you are pretending to be present. It cannot. It takes place when you are quiet enough inside to feel."

"How you define relationship is different from anything I've ever heard," I said.

"Of course it is. That's why relationships haven't been deeply satisfying to you. You've glided along the surface of life believing you were under water. First, relationship has nothing to do with good or bad or right or wrong. Relationship is connection, whether in conflict or in love. From the perspective of relationship as a separate entity, it does not discriminate or judge.

"Relationship is engagement. It is full involvement of your whole self, even the part that is confused, lost, or scared. It is satisfying. It is real. It can last a moment, an hour, a lifetime. It can be a way of life, a commitment to a way of living daily with each person you meet."

Sara sat down on the ground, cross-legged. With a stick she carved a symbol in the soil, but the soil remained undisturbed, intact.

"If you believe it, everything in life is about relationship," she said quietly.

"What does your description of relationship look like? How do I know when I'm completely engaged in relationship or simply being with someone out of obligation, habit, the social thing to do, or fear of hurting feelings?"

Sara looked into my eyes with an expression that demanded I pay more attention to my own answers from within me.

"How do you want your connections with other people to be?" Sara asked. "How do you want to feel? What brings life to you? What is real for you?"

She paused.

"Whatever you answer, it will be true for everyone else as well," she said as she brought her body to a standing position.

During a natural silence between us, I thought of a man I'd recently met who was an administrator with the University of New Mexico. I wanted him to like me. I wanted him to like what I was saying. I wanted him to hire me.

My work history had been filled with feeling intimidated by administrators and "professionals" who wore suits and ties.

As we sat together for the first time, with a large mahogany table between us, he told me about the university programs and the difficulty he was facing with the institution.

His tone of voice was monotonous, and I found I wasn't listening to his words. He and I had no relationship yet. He was simply talking.

He finished outlining his duties and without a moment's pause or break in talking, he asked, "So tell me about you. What do you do?"

I heard his question but something was missing. I thought of giving an answer but instead, I sat back in my chair and felt the pretense hanging between us.

I sat for another minute in silence, shifting my weight in the chair to feel centered. I looked directly into his eyes, past the administrator, past the university employee, and through the distance between us. Ignoring his question, and in a tone of wonder and innocence, I asked, "What satisfies you in your life? What do you want to happen with your work here?"

His face came alive as he smiled. His body shifted to face me directly, our eyes met, and as we engaged we both became more animated, alive.

His answer was instant and personal. What I heard was inspiring. He told me of his work with young people, his family, his love for his children. He told me a deeply personal story about his relationship with his young son. I liked him. Everything in the room softened.

He asked me again, this time with enthusiasm, "Tell me about you. Where are you from? What do you do?"

"Bruce, come back, that's a good story, but you're not here. Stay in relationship with me," Sara said, again interrupting my thoughts. "This is what not being in relationship looks like."

"I was thinking about a time when I did exactly what you're talking about," I replied.

"I know," Sara said, "but you leave relationship completely when you're off in the past, for whatever reason. If you are in your mind, you're not here. You're disconnected from yourself and from what is going on around you. You don't get to do that anymore. Think your thoughts, but leave your awareness here. You have to. It is dangerous not to be aware of everything at all times."

"What could be dangerous?" I asked, as if I didn't know.

"I'll tell you at another time, when you're able to hear it," she replied with a smile.

"Wait," she said with a feigned startled look. "Be quiet a moment. I think you can hear it." With a voice of authority Sara demanded that I recall when I was twenty years old. "Remember your first courageous act with your father, the action that made your relationship happen with him. Remember it!"

"What courageous act?" I asked after a few moments of thought, coming up with nothing unusual.

Sara didn't respond.

"Oh yeah," I blurted out, as if I had just discovered a gold coin in my pocket.

I hadn't thought of that story in decades. Nor had I thought of it as anything particularly significant. Returning home after two years of being at sea on a U.S. Navy aircraft carrier, I settled into an apartment in Los Angeles with my wife, both of us just having turned twenty years of age.

The growing-up years with my father were mostly neutral, with extremes of outrageous fun and outrageous anger. The one theme that had been consistent in his relationship with my brother and I was believing that he had to buy our loyalty with money and things—a belief that was his, not ours. To retain a control I could never relinquish, I often fought with him over his wanting to buy things.

One evening, my wife and I were sitting in our apartment when the doorbell rang. When I opened the door, my father, whom I hadn't seen in several years, stood there holding two large paper bags filled with groceries.

As surprised and happy as I was to see him, I did something that surprised us both. It was unplanned and unexpected. I gazed into his eyes and saw behind the man I called my father and said, "Please leave the groceries in the hallway and come in. Just you."

Startled by the request, his mouth fell open.

"I do not need the groceries," I added. "I want to be with you. That is enough."

He stood there holding the bags. His shoulders softened. The bags dropped a few inches. We looked at each other, our faces only a few feet apart. Our eyes gradually melted into respect for one another. As the moments passed, I noticed tears forming behind his eyes, something I'd not seen before. He placed the bags down just outside the door and took my shoulders and pulled me to him. We walked in together.

I knew that our relationship had changed forever and that remnants of the past had been severed.

"Yes, that's the story," Sara said, calling me back into the present.

Sara's form began to fade in and out as she circled me, floating around my body like waves of colorful electricity.

"I remember an article you wrote for a newspaper," Sara said, as she playfully danced in her luminescent form. "It was an article you were inspired to write after you saw a black man and an American Indian woman being mistreated by a police officer in the street. You wrote the story when you were still in your twenties. That experience determined what the rest of your life would be about. I'll recite it for you from memory."

"You can remember the whole thing?" I asked.

"We always remember those things that bring us life and help our being," she replied, as if her statement was a matter of fact.

I was moved by her recognition of me, the attention she gave to events I had dismissed as trivial—moments of passion that had happened so long ago, seemingly having little to do with my life today.

She noted my tears with a receptive smile. "You see and feel deeply. What you express is not an act of self-importance or pride. Your willingness to feel and see is your gift. You bless others with it. You have always been able to see through the eyes of many, not just your own. You must take this gift seriously. It is important to remember who you really are.

"Listen to what you wrote at such an early age. I will recite it word for word.:

"In my experience with politically, sometimes legally and by government decree, suppressed people, the anger and rage is often all that is left. When, by stated government policies, you have been excluded, dehumanized, rejected, hung, and beaten to death, the stories carry on into the present, where of course the real life stories continue.

"I can differentiate my old rage growing up as a Jewish person not allowed into some clubs, organizations, or schools because I was Jewish. That was strange enough but I learned of compassion. I listened to anti-Semitic jokes when no one knew I was Jewish. I hurt and said nothing. I could get away with almost anything if I didn't tell people I was Jewish.

"I grew up believing men were bad and I was a person in a man's body. Men, I came to believe, only started wars, raped, beat, and battered women, molested little girls and boys, and had no feelings. And I was one of those Bad men. I had a penis and a penis was a bad thing to have. All it did was cause trouble: unwanted pregnancies and sexual diseases. A penis was not to be seen, heard, or talked about, nor even touched for that matter.

"Poor me. A Jewish boy excluded and hated for being Jewish. Big nose, money mad, and controller of international banking. Hide. Hide. Hide. Don't tell anyone you are Jewish. Don't tell anyone you have a penis. Poor me. A man in a man's body. Penis, no heart, no feelings, hard, cold, angry, aggressive, warlike, irresponsible, a demon in underwear and tennis shoes.

"The global myth permeates every man's body, soul, and thought form. But you are a man, you can take it. You are supposed to take it. Don't be wimpy. If you care about all this, if you feel any of this, you are wimpy, soft, and not fulfilling your role as a man in a man's body.

"Poor me. Women have it even harder. They are women in women's bodies. They have to put up with being totally discounted as human beings, rarely taken seriously. They make less money than men. They are pinched, squeezed, and molested by men. They have to work twice as hard to gain respect or power. And men cause all this.

"Poor me. I am Black, Brown, Yellow. I'm out of the loop completely. I am not just excluded, ostracized, and banned from the world, I am beaten, hung, and killed. I am wantonly bombed without regard for my age, gender, or threat to anyone.

"I am Black. I am unarmed. I am a civilian. I am killed along with twenty others of my family in Africa. I was marching. I had no weapon. I am one of hundreds of Black men hung in jail and accused of committing suicide. It is not just my history of generations ago. I am Black today and watch my people, and all people who are non-white, killed indiscriminately because I am different, because I am dehumanized and with color.

"When I am given voice, when I am allowed to speak without being shot, hung, or beaten, I will speak. I will speak loudly and I will be angry. My anger is not only my own. It is your anger too. My anger is yours. You are white. You are woman. You are man. You are child. I am angry for you. My powerless feeling speaks with rage. My rage is the beginning of being specific, direct, and powerful. If it scares you, then feel your scare for it is yours too.

"Women, children, Blacks, Browns, Hispanics, Asians, Arabs, Jews, Men: all of us are enraged. In our perception of being without power, we dominate and attempt to control *others. When you, I, and our friends speak out, and Rage with directness, we free us all. For now, I speak from my heart, rage from my groin, and demand to be heard. I want to hear myself. When I hear myself, my cries grow softer. My voice whispers, I love you all. Be my friend. I like you. Touch me here. I do not wish to hide anymore. And I can be completely out in the open in silence."*

"I wrote that?" I asked, surprised.

"You were angry when you wrote it," Sara replied, "and you wrote it well. You know what relationship means. It is what your life has been about and what it is about. You have no choice."

Sara slowly backed away from me and dissolved like a gaseous cloud dissipating into space. I closed my eyes tightly to double check my own vision. With my eyes closed, I saw the brightest orange sun I'd ever seen even with my eyes open. I was able to look right into it without squinting. The color was fire red and orange, with hues of yellow in the center. It seemed as if I was seeing the sun at its origin, without having to feel the heat or be burned. I noticed how easy and calming it was to see into it.

Instead of turning away so as not to burn my eyes, I was drawn to look deeper into it. The sun was framed by an old, wooden porch doorway with elderly oaks in the foreground.

If I'd thought about what I was seeing and what had just happened with Sara, I would have thought myself crazy. Instead, I felt the effects I was experiencing—the calmness in me, and the hugeness of the vision. The sun continued to bore through all my beliefs and limits of what is possible. My internal vision was so much more satisfying in this moment than any outer life event.

For the first time, I had fallen in love.

10

Seizing the Spirit

I rested on a small, sandy beach along the Rio Grande. Even asleep I could feel the warm sun penetrating my skin, heating every cell and creating unusual light formations beneath my closed eyelids.

A young Mexican man appeared in a dream. He sat down next to my dreaming body and said, "Remember that 'Oh Boy!' list you made? Now, I want you to make a Spirit list."

"What is a Spirit list?" I asked from within the dream.

"I will tell you, but first you must agree to liberate yourself from all judgment or blame you carry within you about anybody, anywhere, from any time in the past, now or in the future."

Even within the dream, I hesitated. I thought about what it would mean if I freed myself from judgment. I could never blame anyone for anything ever again, not even myself. What I was being asked to do seemed not impossible, but unfair, and I said so.

"If I don't judge, and others continue to," I replied, "then I will be the only guilty one and others will still get to blame me. Not fair," I complained. "How come I have to give up judgment to learn what a Spirit list is anyway?"

Hearing my own surliness, I accused, "You came to me in this dream, I didn't come to you."

141

There was a loud silence.

"You don't have to do anything if you don't want to," the man said. "You can keep judgment in your life for as long as you live, and even after. You can blame anyone you like as often as you like. That is always your choice."

"Who are you?" I asked curiously.

"Who do you see?"

"I see a dark-skinned, dark-haired man with an old plaid shirt, soiled jeans, and worn boots. You look as though you have been a farmer or field worker all your life."

"You see much for one who is asleep," he replied, smiling.

"How do you know I'm asleep? Maybe I'm awake," I responded sarcastically.

"I know you're asleep because you have yet to accept my condition to know what a Spirit list is."

"Maybe I'm awake and still refuse to accept your condition," I fought back, undeterred.

"Not possible, *no es posible*," he said, shaking his head back and forth. "If you were awake, you would jump at the chance to know what a Spirit list is. No obstacle would stop you. You would not be judging me now. Your wonder would find you and demand that you know."

He paused, then commanded, "I want you to make a Spirit list."

"If I give up judgment," I asked in a childlike voice, "can I still blame someone for something? Can I complain about how I am treated?"

The dark-skinned man laughed a sweet, understanding laugh, walked over to me, and placed one hand on my shoulder. Electricity soared through me like a waterfall unleashed. I shook all over, zapped clean of any fear of myself. I felt refreshed.

As though in parallel worlds, I knew I was half-asleep on the sand and that I was dreaming. The half-awake part felt the familiar anxiety and the ongoing judgment of myself that I'd carried within me since childhood. Using the awake part of me, I encouraged myself to slip back into the dreaming part to continue the conversation.

It worked.

"Would you like to know what the Spirit list is before you make one?" the slender Mexican man asked again.

"Yes, I would," I replied, surprised at my sudden willingness. "But how do I give up judgment? I can agree to give it up, but I'm not sure I really can."

"Yes, you can," he said, "You have integrity. It matters to you that you do what you say you will do. That is important. You pay attention. That is what the Spirit list is about."

"If you come from the fields," I asked, "picking crops and spending your life around mud, pesticides, meager wages, beer and wine, and moving from place to place every few months, how and what can you teach me?"

His laughter filled my dream. I did not expect him to laugh. I expected him to convince me that my judgment was wrong. I almost awoke fully with the sound of his laughter as he slapped his knees in delight at my seeming innocence.

"At least I make you laugh," I commented, somewhat embarrassed.

"That you do," he said, "and you do it well. *Esta lo haces y lo haces bien.* You make me laugh in both Spanish and English.

"You'll notice that even in your dreams, you have judgment. You bring the thought forms of the waking world into your dream world. At least you are consistent! In your awake state, you take on the thought forms of the world and the people around you, absorbing beliefs that separate you from others and divide your thinking. Now you have a chance to see clearly—beyond petty, trivial, personal illusions."

As he spoke, I was distinctly aware of being asleep and awake at the same time. I could hear his dream words. I could also hear the river and feel the sand beneath my body.

"If you decide to give up judgment," he continued, "you will free yourself from being isolated, separate, and in perpetual fear of being offended by someone, sometime, somewhere. Judgment is a trap. It is a prison. It is never-ending. It's a view of the world that is difficult to maintain.

"To judge and to blame require that you live in a constant trance, programmed like the most intricate computer.

"Judgment has nothing to do with morals, perceived differences, or life history. Judgment is a way of being in the world that requires a particular point of view. You are not a bad person for judging others, or yourself. You are simply stupid."

"There, see," I jumped in. "That's a judgment of me."

"That is not a judgment," he said, smiling. "That is a clear observation."

"What makes what you observe a 'definition' and what I observe a 'judgment'?"

I was still trying to win my point, make my argument and cling to my emotional position—and in the background of my mind, I didn't believe what I was saying.

"There isn't much difference," he replied softly. "What I observe doesn't matter to me. Personally, it does not matter that you see what I see. It does not matter to me that you have the same opinion as I do. On the other hand, your opinion matters to you. You find evidence to support your judgment, your belief, and your side of the story. I do not need you to believe me."

Raising his eyes to mine, he added in all seriousness, "Although it would be to your benefit."

He moved to stand directly in front of me, inches away. Without touching him, I could feel a familiar kind of static electricity all around me. He had my attention.

"Observe," he began, "receive, wonder, take in, rejoice, step back and see what needs to be done, if anything, every moment. Be your own authority. Listen inside. Over and over again, listen inside. Notice when you're not listening and return to listening. Live from wonder now and every moment. Step back from needing to have a place for everything, an explanation for each event and every slight. Live in wonder."

A rock from the canyon wall behind me fell, cracking against other rocks only a few feet from where I had been resting, abruptly awakening me.

Startled and scared, I quickly sat up. I was alone, the sun almost fully set, the sky a bright red. I was quiet inside as the unusually warm river water lapped at my feet.

Just beyond arm's reach, a sheet of paper slid back and forth along the sand, encouraged by a gentle breeze. The paper slowly circled nearer as though beckoning for me to reach out to it. In what seemed like a teasing gesture, it almost slipped from my fingers as I leaned far enough forward to grasp it.

I saw that words, crisp and clear, filled one side of the parchment-like paper completely. The words, in red ink, were handwritten.

The first line read, "*Spirit list: What it is and how to make one.*"

"This is crazy," I said out loud. "This is impossible."

I desperately wanted to see the real person who left the dream paper. I couldn't believe it was simply a coincidence. At the same time, it didn't matter to me whether I saw an actual person or not; the mystery itself was stimulating enough.

I used the setting sun for illumination, appreciating the bright red ink in the fading light.

"*Scan your mind's historical index of names of people that are in your life, or have been in your life since birth. Include family members, old friends, new friends, chance meetings—anyone whose picture or name comes to you.*

"*Set aside your personal beliefs and feelings about them, and allow yourself to see if they are following their spirit. To do this, you must discard judgment about how they are following their spirit, how they behave, and whether you like them or not, even if you severely dislike them.*

"*Instead, ask if they are following a path that is theirs and theirs alone? Are they doing and learning what they need to learn in their own way, that is just right for them, even though their way may not be at all right for you, or even seem logical?*

"Write their name on the Spirit list if they are following their Spirit, no matter what you may feel about them. Then, respect them from your own internal respectful place.

"Even though you may never want to be in their physical presence again, respect them for their journey and their willingness to live completely. I repeat again that their way may not, at all, be your way.

"Suspend your judgment and blame and let them be. Let them be. Let them be. And you are free!

"Respectfully, Leo Garcia."

That night, as I shared this experience with Meigra, I recalled a Leo Garcia I had known in high school. He had entered my life the day after a group of six Mexican teenagers jumped me one night after a party.

Before I could break away from them I was hit several times in the face. I was terrified by the threat to my life. I ran towards my car, reaching it seconds before they did. I jumped in, quickly locking the door behind me. I fumbled for my keys, shaking as I struggled to fit the key into the ignition.

The car started, but my feet were trembling so violently, I was unable to fully depress the clutch to shift into gear. The boys had surrounded the car and were pounding on the windows. With sheer will, and a courage I didn't know I had, I held the clutch in, knowing it could mean my survival. I slammed the gear shift into first gear and with tires squealing, sped away, leaving a dozen hands clutching for my stunned and shaking body.

I sped through the darkened streets of Los Angeles at ninety miles per hour, hoping I'd get stopped by the police. I didn't.

At school the next day, another student, who was Mexican, told me that he'd heard about what had happened the night before. I nervously acknowledged that I was afraid the boys who had jumped me were out to get me and I didn't know why, and that I was cautious and fearful whenever I saw someone who looked Mexican. He could see that I was beginning to judge dark-skinned, dark-haired people who appeared to be Mexican.

My new friend, six inches taller than I, put his arm around my shoulder, an uncommon act for one boy to do with another boy in high school, and said, "I will take care of this for you. I will have them leave you alone. I will tell them you are a friend of mine. They will stay away from you. You're my friend."

I would have cried, had I known how. Instead, we patted each other on the back. I felt his respect for me, for himself, and for people. His name was Leo Garcia.

11

Penetrating the Wild Mind

I took a walk alone the following evening to absorb the events of the previous day. As I walked home, I made a different turn at an arroyo, taking the opposite direction from the one I had intended. It was almost dark.

Instead of a one-hour hike through familiar territory, I was out seven hours, lost in the wilderness—lost in fear. I approached panic several times, and felt body sensations that I suspected would lead to my instant death, alone, without medical help, never to be found again.

Those seven hours reminded me that life is always close to over, yet never-ending.

"Maybe," I thought to myself, "I am on somebody else's Spirit list and I should calm down, trust my senses, and allow the way out to find me. I could live up to myself."

That seemed like an unusual thing to say about myself—that I could live up to myself.

My anxious thoughts were having a dialogue with each other. "One at a time now . . . " I tried to calm myself. "Where is the sun? Doesn't matter, there isn't any; it's night time. Which direction is north? Who knows?"

Then a reassuring voice came in: "There are forces here that want to help you find your way. Rest easy. One thought at a time. Your heart will continue beating and if it doesn't, you will simply die and that will be fine."

This internal dialogue helped me to focus and ultimately choose a direction to travel. I didn't really have a name for the direction, only an intuition. I thought of Jarid, Sara, Leo Garcia, and Meigra.

As I walked, directing my thoughts to stay clear, I found myself noticing every minor physical symptom. "What if I get a kidney stone while I'm out here? I would be here alone in pain, unable to move. What if I get a severe headache? I have no aspirin. What if my fear takes over and I panic and explode into a thousand pieces?"

I listened to my thoughts. Even in the midst of a potentially dangerous situation, I wondered where all the fear thoughts originated. They weren't helping me to be cautious or providing information. Instead, they were taking me to the brink of going crazy, shaking me to my roots, and eroding every bit of calm I could maintain.

As I walked, curiosity consumed a large portion of the fear.

A history of my fear of living, illness, and dying emerged with a clarity that surprised me. I felt as if someone had inserted a computer disk in my visualizing brain that revealed in intricate detail the origin of immobilizing fear.

The disk revealed that early on in life, I had come to believe that my body belonged to germs, viruses, and fate—that it was a home for disease, headaches, backaches, and a variety of illnesses requiring store-bought drugs to numb, hide, and kill any unusual sensation or symptom. I expected to get sick; it's what humans do.

I believed that my mind and my emotions were destined to be frequently depressed, moody, and negatively affected by traumatic life events; that it was inevitable that something awful would happen to me, or had already, when I was little. I expected to devote decades toward healing the hurts, so that I could eventually live in the present without hurting or becoming addicted to some substance or idea.

I was beginning to enjoy these insights. I found myself walking faster, as though my feet knew where they were going. In the darkness, I recognized nothing. There were no familiar landmarks, and the moon lay in hiding behind a thickly overcast sky.

"If there is a God, I thought, she is in my feet."

"She?" I heard myself think.

"Maybe God isn't a she, he, or it. Maybe God is a force, an energy—something totally outside of your personal self that few humans can fathom."

"Uh oh," I said to myself, "you're getting way out there, and you are already really way out here, not knowing where here is."

"If you begin to believe God is someone else and not you, you may abandon yourself and really get lost."

The internal dialogue served as built-in entertainment for the scary situation I was in. I recalled how my inside-mind conversations were often the only meaningful thing happening during most of my school years.

Suddenly, I came to a fork in my path, barely visible in the hazy moonlight. There were two well-worn indentations in the sandy soil heading off in different directions. I'd been walking for several hours and the only map I had to count on was in my feet. I followed them to the left and tripped on the asphalt road right in front of me.

It was a two-lane road with a yellow stripe in the middle, and it was familiar. I realized with relief that I was only five minutes from my house!

That night, Leo Garcia returned to my dream world, but I wasn't ready for him. I was exhausted and wanted to sleep without dreaming anything. Leo showed up anyway. He had work to do, and I was the work!

Just before my mind and body drifted into the intangible world of sleep, I smiled and whispered to myself, "Poor me, why is being alive so difficult?"

"Difficult?" the now familiar dream voice of Leo asked incredulously. "Your view of life is difficult, not life itself."

I was no longer surprised by the other reality that existed while I slept. I was relieved to have the help.

"One alternative is to view the world differently," Leo suggested.

"What?" I questioned in response, as I was pulled deeper into the dream state. "I thought I was viewing the world differently. I'm doing the best I can," I pleaded, hoping he'd pat me on the head and say, "Good work."

Leo was ready. "Doing the best you can is just short of doing it. When you jump out of an airplane, you don't open the parachute the best you can. You open it."

Sheepishly, I asked, "Okay, what would different be?"

Leo's voice boomed with an authority that demanded I stop thinking and listen.

"You don't have to know what you're doing," he said. "You don't anyway. You just pretend you do."

"If I don't know what I'm doing," I asked, "then how do I know what I'm doing, and how can I get anything done?"

I was silent a moment and then added, "I'd look stupid."

"You are stupid," he quickly responded, smiling yet serious. "Assume that not only are you stupid, but you are already judged and people have their opinions about you. Trust that you will be disliked, misunderstood, and dismissed. Know that few people will see you—fewer yet will comprehend what they see. Finally, trust that you absolutely don't know what you are doing and that it doesn't matter."

"It doesn't matter . . . " I began. Leo talked right through me as if what I was about to ask wasn't relevant, and he knew that we both knew it.

"When it doesn't matter to you, you don't have to pretend. You don't have to know anything in advance. You don't have to be seen as wise, in charge, and completely in control. And because you don't have to do any of these things, you are in control. You are in charge."

He waited while I absorbed what he was saying. He could

tell when I had taken it in because I swallowed, as if I had taken the last bite of food.

He summarized, "How you view the world is completely up to you. It is totally your view and your perception, so change your perception and allow the unknown to come to you."

I started to wake up from the dream state but felt myself being drawn back. I tried even harder to see if I could free myself. The more I tried to leave the dream, the greater a force pulled me back. Half-awake, I asked a question.

"What is the unknown?" I asked, "besides the obvious."

"The unknown happens when you step out of the trance," Leo replied. "You remember?"

"I remember."

"But exactly what is the unknown? Where does it come from? Define it."

I thought he'd laugh, but instead he assumed a look of thoughtfulness as though looking for words to describe it.

"The unknown has a particular feel to it," he began. "The unknown is fresh. It is clean. It has never been seen before. No one knows about it. It is unknown. It is where you go when you don't know where you are. It is where you are confused. It has no beginning. It has no end. It has no middle. There are no words for it. It is what the mind attempts to figure out, analyze, understand, structure, and contain. It is sometimes called the unconscious. It is what you run from. It is what fear leads you away from and drives you toward. Yet, you do not go there. And if you are there, you have no way of knowing it."

He stopped to think again, then continued.

"Outside the unknown, there are words to describe it; from within, there are none. There are no handholds, no rungs to climb, no chrome bars, not even an illusion to identify its boundaries.

"Myths arise from it. Fairytales embrace it. Psychology searches it out. Children play in it. Death touches its borders. Life defines it."

There was a timeless pause.

Leo's voice brought me back. "Some people build fences to keep themselves out. You might think that a man who builds a fence around his property does so to keep animals or people out, to protect himself and his belongings. He also builds the fence around himself to keep himself in. His view is limited to the perimeter.

"The unknown reveals itself in your physical symptoms and so-called diseases. They are directly related to how you view your daily life and your world. Those symptoms carry the information necessary for you to change your life. They are the direct link to your edges—to where you go unconscious, into a trance, and lose awareness."

The dream scene changed again, and I found myself floating in the ocean with only an orange life preserver keeping my head above water. Leo was sitting, legs crossed, in a small bright, shiny white rowboat. He held a white oar in one hand as if it were a magical staff.

"You," he pointed the oar handle at me, "live with one foot planted firmly in the past and the other foot planted tentatively in the present. As you know by now, that doesn't work. This is why you have physical and emotional symptoms that inhibit you. This is why you find yourself reacting the same way now as you did decades ago.

"There are no symptoms in the present," he continued. "There is no pain in the present. The present moment has no name for itself. It has no self. It takes a self to feel pain. It takes a self to be diseased."

Using the oar as though it were a pointer on a chalkboard, Leo immersed the tip of the oar a few inches into the water.

"This water," he said, "contains everything you need to know about the sea. All the information is there, right on what you call the surface. You tend to look too deeply, right past the obvious."

"Why would I do that? Why would I want to look past the obvious and make life more difficult?" I asked.

"You are doing it now," he reminded me. "You understand fully what I am saying, but it is easier for you to keep looking than to acknowledge what you see now, and act on it.

"You have favorite places to feel—favorite feelings. These favorite feelings prevent you from being aligned with yourself and being present. Eventually, there will be no favoritism within you. There will be no favorite feelings, only different feelings. All places in you will be satisfying. All will be heard and welcomed and then you will feel at home."

I recalled how much I'd always disliked favoritism, including when I was the favored one. It had never felt right. Someone always had to be excluded and hurt, for favoritism to exist. It was always divisive.

Now, in this dream, I was learning how I was committing favoritism within myself. I had favorite parts of me, while excluding and judging other parts of myself. I was consistently angry with or condescending to one or another internal place. I mentally beat myself up from within. I blamed others, too, for believing, along with me, that life and my own self were too complex for anyone ever to comprehend the truth.

"The only difference between the surface of this water and two miles down, is distance and light," Leo continued. "At the surface, the light illuminates all that you need to see. What exists below, thousands of feet down, exists within you as well."

The water around me suddenly cleared, revealing pristine images of floating seaweed, swimming fish, and multicolored coral reefs. I could feel the current of the water but could not see it.

"Just like people," he went on. "Everything you want to know about someone else or yourself is always right in front of you. You don't need to go digging deeply to discover buried treasures of information or to find the origin of a present time difficulty. Rather, be willing to see what is already revealing itself before your eyes and your senses."

"But what about those repressed, suppressed, painful hidden memories and feelings that reside deep within that I don't even know about?"

"If you don't know about them, how do you know they are there? And if they are there and you don't know about them, what does it matter?

"Pay attention to every physical sensation and symptom within your body," he said, "and you will tap into the major source of information and insight necessary for you to stay awake."

"I do pay attention," I said, as though I needed to defend myself from an attack that didn't occur.

"You selectively pay attention," he replied. "You have always selectively paid attention. You have yet to decide that you're willing to see all the way through to the full truth in you. You tend to see truth only in others."

"That's true," I acknowledged with a half smile.

"This is not a light matter," he replied just short of angry. "It is not funny. There is no respect when you ignore what you see and know."

Without warning, the life preserver deflated as if it had been filled with air, and I began sinking into the water, falling downward into an endless black sea. It all seemed natural. I had no need to breathe, and I wasn't surprised.

As the dream followed my slow descent into darker depths, I recalled a waking-life event that had taken place when I was five years old.

My parents had taken me to the hospital under the guise of having my tonsils checked. As I lay on the table waiting to be examined, a doctor placed a black rubber mask over my face and told me to breathe deeply. He said everything would be fine.

I smelled the strange odor of rubber as it sucked against my face. In terror, I sucked back to get my breath. As my lungs expanded, an unfamiliar chemical odor filled my awareness. My head dropped back to the table as I lost sight of the doctor, the lights, the nurses, and the operating room.

I slipped into a dream state surrounded by thousands of large turtle shells. I began to fall, falling and falling into infinity, an abyss, a tunnel of darkness. I expected to fall forever—to live in a constant state of terror. I could not look directly downward. I wanted to, but I couldn't. I could see only the overlapping of large, live, turtlelike shells lining the route of my descent. I was terrified. I knew I might fall forever.

There was no sound as I fell, no reference point for anything familiar, no nothing. I was a slow-motion free fall through space with an unexpected willingness to drop into nothingness. Falling was everything and seemed to last for hours.

Abruptly, my five-year-old body awoke. My eyes opened. I looked around. I was in a white hospital room filled with beds, curtains, and tables on wheels. I looked up to see a white ceiling. Groggy and disoriented, I tried to sit up but had no strength. A woman in a white dress and a forced smile appeared, pushing a spoon filled with what looked like ice cream in front of my face.

My head shook violently, "No, no, no!"

She pushed the spoon between my tightened lips.

I closed my eyes and fell asleep into another dream, away from the lady in white with the spoon full of ice cream.

"Bruce, Bruce," I heard a voice calling. My mother was leaning over me. She was smiling, and I wondered why. She seemed so unreal. Her smile didn't match the tension in her face.

Everything appeared to be different. The world I was in before being involuntarily drugged no longer existed. My body felt like a different body. Everyone had lied, yet their act of unnecessary deception to remove my tonsils was the catalyst that pushed me into the dimension of dreaming, an inner realm far more interesting than the years of schooling yet to be endured.

A loud cracking sound startled my senses, like white-hot molten lava exploding out of a volcanic cone. Following the shock wave, my childhood dream faded and merged into the present-time dream—Leo beside me, both of us falling together, my body sensations echoing the dream of childhood.

Underwater, Leo's eyes were so magnified that I laughed out loud. Falling into the infinite unknown with Leo was no longer terrifying—I had done this before.

As we descended together, tethered only by a mutual belief, he continued to infuse my open mind with information.

"Life issues do not need to take long periods of time to change," he told me. "It is possible in minutes to do what used to take months and years, if you commit to freeing yourself from learned beliefs that are no longer yours."

I was aware of how absurd we'd seem to someone outside the dream observing us. "This dream is totally out of context with logic, reason, or possibility of even being made up," I thought, dreaming the dream.

"How can I believe all of this information to be true in the regular day-to-day world?" I asked Leo.

"It is not something to believe," he replied instinctively. "You could never prove it. There are some things that are not for believing—only knowing. This information you know. You know it with your body, your intuition, and all the senses that are intangible. Knowing it, you don't need anyone else to corroborate your experience. Your experience is the corroboration."

As we continued descending into the darkening light, I asked one last question. I knew sinking into the depths was my death and that this death was a good death—a death of a way of being in the world. This death would open many windows, many doors.

"How do I do it?" I asked in all humbleness. "How do I free myself from all the beliefs around me? How do I step out of my everyday world without being viewed as mentally unstable, with the real risk of being medicated or institutionalized? How do I make the ultimate decision to free myself from constricting beliefs and all the people who lie in wait, ready to tell me I'm wrong, dissuading me from trusting my own insights and intuition? How?"

"That's a really tough question," he replied, pretending to be thinking about it. "You could ponder that for a year or two, maybe even three. You could even devote the rest of your life seeking out that answer."

Seeing my look of disappointment at hearing his response, he looked at me with an incredulous expression.

"Who's in charge?" he asked. "Who lives in your body with you? Who makes your arms move and your lips open and close. Who is breathing for you? Who takes your pants off? Where are you?"

I coughed into the water, an action I thought impossible, since I had to breathe in, to cough.

"Make the decision to believe your own perceptions and do it," he answered. "You have no more time to work on it, waiting for the perceived safety of everyone liking you, never having to feel discomfort. Be willing to be uncomfortable.

"In a world that demands you stay in it and be swallowed up or be ostracized—like quicksand slowly sucking you in—it takes great strength, will, and faith to step out of it. There is nothing to make you want to be free except your desire to be free.

"As long as you decide to ignore what is going on all around you, as long as you need to blame someone else in your life for anything and you are not willing to feel everything deeply and fully, you will not make the decision. To be free, you must notice everything, all the time, each second, forever.

"Just as there are no accidents, there is no such thing as forgetting. You cannot forget anything unless you choose to forget and there is a place in you that makes the choice to forget. When you forget, you don't have to remember. You leave yourself and justify it."

I saw a glowing, fluorescent ocean floor slowly approaching as we smiled at each other in mutual recognition.

I wondered if Leo would run out of wisdom.

"It's been a lifelong habit," I said, "to be in the world and react to it in the way I've always reacted to it, feeling smaller than the world around me and victim to it. How do I actually, really, really change a lifelong habit of living that way in the world?"

"Habits are not a justifiable reason for continuing to kill your spirit and that of those around you," Leo replied.

"A habit is a chosen path that not only is familiar but also is new each time you choose it again, and again. Habits allow justifications, excuses, and reasons to not be here—to not be present, to not be responsible."

"You keep saying I choose to do this and that as though I am always aware of what I am doing, even if it works against me. Why would I choose to keep a habit I no longer want?"

"Anytime you choose to do something you do not want to do, you are doing exactly what you want to do."

"Huh," I thought, but did not speak.

"Playing dumb to yourself is another habit," he replied. "Fortunately, you have a lot of company to support your habit. Playing dumb to what or why you do anything is a favorite pastime. What if you couldn't play dumb anymore? What if you acknowledged that you are wise and all the information you require is instantly available to you. What would you do then? How would you fit into your world? What if you believed this? You could no longer justify your excuses, reasons, and explanations. You'd be free. Are you ready for that?"

"Well, . . ." I began.

"Habit," he continued, not waiting for an answer, "is a contrived concept with a variety of words to describe why you won't be here, an acceptable excuse for going in circles. Habit is a way of scouting out a situation before entering and, once entered, doing everything possible to deny you are there, pretending to have no way of knowing how you arrived. Conveniently, you name your powerless act a habit. And everyone agrees, having ascribed the same label to their own powerless acts."

I felt myself fidgeting in the dream.

"A good example," he continued, "is how you're able to see what people are really feeling inside beneath the false self, yet believe that what you see in them is yours. Instinctively, you bring yourself in line with them; you join their energy, assuming it's the only way to meet and communicate. In so doing, you completely leave your self. If instead, you brought your real self out and to them . . ."

"What?" I asked anxiously.

"They will change in front of your eyes. You'll be making your own world," he answered. "There is nothing more to explain."

"But . . ." I began, in a tone of voice that revealed everything I was about to say.

"You either do it or you don't," Leo interjected. "You follow your body instinct and intuition or you listen to your ever-demanding mind, lost forever in a twisted circle of thoughts, and evidence to prove those thoughts. When you ignore your body intuition, you will find yourself feeling bad over and over—bad about yourself, drained of energy, tediously hanging by a thread each day."

I was getting lost in what he was saying.

Leo noticed.

"You're not lost," he admonished, "you're again choosing to pretend to yourself that you don't understand, that you're confused, because if you weren't confused, you'd have to be responsible for what you know and see. There would be no buffer between you and God."

He smiled again and slowly drifted out of sight. His last words as he dissolved into the darkness were, "Nothing satisfies your spirit like being free, being here, and listening to the unburdened truth from your universal heart."

"What does that mean?" I silently asked to myself.

"It means," I heard Leo say in a booming voice, even though I could no longer see him, "that no thought is private; thoughts come from a huge collective mind in the sky. It means you must believe and trust your own inner voices, intuition, body signals, dreams. Everything. Step out of all your learned beliefs and theories. Observe everyone, including yourself, from a sense of wonder. Get out of your own way."

12

Tapping the Roots of Insight

I woke up and pinched myself, to see if I was really awake! Then I pinched my arm a second time, just to make sure I wasn't dreaming that I was pinching myself! "Ouch!" I drew blood. It was important for me to be sure I was awake, although as I came fully into my body I noticed that something felt different.

I was hot even though I could feel cold air around me. My skin was warm and moist, and my nose was alternately running and stuffy. My chest felt congested, my eyes were watery and itchy, and my throat was sore and full of mucus. I had all the symptoms of a cold. I'd not had a cold or flu for fifteen years. "Why now?" I wondered.

I remembered the last time I'd had a cold. I'd been sitting alone in my one-bedroom apartment, thinking about my former wife who I had separated from fifteen years earlier. There was no guilt or anger between us, just sadness. Sadness was a feeling I could bask in well, depending on how much time I had to indulge thoughts about what was missing in my life, what could be, and how unfairly I'd been treated.

This was my second full day of sadness, and I was getting bored with sitting slumped in my chair, staring out the window into a beautiful day thinking about things I could be doing if I wasn't so sad.

But I was sad, and I felt powerless to not be sad. I thought about people I could call on the phone who might bring life to me simply by the sound of their voice. If they helped me out of my sadness we'd both benefit. Seemed like a good idea.

My mind's eye scanned a list of names, but I couldn't find one that made me feel better. Even though some of the people were long-time friends, none touched that particular place that wanted satisfying.

I wasn't looking for someone to fix me. I was looking for insight—someone outside me who could pull me emotionally, someone spacious enough to remain unentangled in my story and outside their own sadness enough to make me laugh at my self-inflicted drama.

With no one I could see to call on, I slipped into feeling sad about being sad, then laughed at the absurdity of creating layer upon layer of emotional turmoil, so deep there would be no way for me to climb out of my self-initiated hole.

"If I can't think of anyone outside myself to help me change my mood, maybe I'm to learn to do it by myself. How clever and innovative," I added sarcastically, aware of my ability to create such dramatic mental theater.

I dragged myself out of my chair and began walking back and forth around the apartment, talking to myself. "I can hear myself better if I speak out loud when no one else is around. There's nothing wrong with me if I talk to myself out loud. It just sounds strange to me. Maybe I need more strangeness in my life."

I chuckled as I spoke, aware that my mood was already changing, just by moving around and taking action. I gazed out of the window again, at the trees that lined the property, and talked to them as though they were listening.

"If I can't find anyone outside myself that I believe can hear me, then I will have to hear myself;—I will speak to me and become my own therapist."

I placed two chairs a few feet apart, facing each other, just like they do in a real therapist's office. I picked up my hand-held tape recorder and sat down in one of the chairs, anticipating playing both parts, me and the therapist.

I was having such a good time setting up the scene that I overlooked the fact that I was already out of the original sad mood and I hadn't begun the "therapy session" yet. I flipped a coin to determine which part I would play first. Heads would be therapist, tails would be the client.

Heads came up. I'd be the therapist first.

I selected the chair facing the door, crossed my legs, and assumed a professional demeanor of intense interest with an expression of compassion on my face. I looked at the other chair and imagined my sad self sitting there. Leaning forward, I asked the imagined sad me, "So what is it that's going on with you, Bruce?" My therapist voice was neutral in tone, and full. It had no whine or complaint in it. That stunned me. I was surprised how easy it was to be outside myself. "Where'd the despair go?" I asked the client chair.

I quickly moved over to the other chair, sat down, and instead of answering the question, I erupted into uncontrolled laughter. I laughed so hard, I dropped the tape recorder and fell off the chair onto the floor. The insight was so outrageous I couldn't stop laughing.

"If I can change my mood so easily just by intending it and becoming neutral," I said while still laughing, "then I can do this anytime I want. I don't have to be imprisoned by my moods or beliefs. I can move in and out of moods whenever I remember that I can and am willing to do so."

I danced around the room like I used to when I was a child, saying silly things and being ecstatic over a now-obvious insight.

"Emotions aren't life itself," I said into the tape recorder. "Emotions simply help me move into life more deeply."

"What?" I heard a faint voice inside me ask sarcastically. "Sounds clever and cute but what does it mean? What does moving into life more deeply mean now, here, in the midst of despair?"

"Great question," I complimented the sarcastic voice.

"Emotions run your life," the voice continued. "It is as though you have an emotion of the day, and that particular emotion consumes all your energy and thoughts. Isn't that so?"

Before I could answer myself, the gentle, nudging sarcasm asked, "If this is not the case, how, then, do you use emotions so they don't use you?"

For a few minutes I was quiet. Then I sneezed. And sneezed again. I shivered and felt miserable. I wondered why over the decades, no cure had been found for the common cold, only medications to mask and hide the symptoms. "Maybe I can find a cure for my own cold," I thought. "Maybe colds have to do with emotions."

"Oh sure," the inner voice replied.

"Why do people have colds?" I asked myself. "Why is there an entire industry built for and supported by cold remedies? Why do parents tell their children not to go out in the cold or to get wet in the rain, and give them some form of medicine if their noses run? What is a cold? What does it do? Why is it there? What are the symptoms?"

"That's easy," I said. "I have all the symptoms now. My nose is running. My chest feels tight and congested with fluids. My eyes burn, and they're watering. My throat is sore, scratchy, and mucousy."

I was beginning to form what important scientists call a theory. I noticed two things. All the symptoms appeared between my heart region and my forehead, and they were all related to water or watery substances in one form or another.

I asked myself if all the watery symptoms of a cold could be connected to feelings or emotions that I wasn't expressing in a more direct way. I suspected that there was a connection between waking up with a cold and waking up feeling sad.

As I felt the sadness return, my eyes burned and watered even more and my throat itched. I wandered into the bath-room, looking for a box of tissues.

"Maybe I need to cry, if all the cold symptoms are about emotions and water," I realized. "But that's too easy."

Maybe not. Crying was difficult for me under any condition. I could cry reluctantly in a dark movie theater at a poignant moment, and only if I was alone. I could never cry. I viewed crying like I viewed throwing up—something I would do anything to avoid. The realization that I was afraid to cry was a clue that maybe that's what I needed to do.

"Say 'yes' to things that terrify you!" a voice inside me commanded. I didn't have anything to lose. I was bored with being sad and annoyed by my cold.

I wondered how I could induce tears, if that was what I needed to do to cure my cold. I decided to take a hot shower, which, since the age of seven, had been my way of retreating— a private, steamy, watery place to reveal things to myself, sometimes things I didn't even know I wanted to know.

As I stepped into the shower at three o'clock in the afternoon, the sound of the water filtered out voices and noises of the outside world and created another world, different from the one where I must wear clothes and interact with people. The shower was a secluded space and a time where the water itself soothed, cleansed, and surrounded me with emptiness.

The stream of hot water splashed over my face and shoulders, instantly dissolving tension I hadn't noticed I carried. It was the closest thing to total inner silence I knew. I closed my eyes and felt the hot water unravel everything. I emptied my mind.

I was acutely aware of all the cold symptoms. As the water rushed over my body, I felt a tight, crying type of feeling—a pressing sensation around my throat and chest. I wanted to not acknowledge the symptoms to myself. When I tried to swallow, my throat hurt. I could feel something welling up behind my chest and deep in my throat. My chin and lip quivered. I was scared to let myself feel it, to encourage it to come out fully in sound, or tears, or trembling. I thought if I let it through, I'd die. I wanted to touch the crying sensations and yet there was no book I knew of that taught crying. Once again, I would learn to do this by myself.

"If I can bring forth the saddest, most painful memory I can think of, maybe tears will automatically follow."

"This is sick," another voice in me said. "You're beating yourself up to be sadder?"

I gathered together the best sadness I could think of. I recalled my father's death and how much I missed him.

"That should be a really sad one," I thought. "I'll cry any moment now!"

But there was no sadness, and I didn't cry. Instead, I smiled as I thought of him, treasuring memories of his humor and kindness. I tried another tack. Images of tragic, sad events came and went. What I thought would be painful life dramas to remember and feel, weren't. Surprisingly, events that shook my soul years before had no life or energy in them any more. I found it difficult to feel sorry for myself.

"How will I survive if I can't feel sorry for myself," I joked. No memory or thought worked. Nothing happened. I didn't cry. I had no tears, not even a lump in my throat, yet I could feel a wave of something wanting to move through my chest and throat. I knew this wave sensation carried the pain, the scene, the event, and the catalyst that would bring the tears. I don't know how I knew, I just knew for sure. And I knew it was real. I knew, suddenly, that I wouldn't have to imagine a scene or force the tears. They were simply waiting for me to find them.

I could feel something unexpressed, just out of reach. Still, for the next few minutes, I managed to maintain enough distance from it to pretend it wasn't really there. I knew it was significant because I continued searching for other so-called sad events instead, unwilling to acknowledge the one that was waiting.

Then, with all the courage and internal discipline I could muster, I made the decision that I would be willing to die to feel completely. I knew that to be alive, I had to be willing to die. I had to make the conscious choice to look at the memory I was avoiding and let it burn through the fear of feeling.

I had a choice: to not allow myself to see it, or to call it out. It didn't matter which choice I made: one choice would be freeing, the other familiar and secure.

I made the decision.

It was a big, private decision that no one else needed to know, ever. I decided to allow the background scene to fully come forward into crisp sharpness. I encouraged it to emerge and present me with whatever I was to experience, including the possibility of death, immense pain, or nothing. I wanted to feel it through completely.

I could see the past event way off in my mind's distance. It had taken place many years earlier at the time of my first divorce.

"No," my fearful voice said. "I won't look at it. I won't feel it."

"Do it. Dive in," another voice responded.

"It's too hurtful. I can't bear looking at their faces and feeling their emotions."

"Don't think about it. Do it."

The background scene moved forward, now amplified and intensely clear. In an instant, I saw every detail in the faces of my two children, ages four and six years old, at the moment they saw and heard their mother tell me angrily to leave forever.

In a split second I saw the terror of the end of their world flashing across their faces. Their bright, trusting eyes went blank; their sweet faces turned white. I saw only emotional shock. Their pain shot through me—through the numbness I had felt for eighteen years. My body trembled and jerked as though something long imprisoned had suddenly been set free.

My heart pounded; the lump in my chest and throat grew larger, drawing all its energy together, gathering its forces like a huge ocean wave at its crest, about to break and dissolve into a billion pieces of itself.

The long-waiting emotional wave surged forward out of my heart and chest, up into my throat, and through my face and head. As I felt my children's pain within me, my heart shattered into tears as my body convulsed in sobs. In that moment, the hot water was my solitary friend.

I cried. I laughed. I cried. The tears were warm, and my heart soft. My body shook all over with wondrous relief and expression. I was not in charge of anything. An inner world, previously unknown to me, became my friend.

"Nice going," I heard a humorous voice from inside me say. "Not bad for the first time."

I laughed a soft laugh, one that forms on its own.

My eyes felt relaxed and clear. They were no longer burning. My throat was no longer scratchy. My head was clear, my chest light and spacious. I could breath easily through my nose. In less than five minutes, all the cold symptoms had dissolved.

"So, what did you learn?" I heard a voice ask in a Brooklyn accent. I'd almost forgotten that I'd been conducting an experiment in trying to dissolve cold symptoms.

"That my body is a message bringer, not a disease carrier. I learned that everything physical is related to every other part of my life, especially relationships."

"Good. Not bad. You learn quick for someone so slow," said the Brooklyn voice. "Everything is simple. Nothing is complex. You should be so lucky to remember that."

I sneezed, and came back into the present moment, clearly remembering the dream of a few hours before. Leo Garcia had challenged me to step out of all my learned beliefs and theories. "Observe everyone," he said, "including yourself, from a sense of wonder. Get out of your own way."

Was I ready? "Can I do this?" I asked myself. "Oh, I can't do it today, I've got a cold!"

"Too bad." Leo Garcia's voice was unmistakable. "Do it anyway, even if you don't think you are ready."

13

Respect Defined

I walked into the warm sunlight outside and sat beneath a large cottonwood tree. Looking up, I watched the leaves flickering against the luminescent sun, responding to the soft wind, the sun determined to infiltrate everything in its path.

All was quiet, especially my mind, which was a welcome relief. I imagined what it must be like to be in a spaceship as it reached its apogee, that point exactly between the "efforting" toward its highest reach and the falling effortlessly back toward earth. That point, I imagined, between effort and effortless, is the ultimate moment where nothing known exists.

Nothing matters at the apogee. Peace reigns.

I breathed deeply, and as I relaxed into that feeling, Meigra walked over and quietly sat down beside me. Her face appeared soft and kind. I felt at peace sitting beside her, and cherished the moment.

We sat for several minutes before I started feeling antsy.

"I don't get it," I interrupted. "I don't know what's going on anymore."

"Don't get what?" Meigra asked.

"Oh, just a thought," I replied.

"I don't want to chase you, Bruce. What are you thinking?"

"Sometimes when I look into your face," I answered, "I see a soft, compassionate sweetness. When I see that, I feel relieved. But moments later, your expression can be filled with tension and fear. I was thinking how sometimes I don't look at you for fear of what I might see, knowing that if I see fear, I'll be afraid myself and turn away. If I turn away, I'll still be physically present but I won't really be with you. I'll feel tense instead, and uncomfortable, wondering why you're looking so afraid, believing you must be angry with me."

"Whew! I just wondered," Meigra said.

"That will teach you," I teased.

I was touched by how easily Meigra could move from one mood to another without having to grasp, for dear life, a particular way to be. I knew I had interrupted the silence and brought up what I thought was a trivial thought. I expected her to be irritated by that. Instead, she joined me and went right along with the new place we had entered.

Had Meigra interrupted the silence, I would have been irritated that the quietness had been broken, thinking we'd never retrieve that state of peace again. I always wanted to capture and hold onto such a precious moment, fearful that it could be the last one ever and disappointed when it changed.

"Sometimes, Meigra, I have so much respect for you that I can't handle it. I'm awed by your presence, and your strength and ability to follow yourself so completely. Your flexibility and strength are so big, I often turn on you in a critical way. God, this is embarrassing to tell you, and even more embarrassing to realize I think this at all."

"What you're talking about," she replied, "is respect."

"I respect myself."

"I know you do. What you see in me, the part that sometimes scares you, is also in you but you're not acknowledging it, and that's what frightens you. Acknowledge your own power. Acknowledge your respect for others, your impact on them, and there will be no fear. Whatever you appreciate in me must exist within you as well—that's the only way you could recognize it. It's all about respect, big respect."

"I give up," I replied. "What's big respect?"

"I'll tell you what it isn't," she answered. "It isn't just about respecting another person or different points of view. It isn't something that can be pretended or required as a social expectation.

"The respect I speak of is bigger than that. It is a place inside you where you're willing to look again at everything. And then look again. It's an internal vision that demands you believe your own perceptions without physical evidence.

"Respect is a willingness to be fully in yourself at all times, with no excuses for being absent. It's a commitment that extends beyond personality and beyond moral beliefs. Most people live life without respect because they're not familiar with it. They don't even notice it's missing. A good example is how children become so familiar with being talked down to, criticized, and told what's right for them. They forget that there is another way. They lose touch with respect, their soul, and ultimately their spirit. They become us.

"When you and I speak from respect simultaneously," she added, "we tap into the same source of information. We communicate differently; we don't waste time and energy taking positions, competing, being right and wrong. We listen well and see the world as right, just the way it is."

"What is that source?" I asked.

"I have no idea," she replied. "It's not of the mind. There's no place to pin an answer. It's like 'Where does fire come from?' I don't mean the fuel, oxygen and heat that allows fire to burn, but where does fire come from?"

"Where does fire come from?" I asked.

"It doesn't matter," she answered. "When you step back from listening to the mind dialogue, the proving of anything no longer matters. It doesn't even matter if I know what I'm talking about. I may not. None of this may be true, and it doesn't matter. If something else is true, I'm willing to hear it. Truth changes all the time. Truth is only my perception of things in that moment."

"How do you know all this?" I asked, still awed by her wisdom.

"I don't know all this," she replied. "The respectful place in me knows. It always knows."

I felt unusually warm all over. I was fearful, yet had nothing to attach the fear to. Meigra noticed without commenting.

"Respect is something you are, not something you do," she whispered. She stood up, tall and unwavering, her bare feet firm against the ground. Meigra's physical presence reflected her words.

My body was now feeling like it was on fire, and I knew there was nothing I could do but be with it.

"Can you teach respect?" I asked. I was curious.

"Yes," she replied, "if you're sure respect is something others want. Some people don't want to live from respect, even though they profess to."

"Why wouldn't anybody want to?" I asked.

"Because respect is sacred," she answered. "It's not just a clever social concept. Respect is sacred."

"It is sacred, isn't it?" I whispered, emotion knotted in my throat, my body heat intensifying.

"I used to be nice," Meigra continued. "I used to be good. I used to be sweet, and want everyone else to just be nice. I was uncomfortable with feelings, anger, conflict, hurt, pain, and every other sense that tends not to feel nice. I had to unravel the niceness to find respect. I had to start feeling everything without giving meaning to what I was feeling. I had to hold myself sacred.

"Instead of fitting sacred activities into a weekend schedule with special friends, I began to see that everything I did each moment must be held sacred. I had to get serious about 'living sacred.' This meant I had to take myself seriously and recognize that respect is mine to embody, having nothing to do with the world around me. I had to be sacred to myself."

I began to perspire openly. Meigra was silent a moment.

"I learned quickly that living from respect separates me from everyone and connects me with everyone," she continued.

"How can you be separate and connected at the same time?" I asked.

"You're not really separate," she replied. "But living from a sacred, respectful place within me, meant that some people could no longer be around me and either found fault with how they perceived me or drifted away. Others discovered the same place within themselves. The connection is when others find the same place within themselves.

"Some children, before they are forced to believe that only the external world is true and real, live in a sacred place, connected to everything and everyone."

I remembered a ten-year-old girl I once knew who was her own person completely. Her actions always originated from within her. The external world was her playground, not her guide. Rachel was completely separate, unconcerned with my opinions, yet in her presence, we felt completely connected.

Rachel was at home in herself. She had no concept of not being herself. She lived in respect. She had the ability to hear criticism and judgment from others but know that it wasn't about who she was. She could be admonished, judged, and questioned by adults around her, but nothing stuck. She was so much herself that when someone found fault with her, she could easily listen with no need to defend, justify, or explain herself. It was easy being around her. She granted herself grace. She didn't require others to.

"When you're respecting," Meigra continued, "there is no doubt about what you do moment to moment: you breathe from your belly. When you're respecting, you're willing to see everything there is to see. The decision to live from respect determines your willingness to teach, every moment, by how you live. Until then, you are not teaching—nor are you living— in respect. Instead, you are attached firmly to those who live outside of respect, and outside of themselves.

"That's why being in a living, dynamic relationship can be so difficult. It requires you to make the internal decision to respect yourself completely and fully—to be at home inside and to live from there. You have yet to make that decision."

"How come?" I asked.

"Because," Meigra replied, "there's only one step to respect and it's final. Take that step and you can't go back, ever. There are no incremental steps, no fragments. There is only the whole. You live from respect or you don't. It is a soul decision, not a human one. The soul needs the fuel of respect. The human does not. A person deciding to live from respect must be willing to step out of the trance of daily life and live differently."

"How would I know if I'm living from respect?"

"Sex is the hugest signal of whether respect is living or not in your life," she replied.

"Hugest?"

"Yes, hugest. That's a technical term," she smiled. "Sex is like the common cold. It causes such great disturbance, and no one has really figured it out yet."

Meigra looked up as though observing a visual thought form in her mind's eye. We were both silent.

"Think of sex and you leave your body," Meigra said in a pristine voice that had a rhythm and pace I hadn't heard before. "Most sexual thoughts originate in the mind, out of collective beliefs, not from body instincts. Sexual thoughts usually take over like a trance cloud of molecules rolling in, seeping through every pore of your skin, seducing your entire being before you notice that your heart and soul have taken leave and you are left with only remnants of your former self, internally drooling to fulfill a desire that originates from outside yourself, even though you perceive that it comes from within."

I felt as though she'd dug a deep well, uncovering some truth that I wanted to ignore and dismiss.

"But sex is a human need. It's fun. It's necessary and makes children happen," I interjected, hearing the whine in my voice of a long ago, learned response.

Meigra looked at me in a way I'd never seen before. Her eyes were deep and steady, locked into mine. I could feel my body vibrate through her gaze, calling me back to myself, to listen with my heart, without thought and, for the first time, seriously.

I was frightened. I wondered if she was going crazy and was practicing some kind of witchcraft I'd seen depicted in movies. Maybe she was taking me over, attempting to completely consume what was left of me. I couldn't see the familiar Meigra I was used to, and her voice was stronger and deeper.

Her look softened, and I calmed down inside.

"Much of sexuality as I know it is outdated," Meigra continued. "There's rarely any connection to respect involved. Sex is a frequent event often performed from habit, accompanying the belief that something is missing from my life. The struggle to make it work and to do it right, to fulfill desire, lust, pleasure, fantasy, and physical ecstasy rarely feels quite right."

"How come?" I asked. "Where did my pictures, beliefs, and expectations about sex come from?"

I knew Meigra was on to something heretical, radical, and totally outside any belief system I'd heard of.

"What are the emotional attachments I have to my sexual beliefs?" I asked excitedly. "And who defined sexuality in the first place? How does anyone's personal view of sexuality serve them?"

My question took on a momentum and life of its own.

"And why . . ." I continued, ". . . does sexuality and all the thoughts and fantasies around it, fill so much of my time? Why has an entire culture, including the various religions, given such emphasis to this one aspect of life? Why do people kill over it?"

"Touched a nerve, eh?" Meigra asked, calmly.

"Sexuality is life itself," she explained, her eyes still gazing into mine. "It is creation. It's a process that's constantly changing. It's about relationship. Most important," she repeated, "It's about relationship."

"Most belief systems freeze sex into right and wrong, good or bad, abnormal, normal, narrowing its definition to genitals and intermittent pleasure. These same belief systems have institutionalized sexuality into books, research studies, statistics, and gender separation. Sexuality, as it is commonly seen and practiced, separates people—it does not unite them. It has become a business, a technical thing. Do you understand?"

I was speechless.

"Sex isn't separate from all other aspects of life," she continued. "Sex is all aspects of life. Everything is sexual. Is my definition of human sexuality any more normal or accurate than yours? Sexuality is a process that has been too programmed and defined by studies and attempts to justify and explain, out of context, an aspect of human behavior. What was once a natural life process has become an academic course of study with an endless requirement for homework."

I squirmed in my chair. I was beginning to feel a sense of relief, and I wasn't sure why.

"Sexuality is about connection, creativity, and presence," she continued, "and has nothing to do with what you've been taught to believe. Absolutely nothing.

"Our culture has beliefs not only about sexuality, but about education, money, marriage, divorce—all in terms of right and wrong. These beliefs form the basis for how you live, act, and behave. Underlying these beliefs is the hidden belief that life isn't quite right yet, that something is missing."

Meigra noticed my nervousness and reached out to touch my shoulder.

"There is nothing wrong with these beliefs," she said, withdrawing her hand gracefully, "except that I become dependent on outside sources telling me what is right and appropriate, and fail to notice that I am dependent. I disconnect from my

own body and insights. I learn to distrust my internal knowledge, and end up feeling dissatisfied, confused, yet always
thinking something is missing. The background of my life
becomes consumed by what I think I don't have sexually and
sensually. Sexuality has become a belief. It has become separated from life, relationship, and spirit."

"Are you able to stay with this," Meigra asked, noticing my
obvious antsyness.

"Yes, of course," I replied, challenged. "But you're changing
the future of the world, or at least, my world."

"Hmmmm," she responded, revealing nothing of her
thoughts.

"Understanding sexuality," she continued, "and being in
charge of it requires listening to your own body and feelings.
being willing to feel your body from the inside, completely."

"How do I feel my body from the inside?" I asked.

"You no longer give word meanings to feelings. Instead, you
allow the feeling to give meaning to you," she answered without pause. "You must follow yourself every moment, with the
only rule being to be aware and to be aware of what you are
aware of.

"It is essential to know your intention and let your intention be your guide," she said. "Ask what your intention is for
living and for each of your actions, no matter how small and
trivial. In the largest sense, what is the most important thing
for you in life?"

Meigra saw my eyes watering. She stopped and a gentle,
sweet, receptive smile formed.

"Sexuality," she softly continued, "is another name for living awake, aware, and in continual emotional movement. It is
not even possible to separate sex from the rest of what you
breathe and do. You need not and cannot label it, dissect it,
translate it, or attempt to do it the way others tell you to,
especially others who have studied it and claim to know the
route to ultimate orgasm. The ultimate orgasm is not of the
genitals."

She reached for my hand and held it softly as she caressed my eyes with hers.

"A crazy, possibly totally unscientific view of sexuality is that it is whatever you perceive it to be," Meigra said in a voice so quiet that I couldn't help but hear it. "It is a way of being in the world. It is about relationship. It is about how you connect and relate not only to me, but to all people—children, parents, and especially yourself. It is being able to be present with another human being, to be fully present, real, and totally available . . . the big respect.

"Like nature, sexuality moves in ways that we don't need to fully understand."

14

Leaping the Invisible Edge

"Go to Germany, find Hitler, and tell him to be nice and not hurt people. He will listen to you because you're a little boy and he'll know that you have nothing to hide and nothing to gain." Everything turned dark and black, as though a vacuum had sucked out all remnant of light. There was only silence. No words, no visions. The words were etched into my soul as my seven-year-old body walked up what appeared to be hundreds of wide concrete steps leading to a massive, ornate gray building perched hundreds of feet above the rest of an old, vacant city. Dark cumulus clouds hovered close to the ground, amplifying the silence around me as I sat down to rest—tired, lonely, and afraid. Even though afraid, I knew I was to be here. I saw only varying shades of gray and huge concrete blocks forming walls and arches. There was no life anywhere—no people, no animals.

I was completely alone.

I stood facing two enormous, ornate wood-paneled doors with uniquely oversized brass handles just within my reach. I pulled one handle down and with the strength of my entire body, I leaned up against one door, pushing it just enough for me to squeeze through the opening.

I stepped into a room that appeared to be as big as a stadium. I knew any sound I'd made would have echoed throughout the circular hall. A broad spiral stairway circled the perimeter. Cautiously I walked toward the stairs, my body turning slowly as my eyes consumed every detail, taking in a 360-degree view, searching for movement of any kind.

I began to climb upward stair by stair, an endless series of stairs forming in front of me, unable to see the next floor ahead. It seemed as if I had been climbing a long time before the stairs emptied into a dark, carpeted hallway that echoed even without sound.

Another heavy, thick wooden door hung tall and foreboding to my left, a large swastika carved into its center. I stood motionless, facing the door, feeling intimidated by its size. I had the unusual thought that the door carried secrets from both sides of the wall. For a little self like me, I was surprised by my own thought.

Feeling small and vulnerable, I waited in front of the door, not knowing why I was waiting, yet knowing I was supposed to wait there.

Eventually I heard a creaking as the huge door slowly opened, revealing only darkness behind it. I watched. My eyes, open wider than I thought possible, locked onto a shadow figure taking form as light from the hallway revealed the outline of a man. The outline took one brisk step forward, taking on the well-defined image of Adolph Hitler.

There I stood, seven years old, about four feet tall, sneakers untied, shirt hanging out, one pant leg rolled into a cuff and the other dragging beneath my shoe.

I looked up into Hitler's eyes. In a commanding voice I said, "Be nice and stop hurting people."

Rapidly the vision faded as everything went black.

Now, decades later, as I walked late at night along the Gorge Bridge seven miles north of Taos, I recalled that dream. It had been the childhood dream that had defined the theme of my life—finding ways to connect with others when no connection seemed possible. The bridge I was crossing connected the sheer cliffs that contained the Rio Grande as it slowly cut through the high-desert earth hundreds of feet below me. I was alone in the light of the moon. No cars passed through here at two o'clock in the morning. The setting was eerie. I felt eerie. I was scared again. I knew I could become lost in my fear and flee in panic, or use the fear to learn how I scare myself every day with one thing or another. This was the place to practice.

I was also alone because I couldn't be with anyone. My perspective of being alive was changing too rapidly each day. The quiet night, mixed with the natural fear of being alone in the middle of nowhere, brought me to the dangerous edge of being more aware than I believed I could be. I couldn't hide from myself here.

I stood in the middle of the span of the windswept bridge, high above a place where my life could end, looking straight down into the dark river below, with only a piece of thin metal separating me from one quick leap. I had thoughts of just simply jumping, not from despair, anger, or hopelessness, but simply to jump.

"Just jump," I heard an neutral inner voice say. "Jump. Don't think about it. Do one thing in your life without thought, logic, or knowing what the outcome will be. Do instinct. Jump."

I stepped back a few feet from the railing, nervously laughing at myself, knowing I could do whatever I wanted. "If I jump," I thought, "I'd probably come right back to where I am now in time, and never know I'd jumped in the first place. So why do it at all?"

I moved close to the metal rail again, this time with the excitement of not knowing for sure whether or not my instinct and sense of wonder would hurl me over the bridge to the rocks and water below.

"What if I don't die, though," I wondered, "but instead, land in some twisted way on a rock, with lots of broken bones, alone, in pain, cold, scared, and worst of all, alive. What then?"

I recalled having this kind of mind dialogue with myself as a child, intentionally painting the most grotesque mind pictures I could imagine, scaring myself so much I'd run home and hide under the bedcovers. I'd often push myself to the brink of terror, knowing I was doing the pushing, then wallow in the imagined terror I'd created.

Standing on the bridge, I quieted my mind and allowed my eyes to consume the moonlit canyon walls below me, imagining the ancient information that lived within them. I soon forgot where I was and how scared I should be, hearing unidentified sounds way off in the distance. The sound of the river below was the only constant. Since it had been there for many thousands of years, I felt consoled.

"What if I expand my view of 'normalness,'" I playfully thought as my mind cleared. I encouraged myself to follow these incoming thoughts so as to not get lost in the circling fear. "Maybe there is another way to be alive. What if all physical body forms—including the bodies of so-called retarded, mentally gifted, and physically disabled people—were considered normal and natural and the people who believe that some people's bodies are abnormal and dysfunctional are the abnormal ones?"

I wondered why I needed to see people who were emotionally or physically different from me as incomplete or abnormal. I thought of a man I knew who, at age eighteen, had landed on his neck during a gymnastics meet. He had been a quadriplegic, lying on his back in a hospital bed, ever since.

His movements were limited to turning his head left or right, speaking, and turning the pages of books by using his elbow and trembling hands. His body had become a resting place, holding his form together while he soared into his dreams, imagination, and thousands of books he joyously devoured, which were teaching him of lighter worlds to travel, where a physical body was not required.

People came to him daily to hear his stories and wisdom. He didn't need his body the way I needed mine. He was a great teacher disguised in a disabled body.

I felt the open space around me, the night sky, the fear—the potential risk of taking a shortcut off the bridge. All of this heightened my awareness. I knew I had to be fully awake to everything or I'd easily succumb to fear, even follow the instinct to jump.

The air was cool. I had no place else I needed to be except where I was. I could be on the bridge forever if I chose. "That's always been true," I said out loud.

I observed the quality of my thoughts and the brief life vignettes that moved through my internal movie theater. I was relieved that nothing needed to make sense, be logical or justified.

As the moon created a hole in the sky, I sat down on the bridge, my feet dangling over the edge, seemingly a million feet above the river.

Out of the silence, I felt my heart beating and a warmth radiate throughout my entire body, traveling everywhere at once. I heard the sound of an owl in the distance and the flapping of wings around me, but saw no bird. I saw shadows everywhere, shadows that may have been out to get me or, more likely, were part of the landscape—things that moved in the night while I usually slept.

As I gazed into the darkened canyon, I thought about my conversation with Meigra about teaching respect. I realized that every contact I have with someone, even the seemingly trivial contact, has the potential to change my life forever. Mr. Ohly had taught me this in a most indirect way.

I was surprised to be thinking of him. I hadn't thought of Mr. Ohly in thirty years. Now, in the middle of a bridge over the Rio Grande at two in the morning, with my feet dangling hundreds of feet above the rocks, he appeared.

Mr. Ohly was the first teacher to touch me. He touched me with his hand. It wasn't a sexual touch. It was a touch that changed me in a lasting, meaningful way.

I was thirteen years old, in the eighth grade. I had already submitted to nearly a decade of daily school, patronizing teachers, and a system of approval by letter grade. I believed, and was told, that life would happen later, not then—that the real world began after graduation—which suggested to me that what I was doing before age eighteen wasn't real and didn't matter.

I was unaware of any other choice but to go to the classroom every day, and get through each semester whole, not suspended, and with a passing grade. I wasn't aware of anything missing in my life; I thought that what I was doing was life. But on this particular day in the thirteenth year of my life, something changed.

I was hunched over my desk, like twenty-five other people in the class, totally lost in the words I was writing for Mr. Ohly. I was doing my work like I did my work every other day. I was simply getting it done, hoping I would please the teacher.

Mr. Ohly, a stocky man with gray hair, quietly and slowly walked up and down the aisles observing each of us.

As he approached my row, I felt his presence. "Soon, he'll be standing beside me," I thought anxiously, "looking for something wrong with what I've written, something to correct."

My body tensed, anticipating his arrival, and my neck involuntarily compressed into my shoulders. I was so used to being judged that I no longer even noticed, as I froze in anticipation. My shoulders tightened—a symptom that had become an integral part of my life.

I pretended interest in writing as he approached my desk. I wasn't breathing—a habit I'd acquired while in kindergarten, under similar circumstances. I waited for the criticism or the obligatory "Nice work, son." There wasn't any. No sound at all. Silence. His shoes remained in place; the heat of his presence sent my thoughts reeling.

I felt Mr. Ohly's hand touch my shoulder gently. His huge, warm hand with big, soft fingers rested on my shoulder as my body melted into softness. The feeling was alien to me.

I felt as I imagined a rubber band might feel after being stretched all its life, then suddenly being released to rest back into its natural state, free from having to hold anything together or apart.

After a few seconds, Mr. Ohly just as gently removed his hand and moved to the person in front of me. I stopped writing. Involuntarily, I took a deep breath, and tears formed in my eyes. I chose not to move the slightest bit for fear of losing the quietness I felt.

"He likes me," I thought. "He likes me." I was warm all over, aware of feeling soft, quiet, and content, sensations I hadn't known existed. I glanced up, holding my head still to avoid drawing attention, and watched Mr. Ohly move around the room. He touched each person as he walked by, sometimes on the shoulder or with a light touch on the head, sometimes simply resting his hand for a moment on a person's back.

He didn't say anything to anyone.

Mr. Ohly's simple touch showed me what was there to feel— a home within me. I didn't consciously know it then, but my body did.

In that moment, I awoke to an awareness of when I am not feeling soft, quiet, and receptive inside, three qualities that, I later learned, were absolutely necessary to see the world clearly. Power and strength originate from those soft, quiet places. Mr. Ohly's touch showed me what it feels like to be at home in myself. I learned to notice when I'm caught in the opinions and expectations of others, and the necessity of finding a way, at any risk, to return to myself—a place inside where I'm at ease in silence.

Mr. Ohly, without words, in silence, had taken me to my heart.

A slight breeze came up, drawing my attention to where I was sitting on the bridge. The Mr. Ohly memory blew away with the movement of air, leaving me with my hands holding gently to the bridge railing. As though some energetic window had opened, I saw the link between all life events, the absolute order of everything that has ever happened or will happen.

Strangely, and somewhat precariously, I let my tired body lie back onto the bridge walkway where I drifted into sleep, only to wake with the early morning light accompanied by the sound and vibration of a car driving across the bridge at high speed. As the car drove past me, my tired, half-open eyes read the rear bumper sticker and I smiled, contrasting its message with the one of Mr. Ohly: *My Child is an Honor Student at Santa Fe High School.*

"The ultimate in advertising," I thought as I sat up, "the advertising of smartness, ranking children into categories, dividing them from one another."

The car disappeared into the desert horizon, captured by the ever-reddening landscape.

Suddenly, a sadness washed over me as the image of the bumper sticker message played over and over in my mind. I wondered why something so seemingly innocent was having such an impact on me.

In my partially awake state, without the usual self-censorship, I felt the implication of the message. Children are being artificially divided into a hierarchy of special and not so special, created when they're labeled honor students, gifted students, developmentally disabled, attention deficit disordered, hyperactive, and dozens of other categories.

"Why is it necessary to name and label our children—to have neat categories for them?" I asked no one in particular. "Why separate them from each other? Why advertise children as smart on car bumpers as though they were boxes of cereal?"

"Aren't you being at little picky?" I heard a voice say from behind me.

"What? Who said that?" I blurted out, so startled I nearly folded backwards over the bridge railing.

"I said that," a familiar voice said. I quickly turned and found myself staring into the face of Jarid. He was sitting, cross-legged, directly behind me, leaning against the bridge railing, apparently enjoying my startle. His face wore a smile that teased me into a sense of wonder and disbelief. I could see that he enjoyed my initial discomfort at his ability to appear without warning.

"Where'd you come from? What are you doing out here so early in the morning? How'd you sneak up behind me? How did you know I was here? What's happening? How come you're talking to me so . . . so . . . so . . ."

"Clearly?" he answered for me.

"Yeah, clearly. You're right here in this world with me. How come you didn't speak like this before?"

"You couldn't have heard me if I simply appeared normal and familiar to you," he answered. "You had to be forced to stretch yourself to hear me, especially when I didn't fit your picture of everyday life. You either had to expand on your own or write me off as another form of the mentally disabled."

He smiled and said, "You passed."

"Gee, thanks."

"That time," he added.

His smile remained constant, as though he were waiting for me to settle down to be with him. Instead, I paced around, walking back and forth across the highway from one side of the bridge to the other. Not knowing how Jarid got there was scary, but a thrilling kind of scary. His presence energized me.

"This doesn't make sense, Jarid," I said in a slightly shrill voice. "How'd you get here without my seeing you?"

His only response was his ever present smile. Minutes seem to pass before he spoke.

"Most things that happen around you, you don't see happening, so why should this be different," he said in a matter-of-fact tone.

"That's a clever answer, but what's really going on here?" I asked again.

"Do you really need to know?" he asked back.

"No."

"Good. That's progress."

I sat down on the cold concrete facing him, the river flowing far beneath us. I smiled too.

The scene seemed completely out of context—the two of us sitting on a bridge alone, the sun slowly rising, talking as though we were at a table in a local coffee shop.

"It's been an odd night, Jarid, but you probably already know that, right?"

"Every night is an odd night if you expect it to be like the one before."

"Yeah, but this one was more odd."

"Oh, there are degrees of oddness?" he asked, laughing, enjoying his own humor. "Something is odd to you only if it is the first time you have experienced it. The second time it's unusual, and the third time it doesn't matter. The third time you have no label for it; you have no need to name it. You could be more efficient, simply bypass the first two and look at everything that comes to you each day with a sense of wonder. Eliminate the concept of odd all together. Saves time."

"Okay, it doesn't matter how you got here. I can let it be for now. But it still seems odd that I'd react so much to a silly bumper sticker that says *My Child is an Honor Student*, especially when I'm out here in the middle of nowhere with such vastness around me and the magic of you showing up."

"Maybe that's not all you're seeing," he said in a tantalizing tone. "Maybe your eyes are seeing the words, and your heart and intuition are recognizing the true message within the seemingly innocent phrase."

Jarid reached toward me and placed both hands on my shoulders. With the look of a cat about to pounce, he said, "Just maybe you judge yourself too quickly for being trivial when you're actually seeing the truth."

"It is trivial," I insisted. "Who cares about a message on a bumper?"

Jarid's face grew serious, more intense.

"I should know about people being labeled," he began, "and

sent off to institutions and shrinks to be fixed, worked on, and scrutinized. Because I saw things that these professionals didn't see, I was labeled odd. What I called visions, they called hallucinations. What I called guides and angels, they called nonexistent voices.

"It is limiting, dangerous, and wrong to label people anything. Labeling separates and sets up divisions: good and bad, better or worse. Labels allow us to kill and abuse one another's bodies and spirits. Labels are convenient for those who need convenience, slick answers, and the self-satisfaction of proving our beliefs. Believing anything else becomes inconvenient, uncomfortable, and terrifying."

Jarid stood up. Without bending his knees, he reached down to touch his toes with his palms, spun around a few times, and began to sit but remained standing instead. Only Jarid would do that. Only Jarid could do that.

"Labels," he whispered in a soft voice, "are provided by those who do the labeling. Your response to that simple bumper sticker is not trivial. It is everything."

"I feel like it's more than trivial, but I'm not sure I want to believe what I suspect," I said. "If I believe what I know, I'll have to reveal myself."

"Careful," Jarid said, smiling. "You might have to be real and really be here in this world, even take a huge risk—like believing yourself."

He spun around in place, stopping with his nose a few inches from my face. His eyes burned into mine. "What would you see if you couldn't not believe yourself?" he asked.

"If I couldn't not believe myself?" I repeated, giving myself time to absorb both the vague and the obvious meaning of his question.

"That's pretty good, Jarid," I said, dazed by its implications.

I was enlivened by how he was showing me how to move beyond where I thought I could go.

"I see that children labeled 'Honor Students' are thought of as special, different, and brighter than others," I said without hesitation. "Why? What does it matter, and what are bright and smart? And once I've defined them, so what?"

Jarid reached for a bottlecap resting by his foot. He picked it up and gazed at it as if the cap were a rare stone. He turned it slowly, observing the reflection, and began weaving a fantastic, unimaginable story about the lifetime of that specific bottlecap. His story was so bizarre, it enhanced my own observations.

"Being bright and being smart have little to do with grades, passing tests, or homework. Actually, being bright has nothing to do with school at all. Being bright is the ability to see people, things, and life forces with a sense of wonder, exploration, and almost giddy excitement.

"Being bright is a way to be in the world. Being bright means I ask questions, explore, laugh with myself at the absurdity of daily conflicts, and have no need to restrict or limit the world to fit any category. There's room in the bright mind for everyone and everything.

"With brightness there's no such thing as exclusion, judgment, or self-righteousness. Being bright allows me to open up my awareness to include all people, all ideas, ideologies, lifestyles, cultures, and ways of being, and includes wanting to know about everything and everyone in the world."

Jarid leaned over to put his head through the metal railing so he could spit into the canyon. Some of the spittle dribbled down his chin. I had the thought of how unbright a picture this was.

"Brightness attracts people," he added. I wondered if he was purposely dribbling to double twist my perception, and to demonstrate how appearances have nothing to do with what might really be happening.

"Brightness is like an energy force," he continued, "a vitality that no one can define as belonging to any one group of people. Brightness is everywhere and in everything. Brightness happens when you step out of your limited view of the world. It is when you embrace, if only for moments, all people and all ideas, and especially when you fully embrace yourself. I'm bright not so that you'll honor or label me. I'm bright because I'm most alive at that moment. That is when I realize that everyone in the world belongs here just as they are. Labeling children gifted, slow, medium, and fast serves no one."

"It doesn't," I affirmed instinctively.

"It does for the labeler," Jarid insisted. "All those people who define others for their own comfort get to set themselves apart. The labeler gets to be the judge. She and the labeled one believe the parts they play. One plays the wiser, knowing decider of what is true, and the other plays the lesser, sub-missive, confused soul awaiting approval and definition from the outside. If only one steps out of her self-inflicted identity, chaos may follow but both will be free."

Jarid put his hands behind his head and slowly turned from side to side, stretching his shoulders and arms. His movements were deliberate and thorough, as though he could sense each muscle and joint in motion.

"It is best," he continued as he stretched, "when everyone gets to appreciate themselves for whoever they are, without outside forces telling them who they are. Being alive is a process of learning, and in its natural state, learning does not have to be taught. It can't be taught."

"Yes, yes, yes!" I agreed, embarrassed at my enthusiasm.

"Our present belief," I said as I joined him, "assumes that learning needs to be taught, that if I have no external incen-tive to learn, I would not be interested in exploring the world, other people, or how it all works. But I would rather be real, be around others who are real, and bring the realness out from wherever it hides."

"Maybe," Jarid added with a smile, "the bumper sticker could simply read: *My Child is Herself.*

"Or no bumper sticker at all," I said, believing my final statement to be the cleverest of all.

"Hmmm," Jarid reflected, "that would be brave. No need to tell anyone. Hmmm. That would, indeed, be brave."

15

Descent into the Unfamiliar

It was mid morning as Jarid and I parted. The sun was bright above us, heading toward its high-noon high point.

We were finished for now. There were no more words. With the grace of a cat moving through darkness, Jarid stepped off the narrow curb that had been our platform of magic since sunrise, directly onto the bridge roadway.

Standing a dozen feet away, he looked back toward me with an expression on his face that made me laugh. I interpreted his look to mean, "You think what just happened was something; wait until you see what happens next!" His alll-knowing smile completed his implied message of warning. Jarid turned to face potential oncoming traffic and stuck his thumb out, expecting to hitch a ride in one of the few cars that sped by occasionally.

Before I turned to walk in the opposite direction, we looked at each other one more time, with just a glance of recognition informing me that whoever I thought I was, I wasn't.

Jarid's clothes and physical appearance had me convinced that few drivers in the world would voluntarily stop to allow his unfashionable figure into their car for any reason, much less offer him a long ride somewhere. I imagined him standing there for days, waiting for a ride.

The first vehicle to approach the bridge was a large, four-door family car. A well-dressed, elderly man and woman sat in the front, the woman at the wheel. My first impression was that they were tourists from the East Coast, and my first thought was that they would most certainly avoid any person who appeared slightly out of the ordinary. Jarid was way over that line.

Imagining what the couple was probably thinking, I was embarrassed for Jarid. Simultaneously, I was feeling absolute respect for him and his ability to not deviate one second from being who he was. Jarid was so much able to be Jarid that I realized my embarrassment was for myself. My stomach tightened as I recognized the public identity I projected to look good, appropriate, and acceptable, another of my shadows that distanced me from being real—from being a Jarid. That awareness saddened me.

The big white car with leatherette seats slowed as it approached Jarid's outstretched thumb, then eased to a stop directly in front of him. The man on the passenger side rolled down his window as the woman leaned over him, smiling.

"Where ya going?" she asked, her voice friendly and full of life.

"Same direction you are, ma'am," Jarid answered with a smile.

"Hop in," the couple said simultaneously. "We're going in that direction too."

Jarid smiled graciously. Then, pivoting on both feet, his body etching a circle, arms outstretched, he faced me one last time. Slowly, he bent forward to bow in my direction as a knight before a king, exemplifying grace, and the humor of perspective.

I laughed at his gesture as he stood tall again, turned away, and opened the rear door of the sedan.

He had one more smile and a last word for me. His eyes held me still as he said in a voice just loud enough for me to hear, "How would you treat people if you didn't know who was the chosen one?"

He slipped into the back seat and closed the door.

The couple drove off, heading west with Jarid secure in the back seat. My mouth hung slightly open, incredulous. A few tears rolled down my face.

I walked the length of the bridge toward my car. The world felt different. Everything appeared uncommonly clear, yet completely unfamiliar. I noticed that my sense of time seemed different, and that I didn't have the usual curiosity about what time it was. It wasn't as if time had stood still—there just wasn't any.

The hot sun brought in a mood memory of how, as a teenager growing up along the warm beaches of Los Angeles, life was part of a continuum—something that had already taken place and all I had to do was walk through it. I lived time. I was time. I knew at sixteen that time didn't really exist. People just made up time to explain what they could never know. They felt better knowing that they had been somewhere, were somewhere now, and would go some- where else later. The concept of time was a convenient way to create neat little intangible boundaries of proof that something meaningful was going on in the world of work and learning.

Now, decades later, from a time point of view, I know that, just as I feared leaving home to go into the world on my own as a teenager, I often fear going into the world in front of me, on my own, again, again, and again each day.

The quality of the fear is the same: only the masks for pre- tending it isn't there have changed.

"That's a pretty silly way to live," I thought as I reached the end of the bridge and stepped onto the sandy soil. "But the daily world I live in now is no different than the one I lived in at ages eighteen, twelve, or eight. Age numbers are arbitrary symbols assigned to a point in time in my physical life span. Where do I find any number marked out in space? I can only speak and write age numbers, I can't see them anywhere. Age is a thought. It's a belief. It's not really real."

The sun burned hot into my face as I wondered where all the thoughts were coming from.

"Maybe I'm crazy, or maybe what I'm thinking is too profound to be crazy," I said. "Just maybe I'm supposed to be exactly where I am with myself, even if I don't believe what I just said."

I sat down on a warm rock next to my car and spoke out loud into the desert. "Time, time, time. When I was five, I had no idea what I would feel like at fifteen. When I was twenty, I had no idea what I would feel like at forty. I have no idea what thirty years from now will feel like. So, maybe it shouldn't matter. Maybe even memory is a thought I give a time dimension to. Maybe memory is happening now!"

I couldn't seem to stop my crazy-sounding thoughts. I wondered if I could die under the pressure of self-awareness by accidentally unraveling too many secrets and dissolving into a puddle of water.

This was too much. There had to be another way to live in this world where I didn't have to think so much, where old emotional patterns didn't exist, and where I could change my perception of things at will.

I decided to throw a pencil in the air and drive in whichever direction the lead tip pointed when it landed. I'd drive until the events unfolding in front of me told me to stop. No matter what, I'd trust something I'd never fully trusted before—my intuition and instinct.

I realized that the only way to change my perception and live differently in the world would be to make myself available for events to present themselves to me, instead of trying to make things happen. I would take a risk and open up to something radically different.

I established an internal commitment and tossed the pencil in the air. It landed with the tip pointing east. I got in the car, started the engine, opened all the windows, released the brake, shifted into first gear, and headed east, back over the bridge toward the mountains and Indian land.

Within a few minutes, I saw a blinking red stoplight ahead, hanging from a cable stretched between two telephone poles. The crossroad at the intersection was Highway 68, a north-south highway dissecting northern New Mexico.

About a hundred yards before reaching the traffic light, instinct grabbed the wheel. Without consulting a map to determine where I would be heading, I turned right onto what seemed to be a frontage road leading off into the depths of nowhere.

Immediately, I was confronted with a maze of potholes scattered in a chaotic design along the disintegrating asphalt road, allowing no margin for error. I slowed to fifteen miles per hour, carefully maneuvering over and around the obstacle course of holes, guiding the tires wherever remnants of pavement remained, excited by the challenge. As much as I wanted to look up and out into the infinite horizon, the road directly beneath and ahead of me demanded one hundred percent attention—an inner discipline I'd often ignored. My choice to go where I had never been before required complete awareness if I wanted to avoid a broken axle or a severely damaged tire.

I thought of what it must be like for soldiers walking through a minefield, feeling both terror and anticipation, knowing each next step might be the last.

The specific attention needed to avoid the mysterious depths of each water-filled hole kept me on edge and, simultaneously, completely awake. I glanced at a saying I'd taped to the dashboard weeks earlier: *Let the path form beneath your feet.*

Several miles in, the road smoothed out, unexpectedly free of potholes. Intent and focus gave way to relief as I was able to look out into the horizon, consuming the color and breadth of vision before me.

The newly paved road was just wide enough for two cars to pass in opposite directions without touching if both drivers were well coordinated. There was no painted center line to separate them.

To my right, toward the west, I could see distant rain clouds hovering over mystical mountains seemingly hundreds of miles away. On my left, to the east, appearing to be only a few miles distant, Indian land mountains loomed, forming a natural barrier to whatever lay hidden on the other side. A huge cloud in the configuration of an eagle about to touch down hovered over the mountains, enticing my imagination.

The road gently curved east, cutting a narrow pathway through the desert hillside, hiding the sunlight until I entered the wider horizon. Suddenly, and for only a few seconds, the road disappeared downhill, leaving me unable to see, for certain, my direction. The sensation of a lost road reminded me of the last moment before a roller coaster drops down from its highest point into a bottomless fall.

The sudden downhill turn of the road dropped me into faith—faith that the highway department knew what it was doing and that the road would still be there even if I couldn't see it. The pavement eventually appeared in view, giving me the courage to leave it entirely now and then, to investigate dirt side roads. I followed my intuitive impulses, seeking the unusual adventures promised by uncharted territory. Each road dead-ended within a few miles at the Rio Grande gorge, or simply ceased to exist, dissolving into the desert sand and sage.

I decided to remain on the paved road well into the late afternoon, until a hint of setting sun began to color the sky. As the rearview mirror reflected the sunset, I imagined I was driving away from a sky on fire, burning brightly into the ascending night.

Ahead, in the direction of the mountains, I saw a column of bluish white smoke rising from what I thought could only be a campfire or cabin fireplace. It seemed unusual to see smoke on a warm, late-summer day. The desert terrain was sufficiently warm without the need for an indoor fire.

As I drove directly toward the smoke, my busy mind began to imagine the potential mystery that might await. Maybe, I thought, I'd come across long-lost tourists who'd left the main road weeks ago and were down to their last meal, and I'd be the one to save them. Or, perhaps the smoke was rising from an extinct volcano hidden under the desert floor.

I was close enough now to see clearly the column of smoke drifting upward from its origin—a fire outside a small, sand-colored, old adobe home. I could make out the forms of several people sitting on a ground-level, wood slat porch near the fire.

As I approached a dirt driveway extending out about fifty feet from the house, I came to a complete stop, my attention focused on the strangeness of what I was seeing or thought I was seeing. It seemed so out of context, a small group of Indian or maybe Hispanic women, dressed in brightly colored skirts and blouses, sitting on the porch only a few feet away from a small hole in the ground with a wood fire burning, all laughing while doing something intricate with their hands.

Nobody looked over in my direction even though my presence was obvious. I had the thought that maybe they already knew I was coming, that they had no need to look with their eyes at the car with a dumbfounded human being in it, staring at them.

I knew I was to drive up the short, rain-rutted driveway, park, and simply walk over and join the women in whatever they were doing, even though I wasn't knowingly invited.

My rational mind tried to dissuade me from that idea. I thought it would be intrusive. They didn't know me. They might be scared of a curious-looking white man walking toward them. They'd throw things at me and tell me to get off their property.

I justified all the reasons and excuses I could find to avoid following my intuition, especially since that same intuition had led me down a half-dozen dead-end dirt roads earlier in the afternoon.

"There is nothing more to explain or justify," I heard a voice inside me say firmly. "You either do it or you don't. When you don't follow your instinct, you find yourself feeling bad over and over and over again. You feel drained of energy and hang by a thread each day on old beliefs, seeing nothing new. Remember your internal commitment."

I put the car in reverse and backed up a few feet on the road so that I could drive forward into the driveway. I parked, and before opening the door, observed the four women through the open window as they continued to laugh together, noticing their hands deftly working with brightly colored fabrics that matched the colors of the skirts they wore.

I was suspicious: none of the women looked over in my direction, not even for a glance. My initial concern that they'd be startled by my presence changed into my own fear of why my presence didn't seem to matter to them at all.

"Do they know something I don't know?" I wondered.

"No doubt!" a sarcastic inside voice answered just as quickly.

The mystery I'd asked for was here. On instinct alone, I'd followed an unknown road to find this place, and now an unfamiliar sensation was drawing me toward a scene that was completely unpredictable. I froze in place with the terrifying thought that by listening to my intuition and instinct alone, I could be committing suicide.

"So?" replied a voice inside me, shattering the fear into a smile.

I opened the car door, stepped out and, at the last moment, decided to leave the door unlocked and slightly ajar in case I had to make a clean getaway. Even more cautiously, I leaned into the car to insert the key in the ignition for a quicker escape, just in case.

The magic of the moment became more profound than my background thoughts of doom and mysterious dark forces waiting to eat me alive. I turned toward the four women, expecting to see at least one pair of eyes looking in my direction. They must have noticed me, a complete stranger, miles off the beaten track, hovering by my car, staring at them.

I observed no recognition at all of my presence.

Slowly I walked toward the colorfully dressed women, taking in everything about them and around them, my curiosity filling the empty space between us. Whatever fear I felt was my own familiar response to unusual, unknown, and unpredictable situations—not unlike every other day of my life. But this day was to be different.

16

The Fire Bridge

As I neared the women, I noticed two of them were sewing squares of colored fabric together, creating skirts similar to the ones they wore. The other two were beading bracelets. My visual impression was that two of the women were Indian, one was Hispanic, and the fourth Anglo. There was an unmistakable harmony among them.

I approached, feeling welcome, even though no one had greeted me and no eye contact was offered. Each woman's face carried a hint of smile that brought out a quality of calm I'd never felt. If I had spoken, I would have disturbed the spacious peace and quiet content I was experiencing.

At another time in my life, I might have thought myself rude for staring at their faces. But I wasn't really staring;—I was immersed in their presence. Somehow I knew this was all I was to do and this would be the formal introduction. Their faces carried so much more than personality; they were filled with who they were and who they weren't. There was no facade, no false front—no self-image to project.

Their expressions softened any questions I might have had. The women appeared to be completely satisfied at simply being alive, doing exactly what they were doing. My stomach tightened as I compared myself to them, believing that I had probably never been as at peace inside as they appeared to be.

205

Tentatively, I sat down on a brightly colored canvas chair. It was wobbly and unstable, yet it served as a place to rest my body. The energy and lightness around these women were so satisfying that any discomfort I was experiencing went unnoticed.

I watched them stitch and bead for over an hour before I caught the eye of what appeared to be the oldest of the women. Her ever present smile was comforting beyond anything I'd known, doubly so as her eyes touched mine for just a moment.

In that brief moment of feeling her eyes in mine, a strong crying sensation filled my throat. Her momentary gaze received me so completely that my entire lifetime of hiding behind some self-sustained identity suddenly wasn't necessary. Not only was this woven cloak of social image unnecessary, it was impossible to hold in the presence of her gaze. As the cloak fell away, I could no longer pretend that I knew who I was and what I was doing.

The fire I had seen from a distance burned in a shallow hole carved out of the soft soil, wet after a full day of thundershowers. The sun had set, leaving remnants of reddish light reflecting in the window glass of the old adobe house. Like a mirror, the darkened windowpane reflected the outline of the rain clouds hovering overhead. "What am I doing here?" I wondered. "I don't do this sort of thing. This doesn't make sense. Who are these people? What am I doing here?"

"There is danger in being willing to actually see what is happening in your life," one of the women said quietly, without looking up from her sewing, a sweet smile on her face.

"What?" I asked, startled by the first words I'd heard spoken. I wasn't even sure who spoke them. The words were so penetrating and raw, that before my mind had a chance to make something scientific out of them, I was immersed in mystery.

"Her name is Lupe," said another of the women sitting at the round, brightly painted wooden table. "She knew you were coming. She has more to tell you."

"I didn't even know I'd be here," I said respectfully. "How could Lupe?"

"Where Lupe lives, nothing is too far away to know if she wants to know it," the woman replied.

"I'm here and I don't know why," I said in a generic tone of voice to people whose names I didn't know.

"There is danger in being willing to actually see what is happening in your life," repeated the voice belonging to Lupe. "The danger is that your life will change, your relationships will change, dreams will become vividly clear, and your everyday world will become less important, soon to disappear forever."

"You don't need to say anything," encouraged the other woman, who I heard someone refer to as Nona. "Lupe simply needs to give you this information. You can do with it whatever you choose."

Lupe's eyes twinkled with the sparkle of wisdom. She wore a red bandana, and the most brightly colored clothes of the four women. She appeared to be somewhere between sixty and a hundred years old. I couldn't tell and it didn't matter.

Her full attention was on her sewing meditation. She spoke only occasionally and in a quiet voice filled with authority.

"You judge yourself for what you see in others," she continued. "Now you must be willing to see what you see, and allow what you see to be true or not true. Either way won't matter. Now when you see the truth, you are afraid to see it and conveniently call it confusion. That won't work for you anymore. You can no longer use confusion as an excuse."

I started to speak, but another of the women quietly cleared her throat, signaling me to be still.

"Your life now calls for you to act, not wait. Your coming here was an action. Had you waited an instant longer before coming here, you would have never found us. You never find anything new by waiting. You must bring yourself into the world so it may come to you. You are waking up and you can never go to sleep in the same way again."

I trembled as Lupe spoke. I even felt nauseous. The sensation soon passed, and I felt my eyes become bright and receptive.

All of the women were sitting quietly, still working with their hands, but now their eyes were focused on me. Lupe slowly pushed herself up from her chair. As her body accumulated the strength to walk, she looked down at me as though I were the only other person on Earth and asked, "What way of being seen by others makes you feel good? That's your identity. That is what you believe you need to protect at all costs. That is who you believe you are, or are not. When you no longer need to be seen in any particular way by anyone, you are free to be real."

Gathering the strength she required, she stood a little taller.

Slowly, and slightly hunched over, Lupe walked toward the screen door that led into the house. As the old door slammed behind her and she was halfway into the house, I heard her say, as though she knew I'd hear her, "Nothing originates from who you think you are."

It was almost dark. The earth beneath my dirt-caked shoes was wet and muddy. The wobbly wooden chair I sat in settled several inches into the saturated soil. I had the premonition that my usual way of living daily life was over, just like that—that I could no longer live a life of worry, struggle, paying bills, not paying bills, fun, no fun, and empty talk. The everyday world I had grown up believing was real was now flat and dead.

I didn't believe my perception of living could change so quickly, even if I wanted it to. Could I change an entire worldview so simply without the usual disaster occurring, such as divorce, death, loss of a job, or some life-threatening disease?

The other three women, laughing, sewing, beading, began bantering back and forth, glancing over at me occasionally with what appeared to be an inclusive intent. They spoke to each other, I later learned, in a blend of Spanish, English, and Huichol, the language of the Huichol tribe of central Mexico.

Hearing the screen door slam shut, I knew Lupe was returning and turned to see her settle into her canvas chair. She pulled the skirt she was sewing onto her lap and continued the stitching.

Without any explanation, and seemingly out of nowhere, Lupe instructed me to build a second fire, from scratch, right away, and on top of the wet soil.

"Why?" I asked instinctively, believing I needed a reason.

All activity stopped. I could feel the air compress with tension at the absurdity of my question. I heard myself ask the question as it came from my mouth and wished I could stuff it back in. I avoided suffering the embarrassment of noticing all their eyes on me by quickly gathering nearby kindling.

As Lupe offered specific instructions for the fire, her hands stretched thread and needle, sewing and weaving into colorful cotton fabric. Her voice and those of the others were light, full of humor, their words precise, like a knife cutting through steel.

They trusted themselves, which allowed me to trust them. Their presence alone filled the entire space. I had no desire to speak. I had nothing to say.

The deep reddish sky darkened to grayish black as I contemplated building up the fire in moist earth at dusk, with the masters of fire observing me, probably wondering whether I could light the match.

"Maybe," I thought, "this is all a hoax and I'm being duped by wise-looking, older indigenous women. I'm being taken in by their image, their language, this setting, and the need to experience something magical and out of the ordinary. Later, I'll realize all this and think myself a fool."

I paused, staring into the fire.

"I won't be able to tell anyone what a fool I am. I'm supposed to know better," I whispered to myself.

I looked up to see the faces of Lupe and the others, and most of my doubts dissolved. Noting the few that remained, I decided that if I was being taken in by these four women, I would feel good about it.

One of the women brought more kindling and logs, setting them by my side.

I fumbled with the kindling. Thoughts of how these women would have had the fire blazing by now, while I had yet to reach for the first match, filled a familiar place in me.

"It's time to begin," Lupe finally announced, reminding me of my Jewish grandmother, who'd tell me to "begin already." Overhead, threatening rain clouds gathered as the darkness closed in.

"We cannot do this ceremony if it's to rain," Lupe said. "The rain would douse the fire and the fire is essential."

"What ceremony?" I asked, being respectful but somewhat frightened.

Nobody looked at me this time. Nobody answered. I was left alone to hear myself.

Lupe was obviously not a person who said things out of discomfort with silence, so I assumed she knew what she was doing.

"You can use paper to help start the fire," someone suggested, whose voice I did not recognize. I was thinking it would be cheating to use paper—that one match and a log would be the skilled warrior way. I fiddled with the kindling, hesitating to strike a match and light the fire, realizing that once the match was lit, I was committed to a fire happening, successfully or not. I realized how important it had been to me, since childhood, to look good and not be seen as incompetent or foolish.

I laughed at myself and, strangely, everyone else laughed at the same time, even though I hadn't shared my insight out loud.

I dragged the wooden match along the side of the damp matchbox. It sparked but did not light. On the second attempt, it flamed. I watched the lit paper curl into itself as the heat of fire consumed it and the kindling began to burn. The fire flickered and smoked.

The young Navajo woman came over and gently kneeled

beside me. "My name is Maria," she said, as she reached into the fire with a charred stick to nudge and reposition the logs.

I was touched by her respectful way of providing guidance. The smoke I had been watching and moving away from for the past twenty minutes instantly turned to flame, casting huge, lively shadows all around us. It was as though the fire had been waiting for her. Oddly, I didn't feel foolish.

As the fire blazed, Maria stepped back from the flames and sat down to be with it. Her face was serene, silent, and calming to look at. As I gazed into the fire, I wondered if fire was intelligent.

No one spoke. From then on, whatever I placed on the fire burned well and evenly.

"I almost gave up here. I do that," I observed. "I have a habit of giving up too soon whenever I do things that are totally unfamiliar to me."

"A habit is a chosen path," Lupe said as she continued to sew, "that not only is familiar but is new each time one chooses it, again and again. Habits give us reasons, justifications, and excuses to not be present, to not be responsible."

She closed her eyes and stopped sewing.

"Habit is an excuse for not taking yourself seriously," she continued. "A habit is not a reason for continuing to kill your own spirit and that of those around you."

Lupe looked up, and her eyes entered mine.

"As long as you choose to ignore what is glaring, as long as you still want to blame someone else in your life for anything, then you are not yet willing to feel full yourself, to be an autonomous being."

Before I could ask what an autonomous being was, my feet slipped out from under me and I fell off the chair into the mud, one foot nearly landing in the fire. The laughter around me dissolved my thoughts of self-importance. The need to protect myself against being seen by Lupe became pointless.

I wasn't even sure what Lupe was saying, but I knew it was the truth. Something was changing inside me.

"How you are in your daily life has changed forever," Maria said softly, looking at me from across the fire, her face radiant. "You can no longer devote time to understanding why and what people are doing, thinking, or trying to work out. There is a place in you that requires the most difficult of inner work. It is that place where you immediately take responsibility for yourself, or you don't."

"I thought I was," I replied defensively.

"You work at it. You try. You struggle. You expend effort. You think you've done something because you've tried. But you still need to be nice, to be liked. The place I speak of is not about being nice or not nice. It is different. It is about being here, alive, real, and committed. It is not about telling the truth. It is being truth."

The fire popped loudly, spewing red-hot sparks just past both sides of my head, so close I ducked.

Maria was patient with my reaction to the fire.

"Being in yourself this way," she continued, "can feel fierce, uncomfortable, hard, direct, ruthless, purposeful—and it is. Yet, it originates from an even higher place of compassion, a compassion for yourself and for everyone around you."

She moved closer to the fire and sat directly across from me, only the flames separating us. Who I thought I was, was being completely reshaped by a woman I'd just met.

"You and others like you," she went on, "have been saturated with constantly working out your past, expressing anger, blaming someone, and feeling victim to something. Now it is time to see what clarity and piercing directness look like—what feeling and expressing the truth from the deepest depths look like. Your dwelling on history distracts you from being here. You must be here now."

"I'm getting to be here this moment," I said.

"It feels right inside, doesn't it?" she said, demanding I not pretend. "And it feels fierce, cruel, and unfamiliar," she added with a smile.

"The good part," Maria continued, "is that this way of being requires treating everybody equally and without bias, including your parents, friends, children, and people we know only briefly, as well as ourselves. It is about staying home inside, or leaving for a few moments only to come immediately back to being home again."

Hours seemed to pass, although it may have been only fifteen minutes in familiar time. We all sat in silence, breathing in the internal, softening effect of the fire.

The silence ended when Maria handed me a flaming stick from the fire. As I reached for it, she let it drop back into the fire.

"There is evil in the world you know," Maria whispered in a most serious voice and without preface, "and it's no longer subtle."

"What?!"

"Did I wake you?" she asked, expecting my shocked response.

"You woke me and you're scaring me. Where did that come from?" I asked.

"I wanted to get your attention."

"You've got it, completely."

"Not completely," Maria replied playfully, as she nudged the embers around. She remained quiet, an obvious way for her to provide a space for something new to emerge. Soon, my fear changed to calm.

"The word 'evil' scares people, you especially," she continued. "It scares you so much that you ignore it in your daily life, so therefore it controls you without your knowledge."

She paused, then added, "The word 'evil' scares everybody, not just you. Evil is a strong word, like death is a strong word. Hearing either one is meant to scare you. When frightened, you emotionally freeze, and you cease to explore the larger meanings of evil and death and how they play out in your daily life. You miss seeing the real purpose of so-called evil death forces.

"Specific mind images are created," she continued, "when you hear the words, and they get your attention immediately. You wake up when you hear them. They startle your complacency. You shy away from the evil and demonic forces and yet they're everywhere, all around you."

"Why are you telling me this?" I asked.

"Because you're here," she answered. "I'm telling you because you often claim to be emotionally lost and stuck.

"There's no more time to blame your inaction and confusion on being stuck. There are real enemies in your life in the form of people, places, and instincts. These are not simply innocent enemies that you can easily identify, even though they take the form of everyday people, events, and desires."

"Then . . ." I began to ask, but Maria went right on.

"The enemies in your life demand that you learn to lead yourself or succumb to a world that leads you in circles, lost forever. The enemy forces must be respected, or else you'll be lost in the despair of your spirit."

"I'm lost now," I said, then added, "What do evil enemies and demonic forces have to do with getting lost and stuck?"

Maria leaned in toward the fire and began to whisper, drawing me closer to her. My head was extended almost over the flames when she said softly, "Listen to me, you can hear this."

I turned my head.

"Think of distortion," she demanded. "What picture comes to mind when you hear the word 'distortion'?"

"I'm looking out a window on a dark, rainy day," I replied. "Water droplets are running down the outside of the glass. The trees and green leaves just outside the window are moving slightly, changing shape, even though there's no wind. Colors are changing constantly. Everything is distorted. Each drop, if I follow it, carries a microscopic magnified image of the trees just outside."

"Does that scene scare you?" Maria asked.

"No, why should it? It's a peaceful scene I've seen hundreds of times."

"Meaning you're familiar with it and it's never hurt you?" she translated.

"Not yet, but it could," I replied, pretending to be light.

Maria paid no attention to the pretense. Instead, she gave me another instruction.

"Think the words 'shadow, distraction, energy forces, mood, perception, dimension,' and 'unknown.' Notice how you feel when you feel into those words. Dream into them. Imagine that all of those words create a distortion of what is really in front of you, of what is really happening, and that you can easily react to each distortion as if it were not a distortion but something to fear. What if something is distorted and you don't know it? How would you behave?"

"If I don't know it," I answered, "I could end up being surprised, betrayed, deceived, and hurt."

"And that has happened many times in your life, hasn't it?" Maria reminded me.

"Many times, but that's part of life," I responded.

"No it's not. It's part of your life. It's not part of mine. That's why you get lost and stuck. You ignore the forces around you that want you to wake up."

"You mean the forces are what you call enemies, evil, demons, and other dimensions?" I asked.

"Yes," she replied, "the forces are less a terrifying and bloody thing than they are everyday moments that come and go with people and events around you. What I speak of is a tangible energy that cannot be dismissed as a fairytale. What I speak of is not a label attached only to obviously violent people or violent governments. Sometimes, violent people are only more dramatic and difficult to fathom than the little ways your spirit may be chipped away at every day."

"I'm getting scared, hearing this," I said.

"Of course you are," she replied softly. "You think of this subject as a bad thing, a hurtful thing, something you want no part of. Isn't that right?"

"Yes."

"You need it, then!"

"I need it?"

Maria selected another burning stick from the fire . This time, when she reached across the flame to hand it to me, she held it tightly for a moment, then released it into my waiting fingers. I held the burning stick, mesmerized by the flame.

"If this evil isn't what I'd always imagined it to be, then what is it? What does it look like?" I asked.

"It always comes disguised. It hides in the shadows," she answered.

"That's what I thought," I said, before she could complete her sentence.

"Be still," Maria said, silencing me with her eyes.

"Shadows are what you're not willing to look at or pay attention to. They're what you ignore by living a busy, uninteresting life. They live in those places you don't inhabit in yourself. When you're asleep in your waking life, the shadows thrive, gain sustenance and, like a cancer, grow larger. You find yourself living in fear and keeping busy, to avoid recognizing you're not living, only attempting to live as others have told you to do all your life."

I swallowed, embarrassed at hearing such an accurate description of myself.

"Shadows have no power over you when there is light," she added, smiling, "unless of course, they hide within the light."

The fire burned brightly, flaring up, illuminating the trees and faces of everyone. I felt myself entering more deeply into a black pool of calm.

"How do I recognize what you're talking about?" I asked. "What does a shadow look like? What does evil look like? I want to know. I'm ready to know."

"It may surprise you," she began. "It's a force that enters and departs every day in your life, mostly without your even knowing it. It comes with people you meet, startling events that appear to happen to you as surprises. It lurks in buildings, cars, and, especially, where you store material things of the past—old furniture, clothes, and items full of history but no life.

"It's a form of energy that provokes you and lives off you like barnacles on a whale. It can grab you and sap you of your strength without your even knowing it, over and over again. It is a force that can subdue and even kill your spirit, day after day."

Maria stared at me, wondering whether I was taking in what she was telling me.

"How do I know when it's present?" I asked. I wanted to hear more.

"The only way you know evil, or know when a shadow is present," she continued, "is by noticing your energy drop: you become tired, and your mood becomes darker. You question yourself. You doubt, and you compare yourself with others, which means you are believing yourself to be less than they are. When you compare at all, you are already split by the shadow. You believe life doesn't really work. You think hopeless."

It seemed as though Maria was defining the origin of conflict between people, and why I'd spent most of my life repeating one mood after another, only to return to the preceding mood on a regular basis.

Maria interrupted my mind's wanderings. "When you're around certain people or places, you find your energy suddenly drained, or you experience an abrupt mood change without warning, or feel zapped by another's words or presence."

As Maria spoke, I thought of people and situations where I instantly become tired or angry, thinking that there was something wrong with me.

"Most of the time, when you're with people, you're not seeing all of them. You miss the behind-the-scenes part of them, the background that is depleting your energy, the unspoken thoughts and expectations that demand you give all of yourself up to them. There is never enough of you."

"Once I see and believe all that you tell me, then what?" I asked. "What do I actually do to get my energy back or change my mood?"

"Even now," she responded with a smile, "you move too fast. You move so fast, you cannot feel your own answer. Listen now with your body, without trying to remember my words. Have faith that what you need to take in, you will.

"Having these people in your life," Maria continued, "helps you fine-tune and define yourself, even slow down, so your senses can bring you information. With some people, your eyes and mind will deceive you. You may register what they are saying and how they appear, but your body feels uncomfortable, tense, or even pained. You typically ignore your sense of discomfort and listen to the social mind of 'shoulds' and obligation, even if these people speak from chronic victimhood, complaining, blaming, and recycling life patterns over and over and over again without awareness."

Maria went silent, allowing her chin to drop to her chest as though in deep thought. She raised her head slightly and spit into the fire. The fire responded with a short hiss and a puff of vapor. Her eyes gazed into mine through the flickering light.

"I must be in love with her," I thought to myself. "If I'm in love, that would guarantee that I'd have more of the same, always." I wanted to hold onto the feelings of being with her so badly that I had to believe that I was in love.

"A second later, I realized how alive and bright I felt, simply being in her presence, especially since she was so absolutely present. I didn't have to bind myself with the social label of being in love, to experience the joy of my feeling. I reminded myself that it wasn't necessary to marry Maria and live with her forever because I liked her so much.

My body softened. With this shift in perspective, I could feel the freedom from a belief not my own run through me, and I could more fully take in what she was teaching.

"When you hear someone's apparently innocent words but they're not telling you the whole truth," she went on, "you will feel an 'ouch' in your body. And most people do not tell the whole truth. They have come to be familiar with being appropriate rather than real, careful rather than thoughtful, and nice rather than clear.

"When you see the spirit of someone beneath their outer-world facade, that is not a judgment, it is a blessing. What you do with what you see determines whether you abuse or serve with your awareness."

"I'm speechless," I stuttered.

"Unbelievable," Maria responded. "Is your mind as speechless as your tongue?"

I thought about that for a moment, then laughed at myself for thinking about it.

"Quiet your mind, even for moments, and you will see exactly what I see. You will know what I am telling you before I speak it. This information isn't secret, available only to those you believe to be wiser than you. As Jarid told you so well, you project me out here so you can learn about this part of yourself."

"How do you know Jarid?" I asked, surprised that she'd ever heard of him. I quickly followed with my own answer. "Doesn't matter. Go on."

"These forces come in many disguises," Maria continued. "They come looking like parents, friends, and strangers, sometimes in the form of lovers. They come into your life looking like partially present beings that tease you with their moments of kindness, insight, and receptivity. You may decide to believe only your eyes and ears and, once again, ignore your intuition, fearful that to believe intuition at all would isolate you in a society filled with those who dismiss the world of subtle perceptions. Yet, when you fear your intuition, it is your own power, not so much being awake, that you are fearing."

"That's right," I said, excited.

"You're really not setting yourself apart from others when you believe your own perceptions; you're learning to listen more carefully from inside, relying less on the opinions of others. You're tapping into your own authority, the most sacred of information.

"When you're emotionally autonomous, you're complete. You are who you are. You are free to sense everything fully."

I didn't even think about asking what she meant. I knew that I knew.

"Power unexpressed drains you," she concluded. Maria buried her face in her hands, having nothing more to say.

17

Track of Time

It was near midnight. The black sky was clear for the stars to shine through. The others had nodded off to sleep, still sitting in their chairs around the table. I thought Lupe was asleep too, since her eyes were closed. Yet, I had the feeling she never slept the way most people do, that she always knew what was going on around her, no matter what state she appeared to be in.

As I watched her, I wondered what it must feel like to be in a body that grew up in an Indian world, where the intangible is tangible, the unseen, seen.

Lupe opened her eyes. Her gaze found mine as I sat by the fire facing her, about five feet away. As though she hadn't been asleep at all, she spoke to me with the freshness of someone who was always awake, needing only rest.

"You take people on as projects," she said, not accusingly but as a matter of fact. "You think you're helping people, believing that if you just do one last thing, give a little more time, offer another emotional nudge, provide a little more understanding, they'll come to like themselves and respect who they are.

"They become your projects. You believe that you're the only one able to reach these people, the only one having the connection and the compassion. Is that not so?"

She didn't wait for an answer.

"You believe it is up to you to fix them because you see the goodness in them. They are receptive to you, you believe. You are totally drawn into their energy—hooked, as you would say—but have no idea you are. For some people, family members especially, you can do this for years, decades, and lifetimes. You do their work for them and they watch you do it.

"You go around and around in their vortex of energy until you muster the power and willingness to step out of the magnetic pull of saving others. They do not need to be saved, except to satisfy your own emotional comfort. You stay in a constant state of being lost yourself, and believe deep down that you cannot save them though you should be able to."

I yawned as if I were tired, but I knew the yawns were my body's reaction to being forced to reorganize my self-identity, to be willing to change by shattering illusions. As uncomfortable as I felt, I welcomed the discomfort. The truth of Lupe's words were freeing me from a way of being that never worked well anyway.

I was embarrassed at how small I felt, yet simultaneously aware of how large I really was inside. I realized that I could be free of needing outside approval when it did not matter to me how I was seen by others.

"Even if my mind tells me that outside approval matters," I thought, "it really doesn't. And if it doesn't, I won't have to justify or defend anything anymore. I can be either foolish or wise. I can be a wise fool!"

"So how do I know who to help?" I asked. "How can I know who will receive the help I offer and still do their own work?"

"You don't need to help anyone," Lupe replied firmly. "You don't need to save, fix, or help anyone. You do need to awaken them. Hit them between the eyes with what they're not paying attention to in their lives. Wake people up. Don't fix them."

"How?" I asked. "How do I know, for sure, whose life to enter into and whose to let be?"

"Feel it in your body," Lupe answered. "With some people, you'll feel a mutual receptivity, almost as if they're calling you into their lives, demanding that you bring perspective so they can not only change old patterns, but also enter into a different perception. You'll feel an opening, a willingness to join you, a willingness to step out of the trance. You'll notice movement."

I realized that Lupe was describing the "Oh Boy!" list Leo Garcia had shown me. "Does Lupe know Leo, too?" I wondered. Before I could ask, she went on.

"With these people, awareness operates in their lives all the time, not just when there's crisis. These people want to be awake, they're willing to do whatever it takes to be free of emotional binds and habits that root them in the past. The people you are to connect with have a burning need to explore, discover, and reach beyond the ordinary. They do not live with blame. They have a view of the world that exceeds ordinary awareness."

Lupe's eyes flickered in the firelight.

"Everything is about respect," she went on. "Everything. Respect in yourself. You have to decide whether respect is something you want from within or from others. You may not want it at all. Many of your kind, so-called seekers of truth, do not want respect and the responsibility it carries, even though they profess to. This is not unusual. To want respect requires a willingness to be fully within yourself all the time. You no longer find excuses for whatever you do or don't do, forget or remember."

My heart was beating faster than usual. I began trembling from what I thought was the cold air, even though I was sitting close to the fire.

"To want respect means you cannot live without it," Lupe continued when my eyes again made contact with hers. "You're not living at all if you do not live in respect. There is no other way to live. Respect separates you from everyone and connects you with everyone."

Meigra and Jarid had said the same thing. I could feel what it meant to be separate and connected, but I couldn't explain it. I knew the meaning would become clear, as mist dissolves to reveal the mountains and trees that had always been there.

"When you are respecting," Lupe continued, "you can never again claim ignorance."

Lupe paused, as though she knew I was about to ask a question that did not need to be asked.

"What do you mean by respect?" I asked anyway, expecting to be verbally attacked.

I was.

"My words ring hollow," Lupe said firmly, "to those whose ears hear only familiar phrases. I cannot do this work for you. Relationships can no longer tolerate abstinence of spirit. The children demand spirit. You must know the spirit again."

"Your words do not ring hollow, Lupe," I replied, surprised at how strong I sounded. "I am willing to learn, and sometimes I ask stupid questions, but within those stupid questions are exactly the right ones for me to ask."

She didn't reply, and I didn't need her to.

Before gazing back into the fire, Lupe glanced into my eyes. She spoke to me as though she were speaking to some force she saw within or around me.

"Do this work fully or not at all. I am not here to entertain you," she said. "I am not here to give time effortlessly so you may squander it with self-doubt. This is no longer an easy path. This path requires even bolder, more potentially devastating moves. There are risks, and these risks bring about clarity of thought and spirit."

"Sounds simple," I said, not thinking of how silly that could sound.

"It is quite simple," Lupe said, unexpectedly hearing it the way I meant it. "The decision to respect and live from respect determines your willingness to teach every moment by how you live. Until then, you are not teaching, nor are you living in respect. Instead, you are attached firmly to those who live out-side of respect, outside of themselves, and off the track of time."

She paused again, apparently waiting for me to ask what she meant by the track of time.

"What is the track of time?"

"The track of time," she answered, "is what you feel when you are being yourself. It is a knowing sensation. Life itself becomes the event, not the daily events you believe make up your life. Everything you consider chaotic has an exact order to it.

"As in the track of time, there is only one step to respect. There are no fragments to it. There is only the whole. It is a spirit decision within you to live life daily as though you were the headlight. This is not a human act. It is a spirit act. Your spirit needs the fuel of respect. The human does not. You can no longer collapse under the pressure of self-awareness. It is not difficult."

I turned to see Maria smiling an inner smile.

Maria whispered, "Remember that the journey is the event, not the event."

I closed my eyes and slept, my head resting on Maria's shoulder.

18

Rescuing the Hero

like waking up from a dream, you don't try, it just happens. I woke up to the early morning sunlight. I was sitting alone in a canvas chair by a smoldering fire, my legs covered with a brightly colored wool blanket. I wondered if I'd just awoken from a dream or into one.

I had never awakened this way. I was alone but not lonely, and I didn't have my usual morning heaviness. I felt defined—detached from the usual anxious thoughts that accompany waking into the morning.

My body had no pain; my neck felt lengthened and spacious. I had the funny thought that it's only when I worry that life doesn't go well, then I wondered why I wasn't worrying.

My morning thoughts were unusually useful. "If I were my own authority," I reasoned, "I'd have to acknowledge myself as a wise person and wouldn't have to continually look for someone outside of me to play the role of wise person. Certainly would be more efficient," I laughed.

"Certainly would," I heard another voice repeat.

"Who said that?" I asked as I looked around, seeing no one.

"Who said what?" the same voice repeated.

"I think what you're hearing is yourself," the voice continued. "You've been so used to behaving as though all your answers come from everyone else that you don't recognize yourself when you speak. How embarrassing."

Just then, the screen door opened and Lupe and Maria stepped out. Gracefully they walked over to their low-slung canvas chairs where they gradually settled in, reaching for their stitching and beadwork from the night before. Their faces carried identical smiles, as though they knew what was going on and it amused them.

I watched them.

"What if I didn't need to have anybody outside of me be wiser?" I asked, looking in the direction of Lupe and Maria, realizing too late that it was a complex question for so early in the morning. I pursued it anyway, just to practice being my own authority with real people.

"What if I didn't need others to be wiser?" I repeated aloud. "Even if they were wiser, what if I didn't need them to be? What if I carried within me a feeling of equality with everyone? What if the opinions of others no longer mattered? What would this kind of freedom be like? Could I handle it?"

Hearing myself, I realized what strange questions these were to be asking someone else.

Their lack of response was the perfect answer. I tapped the side of my head with the palm of my hand, exaggerating the silliness of the question while laughing at myself.

I stood and stretched by the smoldering embers, looking up into the thick, rolling clouds and the hazy sunlight. It was still early; everything felt quiet and asleep. Whatever had happened during the night was still running through my body, revealing information I hadn't even known I was seeking.

Observing the two women being so very present, I felt a wave of respect for each of them rise up in my belly and heart. I noticed, for the first time, that I didn't have them on a pedestal. Instead, I felt the distinct absence of hierarchy. We were able to meet each other with mutual respect. I was relieved that I didn't need to hold them higher.

I thought of how often I'd created heroes and wiser people in my life, only to find that they'd never quite live up to the hero, wise-person status I'd assign them.

"I have to tell you something, Lupe and Maria," I said, as though I were about to make a major announcement. "I just had a huge realization."

"Hmmm," they replied, without looking up from their stitching and beading.

"All my life, I've placed people on pedestals," I began. "I needed to have heroes outside myself, to avoid being my own authority. I held everyone accountable for what I did except myself. My facade of innocence has carried me through life. I, like so many people around me, believed others always knew better.

"I used to hold the belief that being a teacher was far beyond anything I could do and, indeed, would be a sign of wisdom and status, were I to become one. Teachers, like athletes, held hero status because, in my mind, they could do things I couldn't.

"Years later, when I became a teacher and found myself doing what I believed I couldn't do, I discovered that the school had a policy to assign all black and Hispanic children to a program labeled "Mentally Retarded" in order to collect extra school funds from the state. In my naive youth, I called for an investigation and was soon fired and blackballed from being hired at any school again for any reason, anywhere."

"Poor dear," Maria replied. "The hero myth began to fade, I'll bet."

"The next year," I continued, "the heroic image I'd created around the integrity of religion crumbled."

"What happened?" they both asked as if shocked, mocking how serious I sounded.

"A Los Angeles rabbi hired me to direct a camp for young children, and instructed me on the third day of the program to dismiss from the camp the only black child enrolled, a six-year-old person, because a white parent complained of his presence."

"What did you do?" Maria asked, pretending to be incredulous.

"Instinctively, I said no. I reminded the rabbi that, especially since we were both Jewish, the last thing he as a rabbi could do is hurt someone because of his race. I was fired again."

"That will teach you to harbor respect in your soul," Lupe said, grinning.

"The third experience . . ."

"There's another?" Lupe said, her eyes momentarily rolling upward.

"The third experience," I repeated, willing to risk further humiliation, "was witnessing police officers beat up a young American Indian couple—deliberately hitting their heads on the police car door as they shoved them into the back seat. The day after appearing in court as a witness to the beating, I was fired from the Bureau of Indian Affairs program I'd been involved with. Three days later, I was arrested for an incident that never happened—a police effort to harass and quiet me."

"Those incidents," Lupe interjected, "rather than distorting your perception of life, woke you up. You'd been living part of your life through others by idealizing in them what you did not see in yourself. You'd grown up in the belief that heroes were always someone else—people who did things you didn't believe you could do. Those were valuable lessons to help break up your illusions so that you could see what is, accurately and truthfully."

For a brief moment, I wondered if, once again, I would place Lupe on a pedestal and lower myself. I knew I was attributing special indigenous wisdom and hero worship to Lupe because of her skin color and facial structure and my beliefs about Native Americans.

Observing Lupe, I realized it was her presence and actions that touched me. She was not pretending wisdom, she embodied it. She could have been any color, either gender, and of any race, and I would have had the same respect for her.

"There are people who do things because they want the image that comes attached to their act," Maria said without looking at either one of us. "They step aside from acknowledging the impact they have on others, unwilling to take themselves seriously, unwilling to listen to the voice inside them that really does know what to do, yet pretends it doesn't.

"That pretense," Maria continued, "is supported by seeking out so-called experts to lean on while you hide inside, safe in the illusion that someday you'll be healed from one thing or another and be able to come out into the world without risk or discomfort.

"Because your actions originate from who you think you need to be to feel important, you always need a pat on the back from someone outside you. You forever feel just short of being fulfilled; just one more pat on the back will be enough and you'll live life happily ever after, comfortable, serene, and despairing no longer.

"You pretend you're doing something meaningful, entertaining yourself with the thought that someday, somewhere, later, you, too, will be brave. Someday. Later."

Their description of the process inside me was so accurate and precise, there was no room for defensiveness. I was relieved rather than embarrassed.

"Seeing another, outside of you, as more powerful and heroic," Lupe interjected, "allows you to stand beside yourself, instead of in yourself. You rely on the opinions of others to know what is best for you, and you find excuses, reasons and justifications for life not working, which you can then blame on others."

Maria turned directly toward me and, for the first time, gazed into my eyes, her look solemn and clear. With tears and a voice filled with strength and conviction, she said, "I know. I've grown up Indian in a world that is terrified of difference— even more terrified of silence."

Maria reached into the cloth bag beside her, pulled out a yellowed sheet of paper, and handed it to me, saying nothing. She wanted me to read it. I unfolded the brittle paper, careful to hold it in one piece at the folds. I noticed it was dated July 4, 1968, Madera, California.

It was a letter Maria had written decades before, addressed to a Bureau of Indian Affairs administrator for a training school in California. The school, I learned later, was run by an

American automobile corporation, under contract with the BIA, to vocationally train American Indians and encourage them to leave their reservations and get jobs in large cities. Reservation land would then be left free for development by white developers. The women stopped what they were doing and listened as I read the letter aloud.

"It's been two hundred years since the Indian has been given a chance to speak her mind. Well, this Indian is going to speak up. White people just don't understand Indians. You white people put us in government schools and try to judge us by white mans' standards. We feel deeper about things than white people could ever know. Indians are people! I demand to be treated as such.

"Indian values are different from that of the white neighbor. Once my people lived in teepees and rode around on horses, killing wild game with bows and arrows. I don't do that now, just as you no longer ride horseback through your streets. Please don't ask the question am I a real Indian? Yes, of course I am. Are you a real white person? What does it matter? You do not have to know me well to respect me.

I do not need people to rule me. I need people to help me help myself. Regardless of how you try to shape and mold me, you're always going to end up with an Indian. I'm not a television image. I feel. I cry. I laugh. You've taken my land and my culture. I will keep my spirit."

The last sentence was written in red ink. When I looked up from the paper, I saw Maria looking away, possibly embarrassed or apologetic.

"I wrote that when I was eighteen years old," she said in a clear voice. "I was angry then. I didn't understand why white people were so mean and hateful, why they treated Indians so badly. There was so much disrespect, and I felt powerless to change anything. For a while, I hated white people. I hated the people who seemed to have so much power over my life.

"One day I awoke from a dream, realizing I was to respect myself even if everyone around me didn't. I could no longer wait for others to see me. I had to see me. I was challenged to the highest degree. I had to do what I didn't believe was possible. I had to respect those that had no respect.

"I began to see behind patronizing and hateful words. I saw that the white people putting me down didn't respect themselves, and I'd been getting trapped by their words, filling myself with anger, draining my power. So I changed my behavior. I had to become their teacher. I had to become my own teacher. The energy of my anger became the guide to lead myself—to having a larger vision of all people. From that moment on, I've lived from respect."

"What happened with the white people in your life?" I asked. "You changed, but what about them?"

"Strangely, the white people around me changed too. They learned to respect themselves, as I lived from respect myself and offered respect to them. They didn't know me, but they liked me. No matter what their mind and beliefs had told them about Indians and people different from them, their spirit responded to the integrity of my respect."

She paused.

"I discovered myself that day," Maria added, "and since then, I can no longer blame others. I don't need to, anymore."

I felt alive being around Maria's bright presence. She reminded me of my picture of an Amazon woman. She was neither female nor male. She was simply strong. She didn't need me to like her, so I could like her with ease.

"No matter how different our lives are," Maria said softly, "those differences are only an illusion, designed to make us weep with ecstasy, recognizing that illusion, or dissolve into the loneliness of believing the illusion."

Maria turned away from me and resumed her beading.

19

The Trickster Mind

I was aware, for the first time in my life, of a new place within me. I found I could completely change lifelong emotional dilemmas and the endless carousel of daily problems to days of wonder and freedom from debilitating emotional weight.

"To appreciate my own heroism," I said to myself, "I must lead myself. I must be in the world as it is, not as I believe it should be."

"That is an excellent start," Maria said. "Realities, not potentials. And you're talking to yourself again!"

"Everybody else talks to me," I replied, appreciating my own cleverness. "Why shouldn't I talk to me?"

Without warning, a gust of wind slammed into my body, carrying a force large enough to blow me off the stool I was sitting on. Nothing else in the immediate area was disturbed by the wind. No one even seemed to notice. The usual giggles followed as I pulled myself up to sit back on the stool.

The incisive power of the wind stunned me. It felt like someone had opened a door and I could see into another room, larger than the one I was in. A voice inside me, the one I often attributed to trivial thoughts, instructed me to get paper and pen and write down the following words:

"You really do know exactly what to do in every situation,

but believe you don't. You're easily seduced by a familiar thought that pulls you, with your consent, into acting on impulse and habit. Intrinsic internal panic at the root of impulse and habit is so familiar that you believe you'd only be pretending if you didn't panic. And since you'd only be pretending, you might as well be afraid again, and panic as usual.

"If, instead, you purposely intend to take a different action, even if you didn't believe you can, you would change an entire life pattern of being victim to mere learned and conditioned ways to respond."

Another gust of wind, this time less intrusive, pushed against me just enough to alert me in advance to the need to balance myself and root my feet into the earth.

"It's up to me to initiate new ways of behaving and responding," I said to Maria. "Intellectually, I've known that for years, but to initiate responding differently in the midst of despair, crisis, or self-doubt requires real courage, if not stupidity. Either way, I've got to do it if I'm to free myself of life's daily cycle of anxiety and distress. It's such a powerful act, especially having never done it before."

Suddenly, everyone seemed to disappear. Everything around me went out of focus, becoming distorted. I thought I was passing out, that my heart was about to stop beating. Fear rushed in abruptly like a giant wave, projecting scenes of impending disaster.

My mind sought logic, anything to make sense of what was happening. Nothing eased the images streaming in. I feared that at any moment, I'd explode into panic, go crazy and run until my body disintegrated. I was afraid of being afraid.

I had no familiar reference point. I was on the edge of being completely immobilized, giving up, and being struck down by terror. I had only an instant, and I knew it. I was about to succumb to the belief that I was powerless and I'd die of fright for sure. I felt seduced by a murky swamp of thoughts, slowly sucking me into a scary darkness.

I made a decision. Instead of trying to make the fear go away, something I'd attempted unsuccessfully since childhood, I'd do something different. I'd use the fear. After all, the fear was being created by my thoughts, not through my body.

With all the emotional strength I could gather, and with a clarity that was frightening in itself, I infused another voice into my thoughts. "It's all right if I die now," I said convincingly. "It's okay to let happen what needs to happen. It doesn't matter."

Instantly, my body relaxed. Everything quieted. Panic dissolved. I shifted into a state of wonder. What had been distorted and out of focus remained distorted and out of focus, but now seemed normal.

As I sat wondering what was going to happen next, I heard a voice disguised as an innocent thought.

"You can't hide in the shadows anymore. You have to come out."

"What are you talking about?" I asked, frightened, and loudly enough to be heard by Lupe and Maria if, in fact, they were anywhere near. "What are you talking about?"

"Trickery is what I'm talking about," the voice replied. "There is a trickster in you—it is that part of you that you don't recognize. It thrives in your false innocence and ability to hide behind your own shadow. Even in this moment, everything around you is exactly as it was a few minutes ago, except the trickster is at work and your self-observer has taken a vacation. Your willingness to be aware, the integrity that is you, sleeps. Therefore you think you don't know what's going on."

"I'm confused," I replied.

"No you're not. Your mind tells you you're confused, and the trickster lives within your mind. That's its home. When you believe yourself to be confused, you either give up, straddling the edge of clarity, or you are forced to define yourself. You are called to sift out all the voices of the past that are not yours, the ones that hold you prisoner to the beliefs of others that you've taken on as your own. When the trickster in you is at work, you become lost, stuck, and confused. That is the nature of the trickster mind.

"The trickster is what stops your movement in life and leads you from one mood to another. She . . ."

"She?" I asked

"She, he, doesn't matter," was the reply. "This isn't about gender. There isn't any gender.

"The trickster mind doesn't allow you to believe all the voices and thoughts inside you. It teaches you to believe only the self-doubting voices, the ones that tell you life is difficult and scary, and that you're never quite good enough."

"Okay, I'm not confused. I just want to understand what you're telling me."

"You're too close to yourself to see clearly," the voice said in a patient tone. "Step back from looking so hard. Soften your gaze. Widen your sight. Surround yourself with empty spaces—a dark hole of awareness.

"The trickster mind lives in those parts of your life that you ignore and consistently discount as unimportant and trivial."

"I think I understand," I said.

"The trickster mind will force you to seek understanding forever," the voice said, "thereby avoiding action of any kind. Understanding is part of the big trance. Seeking to understand is an endless task designed to provide full-time employment for the mind. Locating the origin of things is fuel for the mind, and origin doesn't matter anyway.

"Awareness, however, forces the mind out into the open. In the open you are able to see what needs to be done, moment to moment. You can act.

"People who are entrapped by the trickster mind appear to be in a coma, operating on automatic. You cannot make connection with them. They seem to be distant creatures, and when you're in their presence, you feel alone, afraid, even alienated. They are the people who are pre-programmed, absolutely sure of right and wrong, determined that they and everyone else around them must behave as expected. They cannot deviate from their programmed pattern without great pain."

"Are you talking about me?" I asked. "If so, it's true only some of the time." I felt better saying that. It softened the effect on who I had to believe I was.

For a moment there was no audible response.

"The people who are lost in their minds—the home of the trickster—follow authority as though in a trance," the voice continued. "They thrive on rules, laws, policies, and right and wrong exactly defined. They fear the unknown, the unpredictable, and the insightful nature of humor. Humor gives us perspective on the meaninglessness of the mind's directives. To feel the laughter and relief of humor is to see our absurdity. Those people lost in their trickster mind see each moment of their entire life before them as predetermined with an intention that leaves no room for movement."

"How do I recognize the trickster in me?" I asked.

"Sometimes you can't," I heard Lupe's voice answer.

"How, how, how did . . ?" I stuttered. "What's going on? Where are you?"

As abruptly as everything had gone out of focus and disappeared, Lupe and Maria reappeared in crisp, colorful contrast, in sharp focus, defined, as though nothing unusual had happened except that maybe I'd blacked out for a moment. The house, the trees, the porch, and the furniture emerged into bright clarity, as if through an automatic zoom lens. The world around me returned to how it had been moments or hours earlier.

I looked at Lupe. She was laughing so fully her body shook.

"If you're scared," she said, "you can crawl into bed, get under the covers, pull a blanket over your face, and know that you will then be completely safe, or, if not safe, at least warm."

I laughed, surprised at the absurd answer, at the absurdity of everything.

I didn't question the realness of what was going on. I simply shrugged my shoulders, deciding to believe even my disbelief.

When Maria spoke, her voice carried the same inflection as the voice I'd been listening to inside. "You'll be able to identify trickster mind easily," she said, "if you've always wondered about the world around you that you can't see, touch, smell, or buy."

"Why?" I asked. "How does wondering help me recognize the trickster mind?"

"It's what you don't pay attention to in your life that runs your life," Lupe answered. "If you aren't always in a state of wonder, you're not paying attention."

"The mind cannot live in the shadows if you wonder about the meaning of things," Maria added. "The trickster, as I call it, cannot hide in the habits of the past when you have the ability to wonder how the particles of dust, illuminated by the sunbeam through your window, remain suspended. The trickster has no interest in curiosity, or the aliveness of wonder. It simply doesn't care.

"The mind cannot thrive in the background, depleting your energy, if you question what life would be like without your daily habits and, what is most important, if you lead yourself in the directions you must go each moment."

"I'm on the periphery of understanding," I responded. "I may even understand and not know it."

I paused, wondering what I'd just said.

"I do understand," I added. "I feel it."

"Yes," Lupe interjected in a respectful voice, "that is a good observation. You do."

"Yes, yes, yes," I agreed.

"The trickster mind," Maria added, "can be recognized by the limitations and fear it lives within, believing the world to be limited and fearful."

Her energy was brighter, apparently because I was now able to hear and comprehend what she was saying. Maria could speak without having to monitor herself for me to keep up. I was more easily receptive.

"How do I become aware of my trickster mind? How can I see it?" I asked.

"Bring it into the open so it no longer controls your actions," she answered. "Be aware of and open to every inner revelation and insight, no matter how trivial it may at first seem. Believe everything, including your doubts. Be still. Go very slowly. Be still. Be quiet if only for a minute or two. Listen to your mind's thoughts, and know there is nothing you have to do with those thoughts. No action need be taken. No worry. Simply listen, and notice the thoughts. Notice yourself noticing the thoughts. And be still.

"As you observe your mind trickster writing its own dialogue, that act of observing, in itself, will illuminate the part of you that you ordinarily cannot see. The trickster becomes an insight, a revelation. Your awareness grows. You feel lighter instantly."

"I feel light right now," I said.

"How do you know you feel light," Lupe asked.

"How do I know I feel light?" I repeated, initially thinking the question absurd.

My impulse was to respond in some clever way, to say something sarcastic and witty—an old habit to divert the attention from deepening into a more authentic feeling place. I didn't act on the impulse.

Instead, in the brief moment of silence, I was able to hear Lupe's question, and her respectful tone of voice.

"I know I feel light because there is an absence of tension in me," I answered. "My body and mind are light. I have no thoughts from yesterday or anxiety about tomorrow. I'm here. I'm just being here. There is no feeling of separation from you or anyone else. My energy is alive. I feel it."

"You're also out of the trance you discovered some time ago," Lupe said approvingly, with a smile. "Your willingness to change makes change easy. You are willing to feel. You are willing to listen to your body without having to know what everything means with your mind. This will save your life. This will bring you into life."

I was moved by her words and the respect carried in her voice.

"With your new clarity, absent of trickster mind," she added, "you've momentarily stepped outside who you think and believe you are. You have no restricting identities and learned beliefs about how you must be.

"To help you further in identifying trickster mind thoughts," Lupe continued, "sense your feelings bodily. Be aware of tension or flexibility. Continue to be still—not stiff still, but soft and relaxed still."

"That sounds impossible."

"It is impossible," Maria answered. "Because it's impossible, you have to do it. You don't have a choice. You can no longer pretend to be stupid. You must believe everything."

Maria walked over to where I sat. Standing in front of me, she bent forward at the waist, bringing her face within inches of mine, and purposely exaggerated the silliness of her body position. Speaking in a very slow, elongated speech pattern, clearly pronouncing each syllable, and pausing every few words, she said, "When you pay attention, by slowing down your daily movements and thoughts, you begin to feel and sense things that may initially scare you. Things that make your body antsy and fidgety, things that make you want to flee and run, because your previous pace of living prevented you from noticing those things that existed beneath your daily speed."

I leaned back in my chair to gain some distance, uncomfortable with the proximity of her face to mine, simultaneously giggling at the contrast between her body position and the seriousness of her words.

"By the way you say things, I believe you," I said, "but what you say twists my world into knots. There's a contest going on inside me. One moment I view you as wiser; the next, I view myself as wiser."

"We're both wiser," she replied, then smiled and leaned in closer.

"If you choose not to run," she said, "that will be a good thing. If you choose to run, that will be a decision you are more familiar with. Your work is to respect whatever decision you make and know that the consequences of that decision will be meaningful."

Maria gradually brought her body to an upright position, stepped a few steps backwards, and sat down in her chair, a teasing smile clearly forming. I was now more curious.

"How can I fill in the dark holes of awareness in my life, which is what I assume the trickster mind inhabits?" I asked.

"Yes, that's it, correct," Lupe answered. "You said that well."

Lupe seemed excited to hear such a clear description of what they'd been telling me.

"See yourself doing something you've never done before, but want to," she continued. "Allow whatever that picture or thought is to come into clear view. Focus. Stay with that picture whether it disturbs you or excites you. Open to the internal experience, as subtle and simple as it may appear."

"I want to run and scream," I said excitedly. "I want to run on top of the water at full speed. I want to jump out of an airplane without a parachute. I want to jump and throw my arms up in the air and scream into the clouds forever."

"Observe with an attitude of wonder," Maria and Lupe encouraged in unison. "Allow any doubt to move through you and fade out. Within this realm of wonder, ask yourself a question."

"Ask a question?"

"Yes, like that," Maria answered, laughing. "Ask a question—one that comes from inside you, something you truly want to know. Ask more questions. Be in a state of wonder and innocence. If doubt or self-judgment seep in, bring your attention back to the playfulness of wonder, communicating with what wants to come alive inside you."

"Why?" I asked.

"Why not? Remember the story of your former wife and the silver necklace?"

"That was a long time ago . . . and how . . . ?"

"Doesn't matter," Maria interrupted. "Time has nothing to do with this. That trickster-mind thought form lived within you for decades without your awareness. There is only one way you could have known it was there. You would've had to realize how afraid you were of being betrayed and how you did everything possible to avoid being betrayed again. You had the belief that you weren't supposed to be betrayed and that you could protect yourself against it. An impossibility, I might add."

My wife had announced to me many years ago that she was filing for divorce and that I was to move out and leave our two small children. Months later, I noticed that the necklace she was wearing, one I had given her as a gift years earlier, held a different pendant. The original pendant had held an image, etched in silver, of a wise medicine woman. The new one, a gift from a new boyfriend, had four letters linked together that spelled the word "love."

Seeing it, I grew pale and felt sick. I saw myself as having been betrayed.

"You're thinking about it again," Maria said, "and you're feeling it right now."

"Yes."

"You need betrayal, it is good for you," she said, as though she were offering me a glass of fresh-squeezed orange juice.

"What's good about betrayal?" I asked.

"What's bad about it?" Lupe responded immediately.

"Betrayal is a concept that requires two people," she continued. "One person to betray and another to invite the betrayal. It's a dance. The betrayed always feels duped, hurt, damaged and innocent. In fact, the betrayed one—you—always knew what was coming eventually. You simply ignored the warnings. You ignored everything that would have informed you that the picture you held of your life and the woman you were about to marry had never been real. You were too afraid to see what was in front of you. You lived, as most people do, in an illusion—a trickster-mind thought form."

"But I didn't know any better then," I insisted.

"Yes you did," Lupe insisted more convincingly. "You just didn't listen from the inside. You only listened to the world outside of you, your mind's thoughts. Had you listened inside, you would not have married her, but then again, you would not have learned this lesson. What you call betrayal began when you betrayed yourself by ignoring what you knew to be true.

"Your wife didn't betray you. She woke you up. She broke up your trance image of what life was supposed to be and brought you rapidly falling into the present moment. Your anger at your own ignorance was too much for you to take responsibility for. Therefore you chose to perceive yourself as betrayed—an honorable way out from having to see into yourself first, don't you think?"

"Well, if you put it that way," I said with a smile, "yes."

"I do put it that way," she replied. "It's the truth."

"You have to feel everything completely from now on, every moment," Maria added. "If you don't, not only betrayal awaits you, but a life full of shocking surprises, turbulent events, and enough disasters to list in alphabetical order. You can no longer choose to run without severe consequences.

"Hear this, if you hear nothing else," Maria emphasized. "The world will self-correct for you as you discover the tools to let it."

"Self-correct?" I asked.

"That means knowing that the world works," Maria explained. "The world, just as it is, with all its illusions, violence, and craziness, is working. The world works and self-corrects for you, moment to moment, when you self-correct to meet it—when you remember that the world is in you. Only those who have the deep belief that the world isn't working are lost. If you carry no picture of how the world is supposed to be, it is always working.

"Self-correcting is a technique whereby what you've been taught is real and true comes face to face with what is real. When you cling to no specific belief and become the observer to whatever unfolds in front of you, self-correction takes place."

"What are the tools?" I asked.

"Complete everything, all the way through," Maria replied. "Complete feelings, conversations, and your actions all the way through, every time. Believe everything. To believe every-thing means to trust all the information and voices you hear that come from within you. You can call them guides, angels, intuition, or simply sensations. You must hold them valid even though those around you may believe you to be losing it.

"The only difference between you and the identified psy-chotic street person is that you are selective with the infor-mation you choose to act on. You have the ability to see what-ever you want, anytime, anywhere. How you perceive some-thing is always your choice."

"I know how to do that," I said. "It means, first, I must decide that I want to see everything."

"And to complete everything," they both reminded me.

"Complete everything, believe everything," Lupe repeated with emphasis. "Know that you have the ability to see what-ever you want, anytime, anywhere."

She looked at me with a look that demanded I pay atten-tion. "You're the only one to decide what you see."

We were all silent for a few minutes as my senses reorga-nized around the information.

Maria slipped into the silence. "You can see that event with your wife as a betrayal or as a blessing. You choose. Which one is more fun? For some people, betrayal is more fun. It brings drama to their lives, something to be betrayed about, a traumatic event to live and die over, something to fill time."

She paused a minute and smiled. "You may find blessing more interesting," she said.

It began to rain. I was the only one getting wet.

"You have the choice of either one—or both. Believe what you will until you find something more meaningful to believe. All of this is beyond your imagination anyway. Beyond even my imagination."

20

Snap of Awareness

About forty people stood quietly, side by side, shoulders touching, in a single row, all facing the same direction. At one end of the line I stood, looking outward like the others. Curious about who was in the line with me, I took two steps forward so I could peer down the row of people to see who they were.

What I saw were forty heads leaning slightly forward, so they could see around the person next to them, their faces all turned in my direction, eyes directly on me.

My wife of long ago, a person I'd learned to distrust, stood there. An old friend who had tried to kill me after losing himself in alcohol stood beside her. Peering down the line of faces, I saw old friends, people I'd believed had betrayed me, lied to me, and been cruel, mean, and divisive. I saw faces of good friends who had died years ago.

The variety of people touched every feeling in me at once.

I saw people I'd loved, been intimate with, and many who had taught me important things in life. My life's enemies and friends had banded together. I saw my father, who had died decades ago. I saw children I'd been close to and children I'd disliked. I even saw a police officer who had once roughed me up.

Some faces seemed to light up when I made specific eye contact. A woman who had fired me from a hospital job when I was sixteen, for something I did not do, stood quietly, holding the same expression as all the others.

I saw members of a gang who had beaten me up in high school, and a woman I'd been in love with since the age of three. At the other end of the row, I saw Jarid, Lupe, Maria, the black child, Sara, Leo Garcia, the Boy, Meigra, and someone I didn't recognize yet.

As I looked at all the faces, both friend and perceived enemy, their expressions revealed the same message. Each face carried a faint, soft, kind, knowing smile that I interpreted as asking, "Do you get it yet? Do you see what all the events in your life have taught you?"

I woke from the dream relieved. I did get it.

All the people in my life, in whatever role they played, helped me strengthen my ability to change how I react to the everyday world.

The people who disrupted and disturbed my plans of how I thought life was supposed to go, and their willingness to betray, lie, hurt, love, and shock me, forced me to either succumb to a form of powerlessness and recycled emotions or to find new ways to lead myself.

I could feel it in my body. Everyone who has ever done anything to me or for me has ultimately helped me to learn to rescue myself—to discover that I can rescue myself.

At that moment, the screen door opened and Nona, a white woman and friend to Lupe, came out of the house and announced, "Tomorrow, we'll go into Canyon de Chelly, a sacred area for Native Americans."

She said it was necessary for us to go immediately, because life-changing information was available only at this time.

"Lupe will lead us into the canyon," Nona continued, "and share information she receives from the ancient spirits and the unique energy of the canyon. This is a rare opportunity because Lupe carries within her thousands of years of history and powerful medicine ways."

"No, no," I said, almost loud enough to be heard by the others. I quickly judged myself for having that instinctive reaction. I questioned my right to say no to such a huge idea. I questioned my right to even think "no." I was embarrassed with myself even though I had yet to say anything anybody could actually hear.

An internal debate began. "I am ready to leave here. I am finished for now, but I should go into the canyon."

My thoughts attempted to reason with each other, creating the classic dilemma between two opposing views, both originating from a source within me that didn't have perspective on either view.

One perspective was concerned with what others would think, believing that they probably knew better than I what was right for me. The second perspective was rooted in my instinct and intuition, too new to me to fully trust and believe. I was still learning to recognize the difference between taking an action that was intrinsic and instinctive and one expected of me by others. The latter ensured the least short-term discomfort, but perpetuated a deadening of spirit.

All my thoughts encouraged me to go. "Go with Lupe," they said. "This may be the last opportunity for you to do something like this with a woman who carries generations of knowledge within her."

I respected Lupe and Maria. I liked how I felt around them.

"So why don't you want to go?" I heard Nona ask, interjecting herself into my private thoughts. I realized she must have seen the expression on my face.

"I'm ready to leave, to go home," I answered. "I'm full. I want time to live through all that I've learned these past days."

"This may be the last time Lupe will be taking this trip," Nona continued, sounding more insistent than convincing. "She's in her eighties and may be too weak to ever return here again. She may not be in her body next year."

My first thought was to judge myself as wrong. Who did I think I was, to have my own opinion when in the company of others wiser than I? Every doubt within me rose to the surface. Here I was, confronted with the ultimate outside authority, the wisest of teachers, a respected medicine woman, someone who could teach me things that would change my life. Most probably, this was the last time this opportunity would be available in my lifetime.

And I wasn't sure.

My instinct said to leave. If I couldn't judge myself, if I had to believe my impulse, that's exactly what I'd do. I'd leave. I'd say yes to myself.

I remembered Maria telling me of the trickster mind—that the trickster mind doesn't allow me to believe my inside voices, only the self-doubting ones.

If I continued to seek understanding and the answer for what to do, I'd wander forever back and forth between "what to do's" and "who knows best" in complete and total indecision. I switched my thought process from trying to figure it out to the question of what this decision meant for me.

Like a camera flash illuminating a dark room, an insight, bright and with pristine clarity, shattered my confusion. I knew that even the sweetest and most profound possibilities, presented by the most respected and wisest of souls, may still be illusions, unless I hear my own voice and feel in my own body an answer that is clear, decisive, and unquestioning. A full, unbreakable decision. A snap of awareness that comes from within.

Nona offered more reasons why I should go into the canyon. As she spoke, I heard another voice, one from inside me. It sounded very much like Sara's voice—not an audible sound, more like clear thought made tangible, verbalized.

"Decide," she said, "that you are willing to be your own boss, your own God, your own judge, and your own executioner.

"Know that you will always get what you want. Always. There is no other choice. You cannot *not* get exactly what you want. That is the way the universe works. How else could it be?"

I was listening intently to Sara's voice while hearing the voice of Nona in the background. Sara's words brought me back to myself. They reminded me to take an action, even if wrong, that developed my ability to act from within.

"You can no longer be your small self," Sara said. "You can be, but you cannot tolerate yourself being it, nor should you. When you know how to drive yourself, you don't need others to drive for you, except cooperatively."

I listened, comparing the tone of Nona's voice and that of Sara's. Sara's voice gradually faded, reminding me that "to demand anything from someone else requires a mutual respect. Demand without authority or respect has no meaning." She was gone.

I knew then, without doubt, that the decision to go or not to go was about respect—respect for myself.

For the next hour, Nona tried to convince me to go into the canyon with them. The conversation was getting serious and beginning to feel like a weight in my body, as though the fate of the world rested on whether I said yes or no.

An image of Sara floated through my vision, reminding me to stay light. "Stay light. Nothing really matters this much. Stay light."

A decision was forming. I knew this was not just another decision. It meant I was to step into myself completely. From this moment on, I would be making decisions, all decisions, large and small, from an autonomous place within me, no longer from social expectation, to appease others.

In this moment, I needed all the help I could get.

I remembered a recent dream I'd had. In it, our two-year-old boy was guiding Meigra and I somewhere. He was light and full of energy, giving us directions. The Boy gave me instructions, speaking words Maria, too, had spoken. He said, "You have to complete everything, every moment." With the authority of the wisest of beings, he added, "Fill out all the words and the silence between them."

The dream ended with the Boy standing on the railing of a bridge that spanned a mile-deep canyon.

"He's in a precarious position," I said to Meigra. "He could fall."

"He can't fall," she replied, hearing my fear. "He can fly."

In that moment, my attention was drawn to the silence. Nona, seeing that I wasn't listening, had stopped talking.

"I have something to say, Nona," I began, "which will help you know why I'm not going into the canyon with you and Lupe."

My voice was firm and clear. I was no longer my little self, apologizing, defending, justifying, or explaining. I was respecting. My intent was clear.

"Nona," I continued, "tomorrow, I may wake up and find that I've made the most wrong decision of my life, that I lost the most precious chance to learn of things that I can never again learn anywhere else at any time. I may find that I seriously misread everything and will never recover what I lost, nor heal the wounds of hurting those who were only wanting to help me. I may discover I missed the one golden opportunity, that once-in-a-lifetime chance."

I noticed Nona's eyes watering, and mine as well, as we both felt the power of my decision and the strength of my intent. My voice carried a clarity that I could not doubt or pull back from. I was riding a wave of energy that knew where it was going. I did not have to be right or wrong—I needed only to act. That, in itself, expressed all that I was.

"I must respect myself. I must respect what comes from within me, even when everyone around me disagrees—even if my action disturbs the world I've been used to.

"When I wake up tomorrow, I will feel good, as I do now, that I listened to the voices within me and followed my intuition, even if I believe I should have gone into the canyon with you and Lupe."

Simultaneously, we breathed deeply.

My voice carried a presence and sureness that was unfamiliar to me. I had no emotional attachment to my words. I was speaking to Nona without feeling separate from her or from her point of view. I was speaking to and from myself.

"Maybe what I was to learn in the canyon, from the ancient wise beings and from Lupe, I just learned."

Nona slowly sat down on the floor of the wooden porch and leaned back against the wall. I felt light, soft, at ease, and respectful of both of us.

We looked at each other with sparkling eyes and deep respect. From the outside, someone might think we were lost in staring. From the inside, we were touching each other deeply. I recognized who Nona was, and Nona recognized who I was. We were caring for each other, wanting nothing.

"I am those wise beings," I whispered.

Conclusion

*b*eing real in an unreal world is making possible the almost impossible. It is the most difficult challenge you can ask of yourself. When you begin to live from a real place, you cannot turn back, even if you believe you want to.

Being real enlivens, teaches, leads, and originates from the individual soul and spirit. It brings you home to your body. It is grounded, respectful, earthy, often confusing, sometimes stupid, and sometimes brilliant.

The decision to be real is a serious one that has serious yet welcome consequences. You expand your beliefs and attitudes beyond where you think you can until you're able to see through not only your own eyes, but the eyes of your perceived enemy, as well as the eyes of those with whom you want to be closest.

When you choose to live in a real way, your life will be altered immediately. You draw people to you who value being real as well. Your friends may fade away, relationships will change, your work may change. Simultaneously, your energy will increase, and clarity will be commonplace. What was meaningful yesterday may no longer be meaningful today. You realize you really are the director of each daily scene. You understand and respect that all relationships in your life are there for you to learn about yourself. When real, contests about who is right and who is wrong become boring. Blame always misses the point.

Being real requires a willingness—and willingness is the key word—to live life without blame, anger, or judgment. Some people are not willing, and that is right for them. If you decide that you are willing to live without blame, anger, and judgment, this doesn't mean you're free of them, only that you're able to observe yourself blaming, raging, or judging, which then gives you the option to change your own actions, no matter what the other person does.

In the midst of conflict and emotional crisis, you take action that may, at first, appear as though you've given yourself away and allowed someone else to take you over, and even win. You no longer have to be right or pretend that you know what you're doing. You get bigger in yourself than you believe possible.

You can no longer offer excuses, reasons, justifications, and explanations for your actions or inaction, such as being late, forgetting, being spaced out, being too afraid, or having had a dysfunctional childhood. Instead, you recognize that your every behavior, action, and reaction is completely within your control, always and without exception, and that everything that has ever happened in your life happened for you, not to you. You don't waste energy judging yourself. You keep moving.

When you step out of the circle of falseness, pretense, and shared social and cultural expectations, you recognize the illusion and divisiveness of most beliefs about sexuality, relationships, schools, psychology, and the world around you. You notice the disrespect that commonly exists between adults and children. You may begin to feel the pain, despair, and hurt that most people carry beneath their public selves. Facades burst. You see things you've never seen, you hear things you've never heard. Everything begins to feel unfamiliar. The unfamiliar becomes familiar.

Realness demands an inner discipline that borders on feeling impossible, It requires using fear as a stepping-stone instead of an obstacle. You intend to become your own authority, believing your own perceptions before the opinions of others, with no attachment to being right.

You risk having to lead, to be serious about your purpose for being on this Earth, and acknowledge the impact you have on others. When real, you must also be willing to go beyond the discomfort of having others dislike, condemn, judge, and blame you.

Being real demands one hundred percent awareness of everything you do each moment. Your tone of voice, your physical discomfort, and the endless stream of thoughts that fill your mind become things to observe, not things to ignore or fix.

When you decide to act from a real place, never again will you want a time out to be unreal or to pretend you are a victim of anything. You may often, even daily, slip into old ways of reacting, leaving yourself, or blaming someone for something, but now you notice when you are complaining or feeling powerless. At the point of noticing, it is up to you to shift back into being in charge and at home inside.

If you want to live differently, you step out of the learned program, the trance state in which most people exist today. When you step out, your every action truly originates from within, and it feels right. The daily actions of being real are too freeing, energizing, and alive to permit return to pretense, cultural trance, or the everyday world of busyness, tension, and worry.

Being real requires taking risks you've never taken. More than anything, being real requires softening your heart. To soften the heart is the scariest thing going. It is scarier than the highest roller coaster, or even dying. Softening the heart happens only when you are available for it. You cannot make it happen, only recognize it when it does happen. It takes energy for a soft heart to sustain itself.

Being real is not a technique. It isn't a theory, and it is not of the mind. The mind will only lead you in circles, providing evidence for whatever you want to believe.

To be real is a daily practice that takes place with each and every relationship—each person you meet, each conflict, and each intimate moment.

You will be afraid and free, and welcome both.

The decision to be real will change your life instantly and forever.

For information regarding workshops, presentations, or to reach the author direct:

Bruce Scott
c/o North Atlantic Books
P.O. Box 12327
Berkeley, CA 94712

or

E-mail: SCOTT_BRUCE@hotmail.com

(831) 457-4170